Get Updates and More on Nolo.com

Go to this book's companion page at:

www.nolo.com/back-of-book/DEHB.html

When there's an important change to the law affecting this book, we'll
post updates. You'll also find articles and other related materials.

More Resources
from Nolo.com

Legal Forms, Books, & Software
Hundreds of do-it-yourself products—all written in plain English,
approved, and updated by our in-house legal editors.

Legal Articles
Get informed with thousands of free articles on everyday legal
topics. Our articles are accurate, up to date, and reader friendly.

Find a Lawyer
Want to talk to a lawyer? Use Nolo to find a lawyer who can
help you with your case.

NOLO
LAW for ALL

"In Nolo you can trust."

THE NEW YORK TIMES

"Nolo is always there in a jam as the nation's premier publisher of do-it-yourself legal books."

NEWSWEEK

"Nolo publications...guide people simply through the how, when, where and why of the law."

THE WASHINGTON POST

"[Nolo's]...material is developed by experienced attorneys who have a knack for making complicated material accessible."

LIBRARY JOURNAL

"When it comes to self-help legal stuff, nobody does a better job than Nolo..."

USA TODAY

"The most prominent U.S. publisher of self-help legal aids."

TIME MAGAZINE

"Nolo is a pioneer in both consumer and business self-help books and software."

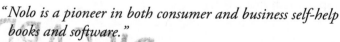

LOS ANGELES TIMES

17th Edition

Home Business
Tax Deductions

Keep What You Earn

Stephen Fishman, J.D.

SEVENTEENTH EDITION	JANUARY 2021
Editor	DIANA FITZPATRICK
Cover Design	SUSAN PUTNEY
Book Design	SUSAN PUTNEY
Proofreading	IRENE BARNARD
Index	ACCESS POINTS INDEXING
Printing	BANG PRINTING

ISSN: 1932-2402 (print)

ISSN: 2326-0092 (online)

ISBN: 978-1-4133-2804-2 (pbk)

ISBN: 978-1-4133-2805-9 (ebook)

This book covers only United States law, unless it specifically states otherwise.

Please note

We know that accurate, plain-English legal information can help you solve many of your own legal problems. But this text is not a substitute for personalized advice from a knowledgeable lawyer. If you want the help of a trained professional—and we'll always point out situations in which we think that's a good idea—consult an attorney licensed to practice in your state.

Acknowledgments

Many thanks to:

Lisa Guerin and Diana Fitzpatrick for their superb editing

Susan Putney for her outstanding book design

About the Author

Stephen Fishman has dedicated his career as an attorney and author to writing useful, authoritative, and recognized guides on taxes and business law for small businesses, entrepreneurs, independent contractors, and freelancers. He is the author of over 20 books and hundreds of articles, and has been quoted in the *New York Times*, the *Wall Street Journal*, *Chicago Tribune*, and many other publications. Among his books are *Deduct It! Lower Your Small Business Taxes*, *Tax Deductions for Professionals*, and *Working for Yourself: Law & Taxes for Independent Contractors, Freelancers & Gig Workers of All Types*.

Table of Contents

Introduction

This book is for you if you're one of the millions of Americans who run a business from home. It shows how home business owners can reduce their taxes by taking advantage of the huge array of tax deductions available to them.

Did you know that, if you have a legitimate home business, you may be able to deduct:

- a portion of your rent or mortgage
- expenses for local and business trips, and
- medical expenses for yourself and your family?

All of these deductions—and many others—can add up to substantial tax savings. The IRS will never complain if you don't take all the deductions available to you. In fact, the majority of home business owners miss out on many deductions every year simply because they aren't aware of them—or because they neglect to keep the records necessary to back them up.

That's where this book comes in. It shows you how you can deduct all or most of your business expenses from your federal taxes. This book is not a tax preparation guide—it does not show you how to fill out your tax forms. (By the time you do your taxes, it may be too late to take deductions you could have taken if you had planned the prior year's business spending wisely and kept proper records.) Instead, this book gives you all the information you need to maximize your deductible expenses—and avoid common deduction mistakes. You can (and should) use this book all year long, so that you're ready to take advantage of every available deduction opportunity come April 15.

Now more than ever, you'll need guidance when it comes to understanding your taxes. In 2017, Congress enacted the most sweeping changes to the tax code in over 30 years when it passed the Tax Cuts and Jobs Act (TCJA), which took effect in 2018. Now, in an effort to stave off economic devastation in the wake of the coronavirus (COVID-19) pandemic, Congress has revised the nation's tax laws yet again, temporarily suspending many of the harshest provisions of the TCJA. We explain these changes including:

- new rules for deducting net operating losses during 2018 through 2020 (see Chapter 1)
- changes to bonus and regular depreciation for improvements to nonresidential real property (see Chapter 5)
- new tax credits for employers who retain their payrolls and provide sick leave and family leave (see Chapter 11)
- new tax credits for self-employed business owners impacted by the coronavirus (COVID-19) pandemic (see Chapter 12)
- temporary rules allowing penalty-free withdrawals from retirement accounts (see Chapter 13)
- rules for deducting business-related meals (see Chapter 14), and
- changes affecting charitable contributions (see Chapter 14).

Even if you work with an accountant or another tax professional, you need to learn about home business tax deductions. No tax professional will ever know as much about your business as you do, and you can't expect a hired professional to search high and low for every deduction you might be able to take, especially during the busy tax preparation season. The information in this book will help you provide your tax professional with better records, ask better questions, and obtain better advice. It will also help you evaluate the advice you get from tax professionals, websites, and other sources, so you can make smart decisions about your taxes.

If you do your taxes yourself (as more and more home businesspeople are doing, especially with the help of tax preparation software), your need for knowledge is even greater. Not even the most sophisticated tax preparation program can decide which tax deductions you should take or tell you whether you've overlooked a valuable deduction. This book can be your guide—providing you with practical advice and information so you can rest assured you are taking full advantage of the many deductions available to home business owners.

Get Updates to This Book on Nolo.com

When there are important changes to the information in this book,
we'll post updates online, on a page dedicated to this book:

www.nolo.com/back-of-book/DEHB.html

Some Tax Basics

Once you start your own business, you can begin taking advantage of the many tax deductions available only to business owners. The tax code is full of deductions for businesses—and you are entitled to take them whether you work from home or from a fancy outside office. Before you can start using these deductions to hang on to more of your hard-earned money, however, you need a basic understanding of how businesses pay taxes and how tax deductions work. This chapter gives you all the information you need to get started.

It covers:

- how tax deductions work
- how businesses are taxed
- what expenses businesses can deduct, and
- how to calculate the value of a tax deduction.

How Tax Deductions Work

A tax deduction (also called a write-off) is an amount of money you are entitled to subtract from your gross income (all the money you make) to determine your taxable income (the amount on which you must pay tax). The more deductions you have, the lower your taxable income will be and the less tax you will have to pay.

Types of Tax Deductions

There are three basic types of tax deductions: personal deductions, investment deductions, and business deductions. This book covers only business deductions—the large array of write-offs available to business owners, including those who work out of their homes.

Personal Deductions

For the most part, your personal, living, and family expenses are not tax deductible. For example, you can't deduct the food that you buy for yourself and your family. There are, however, special categories of personal expenses that may be deducted, subject to strict limitations. These include items such as home mortgage interest, state and local taxes (up to an annual limit), charitable contributions, medical expenses above a threshold amount, and interest on education loans. This book does not cover these personal deductions.

Investment Deductions

Many people try to make money by investing money. For example, they might invest in real estate or play the stock market. These people incur all kinds of expenses, such as fees paid to money managers or financial planners, legal and accounting fees, and interest on money borrowed to buy investment property. In the past, these and other investment expenses (also called expenses for the production of income) were tax deductible, subject to some important limitations. However, the Tax Cuts and Jobs Act eliminated many of these deductions for 2018 through 2025. Investment deductions are not covered in this book.

Business Deductions

Home business owners usually have to spend money on their businesses— for example, for equipment, supplies, or business travel. Most business expenses are deductible sooner or later. It makes no difference for tax deduction purposes whether you run your business from home or from an outside office or workplace—either way, you are entitled to deduct your legitimate business expenses. This book is about the many deductions available to people who are in business and who happen to work from home.

You Pay Taxes Only on Your Business Profits

The federal income tax law recognizes that you must spend money to make money. Virtually every home business, however small, incurs some expenses. Even someone with a low-overhead business (such as a freelance writer) must buy paper, computer equipment, and office supplies. Some home businesses incur substantial expenses, even exceeding their income.

You are not legally required to pay tax on every dollar your business takes in (your gross business income). Instead, you owe tax only on the amount left over after your business's deductible expenses are subtracted from your gross income (this remaining amount is called your net profit). Although some tax deduction calculations can get a bit complicated, the basic math is simple: The more deductions you take, the lower your net profit will be, and the less tax you will have to pay.

> **EXAMPLE:** Karen, a sole proprietor, earned $50,000 this year from her consulting business, which she operates from her home office. Fortunately, she doesn't have to pay income tax on the entire $50,000—her gross income. Instead, she can deduct various business expenses, including a $5,000 home office deduction (see Chapter 6) and a $5,000 deduction for equipment expenses (see Chapter 5). She deducts these expenses from her $50,000 gross income to arrive at her net profit: $40,000. She pays income tax only on this net profit amount.

Claiming Your Deductions

All tax deductions are a matter of legislative grace, which means that you can take a deduction only if it is specifically allowed by one or more provisions of the tax law. You usually do not have to indicate on your tax return which tax law provision gives you the right to take a particular deduction. If you are audited by the IRS, however, you'll have to provide a legal basis for every deduction you take. If the IRS concludes that your deduction wasn't justified, it will deny the deduction and charge you back taxes, interest and, in some cases, penalties.

Make Sure You Are in Business

Only businesses can claim business tax deductions. This probably seems like a simple concept, but it can get tricky. Even though you might believe you are running a business, the IRS may beg to differ. If your home business doesn't turn a profit for several years in a row, the IRS might decide that you are engaged in a hobby rather than a business. This may not sound like a big deal, but it could have disastrous tax consequences: As a result of the Tax Cuts and Jobs Act, people engaged in hobbies are not entitled to any tax deductions during 2018 through 2025, while businesses can deduct all kinds of expenses.

Fortunately, careful taxpayers can usually avoid this unhappy outcome. (See Chapter 2 for tips that will help you convince the IRS that you really are running a business.)

How Businesses Are Taxed

If your home business earns money (as you undoubtedly hope it will), you will have to pay taxes on your profits. How you pay those taxes will depend on how you have structured your business. So before getting further into the details of tax deductions, it's important to understand what type of business you have formed (a sole proprietorship, partnership, limited liability company, or corporation), and how you will pay tax on your business's profit.

> **RESOURCE**
> **Need help figuring out how to structure your business?** Although most home businesses are sole proprietorships, that may not be the best business form for you. If you need to decide how to organize a new business or you want to know whether you should change your current business form, refer to *LLC or Corporation? Choose the Right Form for Your Business*, by Anthony Mancuso (Nolo).

Basic Business Forms

Every business, from a part-time operation you run from home while in your jammies to a Fortune 500 multinational company housed in a gleaming skyscraper, has a legal structure. If you're running a business right now, it has a legal form—even if you never made a conscious decision about how it should be legally organized.

Sole Proprietorship—The Most Popular Home Business Entity

A sole proprietorship is a one-owner business. According to the Small Business Administration, 90% of all home businesses are sole proprietorships. Unlike the other business forms, a sole proprietorship has no legal existence separate from the business owner. It cannot sue or be sued, own property in its own name, or file its own tax returns. The business owner (proprietor) personally owns all of the assets of the business and controls its operations. If you're running a one-person home business and you haven't incorporated or formed a limited liability company, you are a sole proprietor. However, you can't be a sole proprietor if two or more people own your home business, unless you are one of two spouses who jointly own and run their home business together. See Chapter 16 for a detailed discussion about how to legally organize a husband and wife home business.

Other Business Forms You Can Use

Only about 10% of home businesses adopt a business form other than a sole proprietorship. These other forms include:

- **Partnerships.** A partnership is a form of shared ownership and management of a business. The partners contribute money, property, or services to the partnership; in return, they receive a share of the profits it earns, if any. The partners jointly manage the partnership business. A partnership automatically comes into existence whenever two or more people enter into business together to earn a profit and don't incorporate or form a limited liability company. Thus, if you're running a home business with somebody else, you are in a partnership right now (unless you've formed an LLC or a corporation). Although many partners enter into written partnership agreements, no written agreement is required to form a partnership.

- **Corporations.** Unlike a sole proprietorship or partnership, a corporation cannot simply spring into existence—it can only be created by filing incorporation documents with your state government. A corporation is a legal entity distinct from its owners. It can hold title to property, sue and be sued, have bank accounts, borrow money, hire employees, and perform other business functions. For tax purposes, there are two types of corporations: S corporations (also called small business corporations) and C corporations (also called regular corporations). The most important difference between the two types of corporations is how they are taxed. An S corporation pays no taxes itself—instead, its income or loss is passed on to its owners, who must pay personal income taxes on their share of the corporation's profits. A C corporation is a separate taxpaying entity that pays taxes on its profits (see "Tax Treatment," below).

- **Limited Liability Companies.** The limited liability company (LLC) is like a sole proprietorship or partnership in that its owners (called members) jointly own and manage the business and share in the profits. However, an LLC is also like a corporation. Because its owners must file papers with the state to create the LLC, it exists as a separate legal entity, and the LLC structure gives owners some protection from liability for business debts.

Tax Treatment

Your business's legal form will determine how it is treated for tax purposes. There are two different ways that business entities can be taxed: The business itself can be taxed as a separate entity, or the business's profits and losses can be passed through to the owners, who include these amounts on their individual tax returns.

Pass-Through Entities: Sole Proprietorships, Partnerships, LLCs, and S Corporations

Sole proprietorships and S corporations are always pass-through entities. LLCs and partnerships are almost always pass-through entities as well—partnerships and multiowner LLCs are automatically taxed as partnerships when they are created. One-owner LLCs are automatically taxed like sole proprietorships. However, LLC and partnership owners have the option of choosing to have their entities taxed as C corporations or S corporations by filing elections with the IRS. This is rarely done.

A pass-through entity does not pay any taxes itself. Instead, the business's profits or losses are passed through to its owners, who include them on their own personal tax returns (IRS Form 1040). If a profit is passed through to the owner, the owner must add that money to any income from other sources and pay tax on the total amount. If a loss is passed through, the owner can generally use it to offset income from other sources—for example, salary from a job, interest, investment income, or a spouse's income (as long as the couple files a joint tax return). The owner can subtract the business loss from this other income, which leaves a lower total subject to tax.

> **EXAMPLE:** Lisa is a sole proprietor who works part time from home doing engineering consulting. During her first year in business, she incurs $10,000 in expenses and earns $5,000, giving her a $5,000 loss from her business. She reports this loss on IRS Schedule C, which she files with her personal income tax return (Form 1040). Because Lisa is a sole proprietor, she can deduct this $5,000 loss from any income she has, including her $100,000 annual salary from her engineering job. This saves her about $2,000 in total taxes for the year.

Owners of pass-through entities qualify for a new pass-through income tax deduction of up to 20% of their business income under the Tax Cuts and Jobs Act. See Chapter 7 for a detailed discussion.

Although pass-through entities don't pay taxes, their income and expenses must still be reported to the IRS as follows:

- **Sole proprietors** must file IRS Schedule C, *Profit or Loss From Business*, with their tax returns. This form lists all the proprietor's business income and deductible expenses.
- **Partnerships** are required to file an annual tax form (Form 1065, *U.S. Return of Partnership Income*) with the IRS. Form 1065 is used to report partnership revenues, expenses, gains, and losses. The partnership must also provide each partner with an IRS Schedule K-1, *Partner's Share of Income, Deductions, Credits, etc.*, listing the partner's share of partnership income and expenses (copies of these schedules must also be attached to IRS Form 1065). Partners must then file IRS Schedule E, *Supplemental Income and Loss*, with their individual income tax returns, showing their partnership income and deductions.
- **S corporations** must file information returns with the IRS on Form 1120S, *U.S. Income Tax Return for an S Corporation*, showing how much the business earned or lost and each shareholder's portion of the corporate income or loss. Unlike with the other pass-through entities, S corporation owners ordinarily work as employees of their

corporation. This can help them maximize the new 20% pass-through tax deduction (see Chapter 7 for more information).

- **An LLC** with only one member is treated like a sole proprietorship for tax purposes. The member reports profits, losses, and deductions on Schedule C—just like a sole proprietor. An LLC with two or more members is ordinarily treated like a partnership: The LLC must prepare and file IRS Form 1065, *Partnership Return of Income*, showing the allocation of profits, losses, credits, and deductions passed through to the members. The LLC must also prepare and distribute to each member a Schedule K-1 showing the member's allocations of profits, losses, credits, and deductions.

Regular C Corporations—Creating Two Taxable Entities

A regular C corporation is the only business form that is not a pass-through entity. Instead, a C corporation is taxed separately from its owners. C corporations must pay income taxes on their net income and file corporate tax returns with the IRS, using Form 1120, *U.S. Corporation Income Tax Return*, or Form 1120-A, *U.S. Corporation Short-Form Income Tax Return*. They also have their own income tax rates. Starting in 2018, the tax rate for regular C corporations was reduced from a top rate of 35% to a flat tax of 21% on all C corporation income. See IRS Publication 542, *Corporations*, for more information.

When you form a C corporation, you have to take charge of two separate taxpayers: your corporation and yourself. Your C corporation must pay tax on all of its income. You pay personal income tax on C corporation income only when it is distributed to you in the form of salary, bonuses, or dividends. However, you might have to pay special penalty taxes if you keep too much money in your corporation to avoid having to pay personal income tax on it.

C corporations can take all the same business tax deductions that pass-through entities take. In addition, because a C corporation is a separate tax-paying entity, it may provide its employees with tax-free fringe benefits, then deduct the entire cost of the benefits from the corporation's income as a business expense. No other form of business entity can do this. (Although they are corporations, S corporations cannot deduct the cost of benefits provided to shareholders who hold more than 2% of the corporate stock.)

What Businesses Can Deduct

Business owners, whether they work at home or elsewhere, can deduct several broad categories of business expenses:

- start-up expenses
- operating expenses
- capital expenses, and
- inventory costs.

There is also a 20% pass-through tax deduction available to pass-through business entities (any business entity other than a regular C corporation). This section provides an introduction to each of these deduction categories (they are covered in greater detail in later chapters).

Start-Up Expenses

Start-up expenses are those you incur to get your home business up and running—such as license fees, advertising costs, attorneys' and accounting fees, market research, and office supplies expenses. Start-up costs are not currently deductible—that is, you cannot deduct them all in the year in which you incur them. However, you can deduct up to $5,000 in start-up costs in the first year your new business is in operation. You must deduct amounts over $5,000 over the next 15 years. Most home business owners should be able to avoid incurring substantial start-up expenses. (See Chapter 3 for a detailed discussion of deducting start-up expenses.)

Operating Expenses

Operating expenses are the ongoing day-to-day costs a business incurs to stay in business. They include such things as rent, utilities, salaries, supplies, travel expenses, car expenses, and repairs and maintenance. These expenses (unlike start-up expenses) are currently deductible—that is, you can deduct them all in the year when you pay them. (See Chapter 4 for more on operating expenses.)

Capital Expenses

Capital assets are things you buy for your business that have a useful life of more than one year, such as equipment, vehicles, books, office furniture, machinery, and patents you buy from others. These costs, called capital expenses, are considered to be part of your investment in your business, not day-to-day operating expenses.

The cost of business real estate—buildings and building components— must always be deducted over many years, a process called depreciation. Commercial real estate is depreciated over 39 years. However, the cost of personal property used in business—computers, for example—can usually be deducted in a single year using 100% bonus depreciation (available through 2022) or Section 179 of the tax code. Bonus depreciation and Section 179 are discussed in detail in Chapter 5.

Pass-Through Tax Deduction

Business owners (other than those who have formed a C corporation) may qualify for a special pass-through tax deduction starting in 2018 through 2025. This enables them to deduct from their income taxes up to 20% of their net business income. There are certain limitations and requirements that must be met to qualify for this 20% pass-through deduction. (See Chapter 7 for more information.)

Inventory

If your home business involves making or buying products, you'll have an inventory. Inventory includes almost anything you make or buy to resell to customers. It doesn't matter whether you manufacture the goods yourself or buy finished goods from someone else and resell them to customers. Inventory doesn't include tools, equipment, or other items that you use in your business; it refers only to items that you buy or make to sell.

Before 2018, you had to deduct inventory costs separately from all other business expenses—you deducted inventory costs as you sold the inventory. However, starting in 2018, smaller businesses have the option to deduct inventory (1) as nonincidental materials and supplies, or (2) in accordance with their accounting method, enabling cash method businesses to deduct inventory in the year it's paid for. (See Chapter 10 for more on deducting inventory.)

Adding It All Up: The Value of Tax Deductions

Most taxpayers, even sophisticated businesspeople, don't fully appreciate just how much money they can save with tax deductions. Of course, only part of any deduction will end up back in your pocket as money saved. Because a deduction represents income on which you don't have to pay tax, the value of any deduction is the amount of tax you would have had to pay on that income had you not deducted it. So a deduction of $1,000 won't save you $1,000—it will save you whatever you would otherwise have had to pay as tax on that $1,000 of income.

Federal and State Income Taxes

To determine how much income tax a deduction will save you, you must first figure out your income tax bracket. The United States has a progressive income tax system for individual taxpayers. The higher your income, the higher your tax rate. As a result of the enactment of the Tax Cuts and Jobs Act, there are seven different tax rates (called tax brackets), ranging from 10% of taxable income to 37%. (See the chart below.)

You move from one bracket to the next only when your taxable income exceeds the bracket amount. For example, if you are a single taxpayer, you pay 10% income tax on all your taxable income up to $9,875 in 2020. If your taxable income exceeds that amount, the next tax rate (12%) applies to all your income over $9,875—but the 10% rate still applies to the first $9,875. If your income exceeds the 12% bracket amount, the next tax rate (22%) applies to the excess amount, and so on until the top bracket of 37% is reached.

The tax bracket in which the last dollar you earn for the year falls is called your marginal tax bracket. For example, if you have $80,000 in taxable income, your marginal tax bracket is 22%. To determine how much federal income tax a deduction will save you, multiply the amount of the deduction by your marginal tax bracket. For example, if your marginal tax bracket is 22%, you will save 22¢ in federal income taxes for every dollar you are able to claim as a deductible business expense (22% × $1 = 22¢).

The following table lists the 2020 federal income tax brackets for single and married individual taxpayers.

Income tax brackets are adjusted each year for inflation. For current brackets, see IRS Publication 505, *Tax Withholding and Estimated Tax*.

2020 Federal Personal Income Tax Brackets		
Rate	Married Filing Jointly	Individual Return
10%	$0–$19,750	$0–$9,875
12%	$19,751–$80,250	$9,876–$40,125
22%	$80,251–$171,150	$40,126–$85,525
24%	$171,151–$326,620	$85,526–$163,300
32%	$326,621–$414,700	$163,301–$207,350
35%	$414,701–$622,050	$207,351–$518,400
37%	Over $622,050	Over $518,400

You can also deduct your business expenses from any state income tax you must pay. The average state income tax rate is about 6%, although seven states (Alaska, Florida, Nevada, South Dakota, Texas, Washington, and Wyoming) don't have an income tax. (New Hampshire residents pay tax on gambling winnings and income earned through interest and dividends only.) You can find your state's tax rates at the Federation of Tax Administrators website at www.taxadmin.org.

State Income Tax Deductions May Differ

Generally, you may deduct the same business expenses for state tax purposes as you do for your federal taxes. However, there are some exceptions. You should contact your state tax agency for details. Every state tax agency has a website; you can find links to all of them at www.taxsites.com/state-links.html.

Self-Employment Taxes

Everyone who works—business owner and employee alike—is required to pay Social Security and Medicare taxes. Employees pay one-half of these taxes through payroll deductions; the employer must pony up the other half and send the entire payment to the IRS. Business owners must pay all of these taxes themselves. Business owners' Social Security and Medicare contributions are called self-employment taxes.

Self-employment taxes consist of two separate taxes: the Social Security tax and the Medicare tax.

Social Security tax. The Social Security tax is a flat 12.4% tax on net self-employment income up to an annual ceiling that is adjusted for inflation each year. In 2020, the ceiling was $137,700 in net self-employment income. Thus, a person who had that much or more in income would pay $17,075 in Social Security taxes.

Medicare tax. There are two Medicare tax rates; a 2.9% tax is levied up to an annual ceiling—$200,000 for single taxpayers and $250,000 for married couples filing jointly. All income above that ceiling is taxed at a 3.8% rate. Thus, for example, a single taxpayer with $300,000 in net self-employment income would pay a 2.9% Medicare tax on the first $200,000 of income and a 3.8% tax on the remaining $100,000. This 0.9% Medicare tax increase applies to high-income employees as well as to the self-employed. Employees must pay a 2.35% Medicare tax on the portion of their wages over the $200,000/$250,000 thresholds (their one-half of 2.9% (1.45%) plus the 0.9%). In addition, Medicare taxes must be paid by high-income taxpayers on investment income. (See "Investing and Other Income-Producing Activities" in Chapter 2.)

For both the self-employed and employees, the combined Social Security and Medicare tax is 15.3% up to the Social Security tax ceiling.

However, the effective self-employment tax rate is lower because (1) you are allowed to deduct half of your self-employment taxes from your net income for income tax purposes and (2) you pay self-employment tax on only 92.35% of your net self-employment income. But taxpayers who earn more than the $200,000/$250,000 thresholds, can't deduct the 0.9% increase in Medicare tax from their income.

Like income taxes, self-employment taxes are paid on the net profit you earn from a business. Thus, deductible business expenses reduce the amount of self-employment tax you have to pay by lowering your net profit. This makes business tax deductions doubly valuable.

Total Tax Savings

When you add up your savings in federal, state, and self-employment taxes, you can see the true value of a business tax deduction. For example, if you earn $80,000, a business deduction can be worth as much as 22% (in federal income tax) + 15.3% (in self-employment taxes) + 6% (in state taxes—depending on what state you live in). That adds up to a whopping 43.3% savings. (If you itemize your personal deductions, your actual tax savings from a business deduction is a bit less because it reduces your state income tax and therefore reduces the federal income tax savings from this itemized deduction.) If you buy a $1,000 computer for your business and you deduct the expense, you save about $433 in taxes. In effect, the government is paying for almost half of your business expenses. This is why it's so important to know all of the business deductions to which you are entitled—and to take advantage of every one.

> ⓘ **CAUTION**
>
> **Don't buy stuff just to get a tax deduction.** Although tax deductions can be worth a lot, it doesn't make sense to buy something you don't need just to get a deduction. After all, you still have to pay for the item, and the tax deduction you get in return will only cover a portion of the cost. If you buy a $1,000 computer, you'll probably be able to deduct less than half the cost. That means you're still out over $500—money you've spent for something you don't need. On the other hand, if you really do need a computer, the deduction you're entitled to is like found money—and it may help you buy a better computer than you could otherwise afford.

Businesses That Lose Money

Unfortunately, businesses don't always earn a profit. If your losses exceed your income from all sources for the year, you have a "net operating loss" (NOL for short). NOLs are particularly likely to occur when businesses are first starting out or when economic conditions are bad. The coronavirus (COVID-19) pandemic will likely result in many NOLs in 2020. In response, the Coronavirus Aid Relief and Economic Security Act (CARES Act) enacted by Congress in 2020 loosened the strict rules for claiming NOLs that had been imposed by the Tax Cuts and Jobs Act. As a result, there are three separate sets of rules for deducting NOLs, depending on when they occur.

If your business lost money during 2018 through 2020, your loss could provide you with a refund of all or part of previous years' taxes in as little as 90 days—a quick infusion of cash that should be very helpful.

What Is an NOL?

If your business deductions exceed your business income, you have a tax loss for the year. If, like most home business owners, you're a sole proprietor, you may deduct any loss your business incurs from your other income for the year— for example, income from a job, investment income, or your spouse's income (if you file a joint return). If your business is operated as an LLC, S corporation, or partnership, your share of the business's losses are passed through the business to your individual return and deducted from your other personal income in the same way as a sole proprietor. However, if you operate your business through a C corporation, you can't deduct a business loss on your personal return. It belongs to your corporation.

After deducting your tax loss from other income, any remaining loss is called a net operating loss (NOL).

> **EXAMPLE:** Jason incurred $30,000 in losses from his home-based sole proprietorship business for the year and earned $10,000 from a part-time job. His NOL is $20,000.

NOLs for 2017 and Earlier

For NOLs occurring during 2017 and earlier, business owners could "carry a loss back"—that is, they could apply an NOL to past tax years by filing an application for refund or amended return. This enabled them to get a refund for all or part of the taxes they paid in past years. NOLs could generally be carried back two years, and then carried forward 20 years. Moreover, NOLs could reduce taxable income to zero in the carryback or carry forward years. You also had the option to elect to only carry an NOL forward to future years.

> **EXAMPLE:** Assume that Jason from the previous example incurred his $20,000 NOL in 2017. He could carry it back to 2015 and obtain a refund of the tax he paid that year. If he does not fully use the NOL, it is carried forward to 2015 and then to 2018 and future years. He also had the option of waiving the carryback and carrying the $20,000 forward to 2017, where it could offset up to 100% of his income. Any unused amount would be carried forward up to 20 years.

NOLs Under the Tax Cuts and Jobs Act

The Tax Cuts and Jobs Act (TCJA) that went into effect in 2018, eliminated all carrybacks of NOLs. Instead, taxpayers were only allowed to deduct them in any number of future years. Moreover, an NOL could only offset up to 80% of taxable income (before the pass-through deduction) for any year.

> **EXAMPLE:** Assume that Jason from the previous examples incurred his $20,000 NOL in 2018. Because of the TCJA, he could not carry it back to 2016 and obtain a refund of the tax he paid that year. He could only carry it forward to 2019 where it could offset a maximum of 80% of his income. Any remaining amount would have to be deducted in 2020 and later.

Special Rules for NOLs During 2018 through 2020

Due the economic devastation caused by the coronavirus (COVID-19) pandemic, Congress amended the NOL rules for 2018 through 2020. For these years, an NOL may be carried back five years and then carried forward indefinitely until it is used up. Ordinarily, you must carry an NOL back to the earliest year within the carryback period in which there is taxable income, then to the next earliest year, and so on. Also, NOLs for these years may offset 100% of taxable income to reduce the tax liability to zero.

> **EXAMPLE:** Assume that Jason from the previous examples incurred his $20,000 NOL in 2020. He may carry it back to 2015 to reduce his taxable income for that year and obtain a refund of up to 100% of the tax he paid. If he has any NOL amount remaining, it is applied to 2016 through 2019 in turn. Any remaining NOL is applied to 2021 and any number of future years. Alternatively, Jason could elect only to carry his NOL forward to 2021 and future years.

Claiming an NOL Refund

You can only take advantage of an NOL after you've completed and filed your tax return for the year involved. The return will show the amount of the NOL. Thus, you won't be able to take advantage of a 2020 NOL until the 2020 tax year ends and you file your 2020 tax return.

There are two ways to claim a refund for prior years' taxes due to an NOL. The quickest way is to file IRS Form 1045, *Application for Tentative Refund.* If you file Form 1045, the IRS is required to send your refund within 90 days. Additionally, the IRS makes only a limited examination of the claim for omissions and computational errors.

Ordinarily, you must file Form 1045 within one year after the end of the year in which the NOL arose. Thus, for a calendar year 2018 NOL, the deadline was December 31, 2019. However, the IRS extended the deadline for filing Form 1045 for 2018 NOLs by six months until June 30, 2020.

The other way to deduct an NOL is to amend your tax return for the year involved by filing IRS Form 1040-X, *Amended U.S. Individual Income Tax Return.* You have three years after the end of the tax year to file Form 1040-X.

Carrying an NOL Forward

You don't have to carry an NOL for 2018–2020 back five years if you don't want to. You can elect to apply the NOL only to future years. To do so, you must affirmatively waive the carryback on your tax return. You should consider electing the carry-forward option if one or more of the following reasons apply:

- carrying the NOL back will generate little or no tax refund
- you don't need the immediate cash infusion from a tax refund
- you anticipate the NOL deduction will result in greater tax savings in future years—for example, because your tax rate will be higher for those years, or
- you want to reduce the taxes you'll have to pay next year due to cash flow issues if you've made inadequate estimated tax payments.

The decision to carry back an NOL is made on a year-by-year basis. For example, if you have NOLs for 2019 and 2020, you could carry back the 2019 NOL, but elect to only carry forward the 2020 NOL. To waive the five-year carryback of your NOL, you must attach a statement to your tax return for the year. For 2018 and 2019 NOLs, you must make this election on your 2020 tax return. You must attach a separate statement for each year for which you are waiving the NOL carryback, and state that you elect to apply Revenue Procedure 2020-24.

Annual Dollar Limit on NOL Deduction

Another change made by the Tax Cuts and Jobs Act was to limit deductions of "excess business losses" by individual business owners during 2018 through 2025. Married taxpayers filing jointly could deduct no more than $519,000 per year in total business losses. Individual taxpayers could deduct no more than $259,000. Unused losses had to be deducted in any number of future years as part of the taxpayer's NOL carry-forward. The CARES Act completely eliminated this limitation for losses incurred during 2018 through 2020. Thus, taxpayers with very large losses for any of these years can deduct them in full. The excess business loss limit is scheduled to return for 2021 through 2025.

RESOURCE

Need to know more about NOLs? Refer to IRS Publication 536, *Net Operating Losses (NOLs) for Individuals, Estates, and Trusts,* for more information. You can download it from the IRS website at www.irs.gov.

Is Your Home Business Really a Business?

You must operate a bona fide business (in the eyes of the IRS) to take business deductions. This point may seem obvious, but it has gotten more home businesspeople in trouble with the IRS than almost any other provision of the tax law. By declaring your home activity to be a hobby rather than a business, the IRS can, at one fell swoop, eliminate all of your tax deductions for the activity. Because hobbies are ordinarily carried on at home, home ventures are especially vulnerable to being viewed as hobbies by the IRS. That's why it's so important for you to be able to show the IRS that your home activity is a real business.

Proving That You Are in Business

For tax purposes, a business is an activity you regularly and continuously engage in primarily to earn a profit. You don't have to show a profit every year to qualify as a business. As long as your primary purpose is to make money, you should qualify as a business (even if you show a loss when you're first starting out, and even afterward, depending on the circumstances). Your business can be conducted from home, full time or part time, as long as you work at it regularly and continuously. And you can have more than one business at the same time. However, if your primary purpose is something other than making a profit—for example, to incur deductible expenses or just to have fun—the IRS may find that your activity is a hobby rather than a business. If this happens, you'll face some potentially disastrous tax consequences.

> **EXAMPLE:** Jorge and Vivian Lopez thought that they had found an ideal way to save on their income taxes (and enjoy themselves as well). They started an Amway distributorship as a sideline business. They ran the distributorship out of their home. While they had a lot of fun socializing with family and friends, they never came close to earning a profit. They claimed a loss from this business of over $18,000 a year for two straight years. They deducted this loss from Jorge's salary as a full-time petroleum engineer, which saved them thousands of dollars in income taxes. Things were going great taxwise, until the IRS audited the Lopezes' tax returns and concluded that the Amway

distributorship was a hobby rather than a business. This meant the Lopezes could no longer deduct their Amway losses from Jorge's salary, and they owed the IRS over $17,000 in back taxes for the deductions they had already taken. (*Lopez v. Comm'r.*, TC Memo 2003-142.)

Among the activities the IRS has identified as possible hobbies are the following that are normally carried out at home: crafts, stamp collecting, dog breeding, art, photography, and writing. This is a nonexclusive list.

> ## CAUTION
> **Beware of home business tax scams.** Many self-proclaimed tax experts market tax avoidance scams on the Internet and elsewhere. According to the IRS, one of the top 12 tax scams involves setting up a phony business at home and then deducting personal expenses, such as rent or mortgage payments, as business expenses. This scam has been around for years and the IRS is well aware of it—which means you won't get away with it if you're audited. You'll have to pay back the value of any tax deductions you claimed, plus penalties.
>
> Popular home business scams include processing medical insurance claims, online schemes, mail order scams, envelope stuffing, assembling craft items or sewing, multilevel marketing distributorships, and chain letters. Be extremely skeptical about work-at-home promotions that claim you'll be able to reap substantial tax deductions without making a substantial monetary investment in your home business, working at it regularly, or turning a profit.

Your home-based activity can be a business for tax purposes only if you can show that you are engaged in it to earn a profit, not simply to have fun or pursue a personal interest. If you can't prove a profit motive for the activity, you will be considered a hobbyist and forced to enter tax hell.

The IRS has established two tests to determine whether someone has a profit motive. One is a simple mechanical test that looks at whether you have earned a profit in three of the last five years. The other is a more complex test designed to determine whether you act like you want to earn a profit.

> ⚠ **CAUTION**
>
> **Personal investing is not a business.** Personal investing, whether in stocks, real estate, collectibles, or anything else that makes money, is not a business, even though most people do it to earn a profit. See "Investing and Other Income-Producing Activities," later in this chapter.

Profit Test

If your venture earns a profit in three of five consecutive years, the IRS will presume that you have a profit motive. The IRS and courts look at your tax returns for each year you claim to be in business to see whether you turned a profit. Any legitimate profit—no matter how small—qualifies; you don't have to earn a particular amount or percentage. Careful year-end planning can help your business show a profit for the year. If clients owe you money, for example, you can press for payment before the end of the year. You can also put off paying expenses or buying new equipment until the new year.

Even if you meet the three-of-five test, the IRS can still try to claim that your activity is a hobby, but it will have to prove that you don't have a profit motive. In practice, the IRS usually doesn't attack ventures that pass the profit test unless the numbers have clearly been manipulated just to meet the standard.

The presumption that you are in business applies to your third profitable year and extends to all later years within the five-year period beginning with your first profitable year.

> **EXAMPLE:** Tom began to work as a self-employed graphic designer in 2016. Due to economic conditions and the difficulty of establishing a new business, his income varied dramatically from year to year. However, as the chart below shows, he managed to earn a profit in three of the first five years that he was in business.
>
> | Year | Losses | Profits |
> |------|--------|---------|
> | 2016 | $10,000 | |
> | 2017 | | $5,500 |
> | 2018 | $6,000 | |
> | 2019 | | $9,000 |
> | 2020 | | $18,000 |

If the IRS audits Tom's taxes for 2020, it must presume that he was in business during that year because he earned a profit during three of the five consecutive years ending with 2020. The presumption that Tom is in business extends through 2022, five years after his first profitable year (2017).

The IRS doesn't have to wait for five years after you start your activity to decide whether it is a business or hobby—it can audit you and classify your venture as a business or hobby at any time. However, you can give yourself some breathing room by filing IRS Form 5213, *Election to Postpone Determination as to Whether the Presumption Applies That an Activity Is Engaged in for Profit*, which requires the IRS to postpone its determination until you've been in business for at least five years.

Although this may sound like a good idea, it can backfire. Filing the election alerts the IRS to the fact that you might be a good candidate to audit on the hobby loss issue after five years. It also adds two years to the statute of limitations—the period in which the IRS can audit you and assess a tax deficiency. For this reason, almost no one ever files Form 5213. Also, you can't wait five years and then file the election once you know that you will pass the profit test. You must make the election within three years after the due date for the tax return for the first year you were in business—that is, within three years after the first April 15 following your first business year. So if you started doing business in 2020, you would have to make the election by April 15, 2024 (three years after the April 15, 2021 due date for your 2020 tax return).

There is one situation in which it might make sense to file Form 5213. If the IRS has already told you that you will be audited, you may want to file the election to postpone the audit for two years. However, you can do this only if the IRS audit notice is sent to you within three years after the due date for your first business tax return. If you're notified after this time, it's too late to file the election. In addition, you must file your election within 60 days after you receive an IRS audit notice, whenever it is given, or you'll lose the right to make the election.

Behavior Test

If you keep incurring losses and can't satisfy the profit test, don't panic. Millions of business owners are in the same boat, whether they work at home or in outside offices. The sad fact is that many businesses don't earn profits every year or even for many years in a row, especially when they're first starting out. Indeed, over *four million* sole proprietors file Schedule C tax forms each year showing a loss from their businesses, yet the IRS does not categorize all of these ventures as hobbies.

You can continue to treat your activity as a business and fully deduct your losses, even if you have yet to earn a profit. However, you must take steps to demonstrate that your business isn't a hobby, in case you ever face an audit. You must be able to convince the IRS that earning a profit—not having fun or accumulating tax deductions—is your primary motive for doing what you do. This will require some time and effort on your part. It will be especially difficult if you're engaged in a home-based activity that could objectively be considered fun—such as creating artwork, antique collecting, photography, or writing—but it can be done. People who have incurred losses for seven, eight, or nine years in a row have been able to convince the IRS that they were running businesses.

How does the IRS figure out whether you really want to earn a profit? IRS auditors can't read your mind to establish your motives, and they certainly aren't going to take your word for it. Instead, they look at whether you behave as though you want to make money.

Factors the IRS Considers

The IRS looks at the following objective factors to determine whether you are behaving like a person who wants to earn a profit (and therefore, should be classified as a business). You don't have to satisfy all of these factors to pass the test—the first three listed below (acting like a business, expertise, and time and effort expended) are the most important by far. Studies demonstrate that taxpayers who meet these three factors are always found to be in business, regardless of how they do on the rest of the criteria. (See "How to Pass the Behavior Test," below, for tips on satisfying these factors.)

The IRS factors are:

- **Whether you act like a business.** Among other things, acting like a business means you keep good books and other records and carry on your activities in a professional manner.
- **Your expertise.** People who are trying to make money usually have some knowledge and skill in the fields of their endeavors.
- **The time and effort you spend.** People who want to make profits work regularly and continuously. You don't have to work full time, but you must work regularly.
- **Your track record.** Having a track record of success in other businesses—whether or not they are related to your current business—helps show that you are trying to make money in your most recent venture.
- **Your history of profit and losses.** Even if you can't satisfy the profit test described in "Profit Test," above, earning a profit in at least some years helps show that you have a profit motive. This is especially true if you're engaged in a business that tends to be cyclical—that is, where one or two good years are typically followed by one or more bad years.
- **Your profits.** Earning a substantial profit, even after years of losses, can help show that you are trying to make a go of it. On the other hand, earning only small or occasional yearly profits when you have years of large losses and/or a large investment in the activity tends to show that you aren't in it for the money.
- **Your business assets.** Your profit includes money you make through the appreciation (increase in value) of your business assets. Even if you don't make any profit from your business's day-to-day operations, you can still show a profit motive if you stand to earn substantial profits when you sell your assets. Of course, this rule applies only to ventures that purchase assets that increase in value over time, such as land, collectibles, or buildings.
- **Your personal wealth.** The IRS figures that you probably have a profit motive if you don't have substantial income from other sources. After all, you'll need to earn money from your venture to survive. On the other hand, the IRS may be suspicious if you have substantial income from other sources (particularly if the losses from your venture generate substantial tax deductions).

- **The nature of your activity.** If your venture is inherently fun or recreational, the IRS may doubt that you are in it for the money. This means that you'll have a harder time convincing the IRS that you're in business if your venture involves activities such as art, crafts or sewing, photography, writing, antique or stamp collecting, or training and showing dogs or horses, for example. However, these activities can still be businesses, if you carry them on in a businesslike manner. Even if they don't qualify as businesses, they can still be classified as income-producing activities, which is better than being a hobby.

How to Pass the Behavior Test

Almost anyone with a home business can pass the behavior test, but it takes time, effort, and careful planning. Focus your efforts on the first three factors listed above. As noted earlier, a venture that can meet these three criteria will always be classified as a business. Here are some tips that will help you satisfy these crucial factors—and ultimately ace the behavior test.

Act Like a Businessperson

First and foremost, you must show that you carry on your activity in a businesslike manner. Doing the things outlined below will not only help you with the IRS, but will also help you actually earn a profit someday (or at least help you figure out that your business will not be profitable):

- **Keep good business records.** Keeping good records of your expenses and income from your activity is the single most important thing you can do to show that you want to earn a profit. Without good records, you'll never have an accurate idea of where you stand financially. Lack of records shows that you don't really care whether you make money or not—and it is almost always fatal in an IRS audit. You don't necessarily need an elaborate set of books; a simple record of your expenses and income will usually suffice. (See Chapter 15 for a detailed discussion of record keeping.)

EXAMPLE: A computer consultant who sold software on the side (at a loss) was found not to be profit motivated because he didn't keep adequate records. The tax court found that his failure to keep records meant that he was "unaware of the amount of revenue he could expect and had no concept of what his ultimate costs might be or how he might achieve any degree of cost efficiency." (*Flanagin v. Comm'r.*, TC Memo 1999-116.)

- **Keep a separate checking account.** Open up a separate checking account for your business. This will help you keep your personal and business expenses separate—another factor that shows you want to make money.
- **Create a business plan.** Draw up a business plan with a realistic profit and loss forecast—a projection of how much money your business will bring in, your expenses, and how much profit you expect to make. The forecast should cover the next five or ten years. It should show you earning a profit some time in the future (although it doesn't have to be within five years). Both the IRS and courts are usually impressed by good business plans.

RESOURCE

Need help drawing up a business plan? If you are really serious about making money, you will need a business plan. A business plan is useful not only to show the IRS that you are running a business, but also to convince others—such as lenders and investors—that they should support your venture financially. For detailed guidance on putting together a business plan, see *How to Write a Business Plan*, by Mike McKeever (Nolo).

- **Get business cards and letterhead.** It may seem like a minor matter but obtaining business stationery and business cards shows that you think you are in business. Hobbyists ordinarily don't have such things. You can use software programs to create your own inexpensive stationery and cards.

- **Create a website.** Most businesses have some sort of website that, at a minimum, provides contact information. Not having a website indicates you're not serious about being in business.
- **Obtain all necessary business licenses and permits.** Getting the required licenses and permits for your activities will show that you are acting like a business. For example, a home-based inventor who attempted to build a wind-powered ethanol generator in his backyard was found to be a hobbyist partly because he failed to get a permit to produce alcohol from the federal Bureau of Alcohol, Tobacco and Firearms.
- **Obtain a separate phone line for your home office.** Set up a separate phone line for your business (which may be a cellphone). This helps separate the personal from the professional and reinforces the idea that you're serious about making money.
- **Join professional organizations and associations.** Taking part in professional groups and organizations will help you make valuable contacts and obtain useful advice and expertise. This helps to show that you're motivated to earn a profit.

Expertise

If you're already an expert in your field, you're a step ahead of the game. But if you lack the necessary expertise, you can develop it by attending educational seminars and similar activities and/or consulting with other experts. Keep records of your efforts (for example, a certificate for completing a training course or your notes documenting your attendance at a seminar or convention).

Work Steadily

You don't have to work full time to show that you want to earn a profit. It's fine to hold a full-time job and work at your sideline business only part of the time. However, you must work regularly and continuously rather than sporadically. You may establish any schedule you want, as long as you work regularly. For example, you could work at your business an hour every day, or one day a week, as long as you stick to your schedule.

Although there is no minimum amount of time you must work, you'll have a hard time convincing the IRS that you want to make money if you work fewer than five or ten hours a week. Keep a log showing how much time you spend working. Your log doesn't have to be fancy—you can just mark down your hours and a summary of your activities each day on your calendar or appointment book.

Tax Consequences of Engaging in a Hobby

A hobby is something you do primarily for a purpose other than to make a profit—for example, to have fun, learn something, help your community, or impress your neighbors. Almost anything can be a hobby; common examples include creating artwork or crafts, photography, writing, or collecting coins, stamps, or other objects.

You do not want what you consider business activities to be deemed a hobby by the IRS. Because hobbies are not businesses, hobbyists cannot take the tax deductions to which businesspeople are entitled. However, for decades hobbyists were allowed to deduct their hobby-related expenses up to the amount of income the hobby earned during the year. Hobby expenses were deductible as a personal miscellaneous itemized deduction on IRS Schedule A. This meant they could be deducted only by taxpayers who itemized their personal deduction, and only if, and to the extent, they exceeded 2% of the hobbyist's adjusted gross income (total income minus business expenses and a few other expenses). This was not a very generous deduction, but it was better than nothing.

Unfortunately for people who earn income from hobbies, the Tax Cuts and Jobs Act completely eliminated the itemized deduction for hobby expenses, along with all other miscellaneous itemized deductions. The prohibition on deducting these expenses is in effect for 2018 through 2025. This means that taxpayers may not deduct any expenses they earn from hobbies during these years, but they still have to report and pay tax on any income they earn from their hobby!

> **EXAMPLE:** Charles runs a part-time dog sitting activity from his home. This year, he had $2,000 in expenses and earned $4,000 in income from dog sitting. The IRS determines that this activity is a hobby. As a result, his $2,000 in expenses cannot be deducted, but he must still report and pay income tax on the full $4,000 in income he earned.

This tax change could be particularly devastating for the millions of American who work as self-employed salespeople with multilevel marketing companies like Amway, Mary Kay, and Herbalife. The vast majority of participants in these sales schemes lose money and the IRS and tax court have routinely found such activities to be hobbies for tax purposes. Fortunately, there is a tax loophole that allows them to deduct some of their expenses. IRS regulations permit people whose hobby involves selling items to deduct the cost of goods sold from their gross receipts. (IRS Reg. 1.183-1(e).)

> **EXAMPLE:** Arthur is engaged in a hobby selling goods for a multilevel marketing company. This year he purchased $8,000 in inventory and earned $10,000 from product sales. He had $2,000 in other expenses. He may deduct his cost of goods sold from his gross receipts, leaving $2,000 in hobby income he must pay tax on. He may not deduct his other expenses.

Investing and Other Income-Producing Activities

You can earn money without being in business. Many people do this all the time (or try to) by engaging in personal investing—for example, by having personal bank accounts that pay interest or investing in stocks that pay dividends and appreciate in value over time (hopefully). Activities like these—that are pursued primarily for profit but aren't businesses—are called income-producing activities. They are neither businesses nor hobbies and they receive their own special income tax treatment.

Many of the moneymaking activities people engage in at home are income-producing activities, not businesses. The distinction is crucial because income-producing activities receive much less favorable tax treatment than businesses. Thus, you'll want to avoid this classification, if possible.

RESOURCE

Need more information on investment taxation? For detailed guidance on taxation for investments, refer to IRS Publication 550, *Investment Income and Expenses*. Like all IRS publications, you can download it from the IRS website at www.irs.gov, or obtain it by calling the IRS at 800-829-3676.

Tax Consequences of Income-Producing Activities

If, in the course of an income-producing activity, you incur expenses to produce rents or royalties, you can deduct these expenses directly from your gross income (just like business expenses). What are rents and royalties? Rent is what you earn from renting real estate. Thus, landlords who don't qualify as businesspeople may still fully deduct their expenses. Royalties are income from things like copyrights or patents, or mineral leases. If your income comes from real estate or royalties, you list it and your expenses on Schedule E, *Supplemental Income and Loss.*

Expenses incurred from any other income-producing activity—for example, investing—are miscellaneous itemized deductions. In the past, they were deductible as a personal itemized deduction on Schedule A to the extent they exceeded 2% of adjusted gross income. However, as a result of the Tax Cuts and Jobs Act, such expenses are not deductible at all for 2018 through 2025. Thus, for example, an investor in the stock market may not deduct fees for investment advice, accounting services, or the cost of subscriptions to investor newsletters. But such an investor must report and pay income tax on the investment income earned. There is one exception: Interest paid on money borrowed to make an investment is deductible up to the amount of income you earn from the investment. Also, fees and commissions paid directly from funds in an IRA or a pooled investment such as a mutual fund are subtracted from the income from the IRA. The investor only pays tax on the net income from the fund after such expenses are subtracted.

Medicare Tax on Investment Income

A 3.8% Medicare contribution tax must be paid on investment income by taxpayers whose adjusted gross income exceeds certain threshold amounts: $200,000 for single people and $250,000 for married couples filing jointly. If your AGI is below these amounts, then you don't need to worry about this tax. A taxpayer with income above those thresholds must pay the 3.8% Medicare tax on the lower of either:

- the amount that taxpayer's adjusted gross income (investment income plus other taxable income) exceeds $200,000 for single taxpayers, or $250,000 for married couples filing jointly, or
- the taxpayer's total net investment income (which is included in AGI).

> EXAMPLE: Phil and Penny are a married couple who file a joint return. Together, they earn $200,000 in wages and $350,000 in investment income. Their AGI is $550,000. Their taxable amount using the first bullet choice is $300,000 ($550,000–$250,000 = $300,000). Using the second, their second number is $350,000. Thus, they must pay the 3.8% Medicare tax on $300,000. Their Medicare contribution tax for the year will be $11,400 (3.8% × $300,000 = $11,400). However, if their wages were $350,000 and their investment income was $200,000, the first number would still be $300,000, but the second number would be $200,000. In this event, they would have to pay the 3.8% tax on $200,000, resulting in a $7,600 tax.

As the example shows, the tax applies only to people with relatively high incomes.

This tax does not apply to income from an active trade or business (see "Is Income From Your Home Business Subject to the Medicare Contribution Tax?" below). However, people in business must pay a 3.8% Medicare tax on their net self-employment income over similar

$200,000/$250,000 thresholds. Moreover, they must pay a 2.9% Medicare tax on their self-employment income below the threshold (plus Social Security taxes).

Is Income From Your Home Business Subject to the Medicare Contribution Tax?

If your home activity qualifies as a business for tax purposes, then your income from that business will most likely *not* be subject to the 3.8% Medicare contribution tax. The only way it would be subject to the tax would be if both of the following were true:

- Your AGI (from all activities) is over the $200,000/$250,000 threshold amounts.
- You (and your spouse, if any) do not "materially participate" in the home business.

So, if you don't earn over $200,000 (singles) or $250,000 (married filing jointly) per year, you can forget about this tax. If you do earn more than these amounts from all of your activities combined, then you would be subject to the tax only if your home business is deemed to be a "passive activity." A passive activity is one in which you (and your spouse, if any) don't "materially participate" in the business. There are several tests for material participation. The vast majority of home business owners should have no problem satisfying one of these tests. For example, you materially participate in a business if, during the year, you (and your spouse, if any):

- are the only people who work in the business
- spend over 500 hours per year working in the business, or
- spend over 100 hours working in the business, and no one else, including employees, puts in more than 100 hours.

EXAMPLE: Amy, an unmarried investment banker, earns $200,000 per year in salary. She also has a part-time home business selling merchandise online. She earns $50,000 from this business. Amy operates her home business by herself. Because Amy is the only person working at this business, it is not a passive activity so her income from the business is not subject to the net investment income tax. The same result would occur even if Amy had employees working for her home business, as long as she spent at least 500 hours working at it herself.

Types of Income-Producing Activities

Anything you do primarily to earn a profit is an income-producing activity, unless it constitutes a business. You determine whether an activity is done primarily for profit by applying the three-of-five-year profit test or the behavioral test discussed in "Proving That You Are in Business," above—the same tests used for businesses.

Personal Investing

Personal investing is by far the most common income-producing activity. Investing means making money in ways other than running a business—for example, you:

- put your money in a bank and earn interest
- buy stocks, bonds, or other securities in publicly traded corporations and earn money from dividends or from the securities' appreciation in value over time
- buy commodities like gold or pork bellies and earn money from their appreciation in value over time
- buy real estate and earn money from rents or from appreciation in the property's value over time, or
- purchase an interest in a privately owned business run by someone else and earn money from the increase in the business's value over time or payments from the business.

What all these activities have in common is that you are not engaged in the active, continuous, and regular management or control of a business. You are passive—you put your money in somebody else's business and hope your investment will increase in value due to their efforts, not yours. Or, you buy an item like gold, and then sit and wait for it to increase in value.

Personal investing is always an income-producing activity for tax purposes, not a business. It makes no difference whether you invest from home or an outside office. Thus, for example, you can't take a home office deduction when you direct your investments from a home office.

Other Activities

Investing is by far the most common and important income-producing activity, but it is by no means the only one. Almost any activity can qualify if your primary motive for engaging in it is making money, but you don't work at it enough for it to rise to the level of a business. You must work continuously and regularly at an activity for it to be a business.

Trading in Stocks as a Business

People who buy stocks, bonds, and other securities as personal investments are not in business for tax purposes. But professional securities dealers and traders in securities are in business because they are not investors.

Such people are not subject to the restrictions on deductions listed in "Tax Consequences of Income-Producing Activities," above. Thus, for example, a professional stock trader may take a home office deduction (provided, of course, that the other requirements for the deduction are met; see Chapter 6). Professional dealers and traders may not deduct the commissions they pay to buy stocks or other securities; these are added to the basis (value) of the securities for purposes of calculating gain or loss when they are sold. Traders who are sole proprietors list their expenses on Schedule C, *Profit or Loss From Business*. However, they list their income or loss from trading on Schedule D, *Capital Gains and Losses*.

Most people who buy and sell stocks and other securities do it as an investment. Professional stock traders do it as a business. What's the difference between a stock market investor and a professional trader? A trader's profits come from the *very act of trading*; an investor's come from dividends or from the increase in value of his or her holdings over time. The IRS says that to qualify as a professional trader, you must meet all of these requirements:

- You must seek to profit from daily market movements in the price of securities, not from dividends, interest, or capital appreciation.
- Your trading must be substantial.
- Your trading must be continuous and regular.

Any Type of Buying and Selling Can Be a Business

Buying and selling anything can be a business—it doesn't have to involve stock or other securities. If you earn your money from the activity of buying and selling and you engage in it regularly and continuously, you can qualify as a business. For example, thousands of people now have businesses buying and selling items on eBay. However, sporadic buying and selling is not a business, even though it is profitable—for example, occasionally selling items on eBay won't qualify as a business.

Getting Your Business Up and Running

E veryone knows that it costs money to get a new business up and running. But many people don't know that these costs—called start-up expenses—are subject to special tax rules. This chapter explains what types of costs are start-up expenses and how you can deduct them as quickly as possible.

What Are Start-Up Expenses?

To take business deductions, you must actually be running a business (see Chapter 2). This commonsense rule can lead to problems if you want to start (or buy) a new business. The money you spend to get your business up and running is not a currently deductible business operating expense because your business hasn't yet begun.

Instead, business start-up expenses are capital expenses—costs that you incur to acquire an asset (a business) that will benefit you for more than one year. Normally, you can't deduct these types of expenses until you sell or otherwise dispose of the business. However, a special tax rule allows you to deduct up to $5,000 in start-up expenses the first year you are in business, and then deduct the remainder, if any, in equal amounts over the next 15 years. (I.R.C. § 195.) Without this special rule for start-up expenses, these costs (capital expenses) would not be deductible until you sold or otherwise disposed of your business.

Once your business begins, the same expenses that were start-up expenses before your business began become currently deductible business operating expenses. For example, supplies you purchase *after* your home business starts are currently deductible operating expenses, but supplies you buy *before* your business begins are start-up expenses.

> **EXAMPLE:** Diana Drudge is sick of her office job. She decides to start a business as a home-based independent travel agent. Before her business begins, she spends $20,000 of her life savings on advertising. Her business finally starts on July 1, 2015. Because advertising is a start-up expense, she can't deduct the full cost in her first year of business—instead, she can deduct $5,000 of the expenses the first year she's in business and the remaining $15,000 in equal installments over 15 years (assuming she's in business that long).

This means she may deduct $1,000 of the remaining $15,000 for each full year she's in business, starting with the first year. However, Diana's business is open for only six months her first year, so she may deduct only $500 of the $15,000 that year, plus the initial $5,000 she's entitled to. Her total first year total deduction is $5,500.

Obviously, you want to spend no more than the first-year ceiling on start-up expenses so you don't have to wait 15 years to get all your money back. There are ways you can avoid spending more than the first-year threshold amount. These are described in "Avoiding the Start-Up Tax Rule's Bite," at the end of this chapter.

> **CAUTION**
>
> **Your business must actually start to have start-up expenses.** If your business never gets started, many of your expenses will not be deductible. So think carefully before spending your hard-earned money to investigate starting a new business venture (see "Avoiding the Start-Up Tax Rule's Bite," at the end of this chapter).

Common Start-Up Expenses

The vast majority of home business owners (87%, according to a Small Business Administration study) start new businesses rather than buying existing ventures. Most of the costs of investigating whether, where, and how to start a new business, as well as the cost of actually creating it, qualify as business start-up expenses.

Here are some common types of deductible start-up expenses:
- operating expenses incurred before the business begins, such as home office rent, telephone service, utilities, office supplies, equipment rental, and repairs
- the cost of investigating what it would take to create a successful business, including research on potential markets or products
- advertising costs, including advertising for your business opening
- costs for employee training before the business opens
- expenses related to obtaining financing, suppliers, customers, or distributors

- licenses, permits, and other fees, and
- fees paid to lawyers, accountants, consultants, and others for professional services.

Special Rules for Some Expenses

There are some costs related to opening a business that are not considered start-up expenses. Many of these costs are still deductible, but different rules and restrictions apply to the way they are deducted.

Expenses That Wouldn't Qualify as Business Operating Expenses

You get no deduction at all for preopening operating expenses that are not ordinary, necessary, directly related to the business, and reasonable in amount. (See Chapter 4 for a discussion of business operating expenses.) For example, you can't deduct the cost of pleasure travel or entertainment *unrelated* to your business. These expenses would not be deductible as operating expenses by an ongoing business, so you can't deduct them as start-up expenses either.

Inventory

The largest expense many home businesspeople incur before they start their businesses is for inventory—that is, buying the goods (or the materials to make them) that they will sell to customers. For example, if you decide to start an eBay business selling items you buy at flea markets, you would treat the items you purchase for resale as inventory. (See Chapter 10 for more on deducting inventory costs.)

Long-Term Assets

Long-term assets are things you purchase for your business that will last for more than one year, such as computers, office equipment, cars, and machinery. Long-term assets you buy before your business begins are not considered part of your start-up costs. Instead, you must treat these purchases like any other long-term asset you buy *after* your business begins: You must either depreciate the item over several years or deduct the cost in one year using bonus depreciation or Section 179. (Chapter 5 explains how to deduct long-term assets.) However, you can't take regular or bonus depreciation or Section 179 deductions until after your business begins.

Research and Development Costs

The tax law includes a special category for research and development expenses. These are costs a business incurs to discover something new (in the laboratory or experimental sense), such as a new invention, formula, prototype, or process. They include laboratory and computer supplies, salaries, rent, utilities, other overhead expenses, and equipment rental, but not the cost of purchasing long-term assets. Research and development costs are currently deductible under Section 174 of the Internal Revenue Code, even if you incur them before the business begins operations. This tax rule is a particular benefit to home-based inventors.

Organizational Costs

Costs you incur to form a partnership, limited liability company, or corporation are technically not part of your start-up costs. However, the rule for deducting these costs is the same as for start-up expenses. (I.R.C. § 248.) But, if you form a one-member LLC, you get no deduction at all if your start-up expenses exceed $5,000.

Buying an Existing Business

Different (and harsher) rules apply if you buy an existing business rather than creating a new one. The money you pay to actually purchase the existing business is not deductible. Instead, it is a capital expense that becomes part of the tax basis of your business. If and when you sell the business, you will be able to deduct this amount from any profit you make on the sale before taxes are assessed. The expenses you incur to decide *whether* to purchase a business and *which* business you should buy are start-up expenses. Few home business owners (only 13%, according to the Small Business Administration) buy existing businesses, so this rule probably won't apply to you.

What's Tax Basis?

Tax basis is accounting lingo for your investment in property for tax purposes. Generally, your tax basis is the amount you paid for the property plus the costs of any improvements you make to it. You need to know your basis to figure your gain or loss on a sale, whether you sell a single item of property or an entire business. Chapter 5 explains how to figure out your tax basis.

Expanding an Existing Business

What if you already have a home business and decide to expand your operation? The cost of expanding an existing business is considered a business operating expense, not a start-up expense. As long as these costs are ordinary and necessary, they are currently deductible. However, this rule applies only when the expansion involves a business that is the same as—or similar to—the existing business. The costs of expanding into a new business are start-up costs, not operating expenses.

When Does a Business Begin?

The date when your home business begins for tax purposes marks an important turning point. Operating expenses you incur after your business starts are currently deductible, while expenses you incur before this crucial date may have to be deducted over many years.

A new business begins for tax purposes when it starts to function as a going concern and performs the activities for which it was organized. (*Richmond Television Corp. v. U.S.*, 345 F.2d 901 (4th Cir. 1965).) The IRS says that a venture becomes a going concern when it acquires all of the assets necessary to perform its intended functions and puts those assets to work. In other words, your business begins when you start doing business, whether or not you are actually earning any money.

If Your Business Doesn't Last 15 Years

Not all home businesses last for 15 years. In fact, most small businesses don't last this long. If you had more than $5,000 in start-up expenses and are in the process of deducting the excess amount, you don't lose the value of your deductions if you sell or close your business before you have had a chance to deduct all of your start-up expenses. You can deduct any leftover start-up expenses as ordinary business losses. (I.R.C. § 195(b)(2).) This means that you may be able to deduct these losses from any income you have that year, deduct them in future years, or deduct them from previous years' taxes.

If you sell your business or its assets, your leftover start-up costs will be added to your tax basis in the business. This is just as good as getting a tax deduction. If you sell your business at a profit, you can subtract the remaining start-up costs from your profits before taxes are assessed, which reduces your taxable gain. If you sell at a loss, you can add the start-up costs to the money you lost; because this shortfall is deductible, a larger loss means a larger deduction, and therefore lower taxes.

If you simply go out of business with no assets to sell, you can deduct your leftover start-up expenses as ordinary business losses. This means that you can deduct them from any income you have that year, deduct them in future years, or deduct them from previous years' taxes.

Keep Good Expense Records

Whether you intend to start a new business or buy an existing one, you should keep careful track of every expense you incur before the business begins. Obviously, you should keep receipts and canceled checks. You should also keep evidence that will help show that the money went to investigate a new business—for example, correspondence and emails with accountants, attorneys, and consultants; marketing or financial reports; and copies of advertisements. You will need these records to calculate your deductions and to prove your expenses to the IRS if you face an audit.

Expenses for Businesses That Never Begin

Like many people, you may investigate starting a home business, but the venture never gets off the ground. While this is no doubt disappointing, you might be able to recoup some of your expenses in the form of tax deductions.

General Start-Up Costs

General start-up costs are expenses you incur *before* you decide to start a new business or acquire a specific existing business. They include all of the costs of doing a general search for, or preliminary investigation of, a business—for example, costs you incur analyzing potential markets. If you never start the business, these costs are personal and not deductible. In other words, they are a dead loss.

> EXAMPLE: Bruno would like to start his own home business as a fashion designer. He buys several books on fashion, attends a fashion design course, and travels to New York City, where he stays several nights in a hotel, to speak to people in the fashion industry. However, he ultimately decides to keep his day job. None of the expenses he incurred in investigating the fashion design business idea are deductible.

One intended effect of this rule is that you can't deduct travel, entertainment, or other "fun" expenses by claiming that you incurred them to investigate a business *unless you actually start the business.* Otherwise, it would be pretty tough for the IRS to figure out whether you were really considering a new venture or just having a good time.

> EXAMPLE: Kim spends $5,000 on a two-week Hawaii vacation. While there, she attends a one-hour seminar on how to make money by stuffing envelopes at home. However, she never starts the business. The cost of her trip is not a start-up expense.

> **TIP**
> **Corporations can deduct general start-up costs.** A corporation can deduct general start-up expenses as a business loss, even if the business never gets going.

Costs to Start or Acquire a Specific Business

The expenses you incur to actually start or acquire a particular business (that ultimately never begins operations) are not deductible as start-up expenses. Expenses such as accounting and legal fees may be deducted as investment expenses, which are generally deductible only as itemized miscellaneous deductions (I.R.C. § 165; see Chapter 2 for more information on deducting investment expenses). Costs incurred to acquire a specific asset for your future business—for example, equipment—are capital expenses. You get no direct tax deduction for these costs, but you may recover them when you sell or otherwise dispose of the asset.

Avoiding the Start-Up Tax Rule's Bite

You will be adversely affected by the start-up tax rule only if you spend more than $5,000 on start-up costs before your business begins. If you spend less, you can deduct all your start-up expenses during the first year you are in business. You will need to keep track of what you spend and, if you get near the threshold amount, cut back on your spending until your business begins. If you are at or near the threshold and need to keep spending, you could try to postpone paying for an item until after your business begins. Deductible start-up costs always qualify as currently deductible business operating expenses once a business begins. Postponing payment will only work, though, if you're a cash basis taxpayer—someone who reports income and expenses on the date they are actually paid, not on the date when an agreement to pay is made.

If you need to spend more than $5,000, go ahead and do it—you will still be able to deduct those expenses. You'll just have to deduct them over 15 years instead of one. Try to keep your total start-up expenses below $50,000 though. If you go above the limit, your first-year deduction will be reduced by the amount you exceed the limit.

Home Business Operating Expenses

This chapter covers the basic rules for deducting business operating expenses—the bread and butter expenses virtually every home business incurs for things like home office expenses, supplies, and business-related travel. If you don't maintain an inventory or buy expensive equipment, these day-to-day costs will probably be your largest category of business expenses (and your largest source of deductions).

Requirements for Deducting Operating Expenses

There are so many different kinds of business operating expenses that the tax code couldn't possibly list them all. Instead, if you want to deduct an item as a business operating expense, you must make sure the expenditure meets certain requirements. If it does, it will qualify as a deductible business operating expense. To qualify, the expense must be:

- ordinary and necessary
- current
- directly related to your business, and
- reasonable in amount. (I.R.C. § 162.)

Ordinary and Necessary

The first requirement is that the expense must be ordinary and necessary. This means that the cost is common and "helpful and appropriate" for your business. (*Welch v. Helvering*, 290 U.S. 111 (1933).) The expense doesn't have to be indispensable to be necessary; it needs only to help your business in some way—even if it's minor. A one-time expenditure can be ordinary and necessary.

> EXAMPLE: Bill, a home-based marketing consultant, hires a freelance researcher for two weeks to help him write a marketing report for a client. Hiring such assistance is a common and accepted practice among consultants. The researcher's fee is deductible as an ordinary and necessary expense for Bill's business.

It's usually fairly easy to figure out whether an expense passes the ordinary and necessary test. Some of the most common types of operating expenses include:

- home office expenses
- equipment rental
- legal and accounting fees
- car and truck expenses
- travel expenses
- business-related meal expenses
- supplies and materials
- business websites
- publications
- subscriptions
- repair and maintenance expenses
- business taxes
- interest on business loans
- licenses
- banking fees
- advertising costs
- business-related education expenses
- postage
- professional association dues
- business liability and property insurance
- payments to independent contractors, and
- software used for business.

Generally, the IRS won't second-guess your claim that an expense is ordinary and necessary, unless the item or service clearly has no legitimate business purpose.

> **EXAMPLE:** An insurance agent claimed a business deduction for part of his handgun collection because he had to go to "unsafe job sites" to settle insurance claims, and there was an unsolved murder in his neighborhood. The tax court disallowed the deduction explaining, "A handgun simply does not qualify as an ordinary and necessary business expense for an insurance agent, even a bold and brave Wyatt Earp type with a fast draw who is willing to risk injury or death in the service of his clients." (*Samp v. Comm'r.*, TC Memo 1981-1986.)

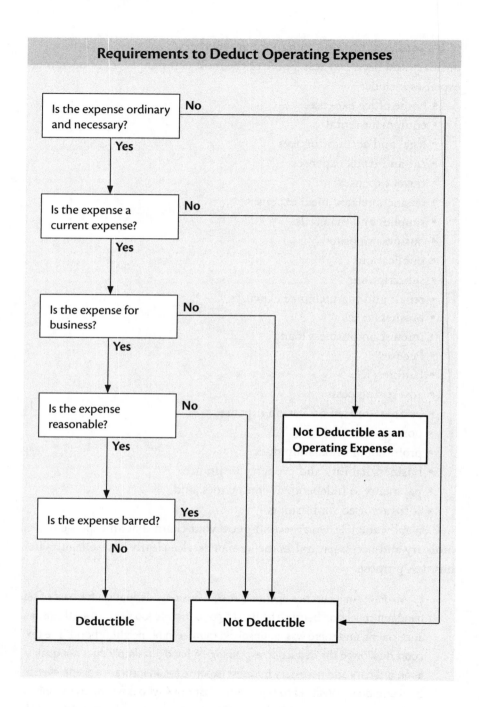

Requirements to Deduct Operating Expenses

Current Expense

Only current expenses are deductible as business operating expenses. Current expenses are for items that will benefit your business for less than one year. These are the costs of keeping your business going on a day-to-day basis, including money you spend on items or services that get used up, wear out, or become obsolete in less than one year. A good example of a current expense is your business's monthly phone bill, which benefits your business for one month. In contrast, buying a telephone for your business would be a capital expense (not a current expense) because the phone will benefit your business for more than one year. Other common capital expenses include cars, business equipment, computers, and real estate. (For more on deducting capital expenses, see Chapter 5.) However, repairs to business property, such as vehicles or computers, are current expenses (see Chapter 5).

Current expenses are currently deductible—that is, they are fully deductible in the year when you incur them. Because all business operating expenses are current expenses, they are also all currently deductible. However, your total annual deduction for some operating expenses (notably home office costs) cannot exceed the profits you earn from the business in that year. (See Chapter 6 for more on the home office deduction.)

Business Related

An expenditure must be *directly related to your business* to be deductible as a business operating expense. This means that you cannot deduct personal expenses. For example, the cost of a personal computer is a deductible operating expense only if you use the computer for business purposes; it is not deductible if you use it to pay personal bills or play computer games. If you buy something for both personal and business use, you can deduct only the business portion of the expense. For example, if you buy a cellphone and use it half of the time for business calls and half of the time for personal calls, you can deduct only half of the cost of the phone as a business expense.

A business expense for one person can be a personal expense for another, and vice versa. For example, a professional screenwriter could probably deduct the cost of going to movies—seeing movies is an essential part of the screenwriting business. But a salesperson could not deduct this type of expense.

Many expenses have both a personal and a business component, which can make it difficult to tell if an expense is business related. Even the most straightforward costs can present difficulties. For example, it's usually easy to tell whether postage is a personal or business expense. If you mail something for your business, it's a business expense; if you mail something unrelated to your business, it's a personal expense. But even here, there can be questions. For example, should a doctor be allowed to deduct the postage for postcards he sends to his patients while he is on vacation in Europe? (The tax court thinks so—it said the doctor's postage was deductible as an advertising expense.) (*Duncan v. Comm'r.*, 30 TC 386 (1958).)

The IRS has created rules and regulations for some operating expenses that commonly involve a crossover of personal and business use. Some of these rules lay out guidelines to help you figure out when an expense is and isn't deductible. Others impose record-keeping and other requirements to prevent abuses by dishonest taxpayers. Most of the complexity in determining whether an expense is deductible as a business operating expense involves understanding and applying these special rules and regulations.

The expenses that present the most common problems (and are therefore subject to the most comprehensive IRS rules and regulations) include:
- home office expenses (see Chapter 6)
- meals (see Chapter 14)
- travel (see Chapter 9)
- car and truck expenses (see Chapter 8)
- business gifts (see Chapter 14)
- bad debts (see Chapter 14)
- employee benefits (see Chapter 11)
- interest payments (see Chapter 14)

- health insurance (see Chapter 12)
- casualty losses (see Chapter 14)
- taxes (see Chapter 14), and
- education expenses (see Chapter 14).

Through these rules and regulations, the IRS provides guidance on the following types of questions:

- If you rent an apartment and use part of one room as a business office, should you be allowed to deduct all or a portion of the rent as a business operating expense? How much of the room must you use as an office (and for what period of time) to convince the IRS that you're using the room for business rather than personal purposes? (See Chapter 6 for information on the home office deduction.)
- Can you deduct the cost of going out of town for a business meeting? Does it matter if you spend part of the time sightseeing? (See Chapter 9 for rules about deducting business travel expenses.)

Reasonable in Amount

Subject to some important exceptions, there is no limit on how much you can deduct, as long as the amount is reasonable and you don't deduct more than you spend. As a rule of thumb, an expense is reasonable unless there are more economical and practical ways to achieve the same result. If the IRS finds that your deductions are unreasonably large, it will disallow them or at least disallow the portion it finds unreasonable.

Certain areas are hot buttons for the IRS—especially mileage, travel, and meal expenses. You will have to follow strict rules requiring you to fully document these deductions. (See Chapters 8 and 9.) The reasonableness issue also comes up when a business pays excessive salaries to employees to obtain a large tax deduction. For example, a home business owner might hire his 12-year-old son to answer phones and pay him $50 an hour—clearly an excessive wage for this type of work.

For a few types of operating expenses, the IRS limits how much you can deduct. These include:

- the home office deduction, which is limited to the profit from your business (although you can carry over and deduct any excess amount in future years) (see Chapter 6)
- business meals, which are only 50% deductible (see Chapter 14)
- car and travel expenses, which are limited depending on the length of your trip and the time you spend on business while away (see Chapters 8 and 9), and
- business gifts, which are subject to a $25 maximum deduction per individual per year (see Chapter 14).

Operating Expenses That Are Not Deductible

Even though they might be ordinary and necessary, some types of operating expenses are not deductible under any circumstances. In some cases, this is because Congress has declared that it would be morally wrong or otherwise contrary to sound public policy to allow people to deduct these costs. In other cases, Congress simply doesn't want to allow the deduction. These nondeductible expenses include:

- fines and penalties paid to the government for violation of any law— for example, tax penalties, parking tickets, or fines for violating city housing codes (I.R.C. § 162(f))
- illegal bribes or kickbacks to private parties or government officials (I.R.C. § 162(c))
- lobbying expenses or political contributions (businesses used to be able deduct up to $2,000 per year to influence local legislation (not including hiring professional lobbyists); the Tax Cuts and Jobs Act eliminated this deduction for 2018 and later)
- two-thirds of any damages paid for violation of the federal antitrust laws (I.R.C. § 162(g))
- bar or professional examination fees
- charitable donations by any business other than a C corporation (these donations are deductible only as personal expenses; see Chapter 14)

- country club, social club, or athletic club dues (see Chapter 14)
- federal income taxes you pay on your business income (see Chapter 14), and
- certain interest payments (see Chapter 14).

Entertainment Deductions Eliminated

For decades, taxpayers were allowed to partly deduct entertainment, amusement, and recreation costs if the purpose was to generate income or provide some other specific business benefit. The Tax Cuts and Jobs Act eliminated all such deductions starting in 2018. (I.R.C. § 274(a).) Thus, you can no longer deduct entertainment expenses like club or skiing outings, theater or sporting event tickets, entertainment at nightclubs, or hunting, fishing, or vacation trips. However, a few types of entertainment remain deductible; see Chapter 14.

How to Report Operating Expense Deductions

It's very easy to deduct operating expenses from your income taxes. Simply keep track of everything you buy (or spend money on) for your business during the year, including the amount you spend on each item. Then, record the expenses on your tax return. If, like the vast majority of home business owners, you are a sole proprietor or the owner of a one-person limited liability company (LLC), you do this on IRS Schedule C, *Profit or Loss From Business*. To make this task easy, Schedule C lists common current expense categories—you just need to fill in the amount for each category. For example, if you spend $1,000 for business advertising during the year, you would fill in this amount in the box for the advertising category. You add up all of your current expenses on Schedule C and deduct the total from your gross business income to determine your net business income—the amount on which you are taxed.

If you are a member of a limited liability company with more than one owner, a partner in a partnership, or an S corporation owner, the process is very similar, except you don't use Schedule C. Multimember LLCs and partnerships file IRS Form 1065, *U.S. Return of Partnership Income,* and their owners' shares of expenses are reported on Schedule K-1, *Partner's Share of Income, Deductions, Credits, etc.* S corporations use Form 1120S, *U.S. Income Tax Return for an S Corporation.* Each partner, LLC member, and S corporation shareholder's share of these deductions passes through the entity and is deducted on the owner's individual tax return on Schedule E. Regular C corporations file their own corporate tax returns.

Deducting Long-Term Assets

D o you like to go shopping? How would you like to get a 45% discount on what you buy? Sound impossible? It's not. Consider this example: Sid and Sally each buy the same $2,000 computer at their local computer store. Sid uses his computer to play games and balance his personal checkbook. Sally uses her computer in her graphic design business. Sid's net cost for his computer—that is, his cost after he pays his taxes for the year—is $2,000. Sally's net cost for her computer is $1,100.

Why the difference in cost? Because Sally uses her computer for business, she is allowed to deduct its cost from her taxable income, which saves her $900 in federal and state taxes. Thanks to tax laws designed to help people who own businesses, Sally gets a 45% discount on the computer.

This chapter explains how you can take advantage of these tax laws whenever you purchase long-term property for your business. You will need to be aware of, and follow, some tax rules that at times may seem complicated. But it's worth the effort. After all, by allowing these deductions, the government is effectively offering to help pay for your equipment and other business assets. All you have to do is take advantage of the offer.

Long-Term Assets

This chapter explains how to deduct long-term assets—business property that you reasonably expect to last for more than one year. Long-term assets are also called capital expenses (the terms are used interchangeably in this book).

Whether an item is a capital expense or not depends on its useful life. The useful life of an asset is not its physical life, but rather the period during which it may reasonably be expected to be useful in your business—and the IRS, not you, makes this call. Anything you buy that will benefit your business for *more than one year* is a long-term asset or capital expense. For home businesses, this typically includes items such as computers, office furniture, office equipment such as telephones and copiers, books, vehicles, and software. Anything you buy that will benefit your business for less than one year is a current expense. This includes expenses such as utility bills, travel, and office supplies.

> **EXAMPLE:** Doug pays $3,000 for office furniture for his home office. Because furniture can reasonably be expected to be useful for several years, it is a capital expense. The $50 per month that Doug spends on utilities for his home office, however, is a current expense.

The difference between current and capital expenses is important for tax purposes because current expenses (also called operating expenses) can always be deducted in the year you pay for them, assuming you're a cash basis taxpayer. In contrast, the cost of long-term assets may have to be deducted over several years. However, many home business owners are able to deduct all (or mostly all) of their long-term asset purchases in a single year by taking advantage of the tax rules described below.

> **TIP**
>
> **Inventory is treated differently.** This chapter covers the tax treatment of things you buy to use in your home business. It does not cover the cost of items you buy or make to sell to customers. These items are called inventory. Inventory is neither a current expense nor a capital expense. (See Chapter 10 for more on inventory.)

Deducting Inexpensive Property: The De Minimis Safe Harbor and Materials and Supplies Deduction

IRS regulations permit you to deduct relatively inexpensive property without worrying about the complex depreciation rules. Because of the low cost involved, you are not required to treat this property as a capital asset. Instead, you are allowed to treat it as a business operating expense that you can automatically deduct in a single year, the same as office rent or utilities. There are two ways to do this:

- the "de minimis" safe harbor, or
- the materials and supplies deduction.

These deductions are particularly helpful for smaller businesses that don't purchase a lot of expensive equipment or other property, which includes most home businesses. Indeed, you may be able to currently deduct all the long-term property you buy for your home business by taking advantage of these rules alone. Moreover, these rules allow you to remove the affected assets from your books and tax returns. This simplifies your tax and business records because you don't have the assets cluttering your books.

We'll start with the de minimis safe harbor since you will likely not use the materials and supplies deduction if you use the safe harbor.

The De Minimis Safe Harbor

The most significant of these new deductions is the de minimis safe harbor for property costing $2,500 or less. ("De minimis" is Latin for minor or inconsequential.) (IRS Reg. 1.263(a)-1(f).) Most home businesses may use the de minimis safe harbor to currently deduct the cost of personal property items that cost up to $2,500 apiece. This can result in a substantial deduction because there is no limit on how many items costing up to $2,500 apiece can be deducted each year.

To use this deduction, you must file an annual election with your tax return—something that is easy to do. When you make this election, it applies to all expenses you incur that qualify for the de minimis safe harbor. You cannot pick and choose which items you want to include. You must also include items that would otherwise be deductible as materials and supplies.

The de minimis safe harbor can't be used to deduct the cost of land, inventory (items held for sale to customers), certain spare parts for machinery or other equipment, or amounts that you pay for property that you produce or acquire for resale.

You can use the de minimis safe harbor to deduct the cost of property you don't use 100% of the time for business. Your deduction is limited to the dollar amount of your business use percentage.

De Minimis Safe Harbor Versus Bonus Depreciation

As a result of the Tax Cuts and Jobs Act, you can deduct most of the same expenses in a single year using 100% bonus depreciation through 2022 as you can using the safe harbor. However, the great virtue of the de minimis safe harbor is its simplicity. All expenses deducted with the safe harbor are currently deducted as business operating expenses. Unlike with bonus depreciation, there is no need to list safe harbor expenses on IRS Form 4562, *Depreciation and Amortization.* You need not create or maintain depreciation schedules for such property items or include them in your accounting records as assets.

Bonus depreciation has some advantages over the de minimis safe harbor: There is no $2,500 per item ceiling on bonus depreciation. Also, if you sell property for which you took 100% bonus depreciation, you only pay income tax on your gain, not self-employment tax. This is not the case when you use the de minimis safe harbor, as described below.

Moreover, property deducted with the safe harbor won't count for purposes of taking the pass-through deduction. At higher income levels (for 2020, $163,300 for singles and $326,600 for marrieds) the pass-through deduction can be limited wholly or partly to 2.5% of the cost of a business owner's depreciable property. This would not include property you've deducted using the safe harbor but does include property deducted with bonus depreciation. (See Chapter 7 for a full discussion of the pass-through tax deduction.) For this reason, if you want to maximize your pass-through deduction, you may wish to avoid using the de minimis safe harbor and use bonus depreciation instead. You elect to use the safe harbor each year, and you can use it some years and not use it others. Alternatively, you could reduce the dollar amount of your de minimis safe harbor election; $2,500 per item is the maximum amount allowed under the safe harbor (unless you have a financial statement; see below). But you can elect to deduct a smaller amount—for example, $1,000 or $500 per item, and use bonus depreciation to deduct more expensive items.

> **EXAMPLE:** Sheila purchases a $2,000 computer she uses 50% of the time for her home-based Web design business and 50% of the time for personal purposes. She may deduct $1,000 of the cost this year using the de minimis safe harbor. The remaining $1,000 basis is not deductible.

However, to determine whether property qualifies for the de minimis safe harbor, you look at its total cost, without subtracting the personal use percentage.

> **EXAMPLE:** Assume that Sheila from the above example purchases a $3,000 computer she uses 50% of the time for business. She may not deduct the computer under the safe harbor because it cost more than $2,500.

What if you sell property you deducted using the de minimis safe harbor? You'll likely have taxable gain because your adjusted basis in the property will be zero. The entire amount of gain you realize from the sale is treated as ordinary business income—that is, it is taxed at your normal individual tax rates not lower capital gain rates. The gain is also subject to self-employment (Social Security and Medicare) tax—this is a 15.3% tax up to an annual income ceiling.

> **EXAMPLE:** John uses the de minimis safe harbor to fully deduct in one year a $1,000 computer he purchased for his home business. His adjusted basis in the computer after the sale is $0. He sells the computer for $500 one year later. He has a $500 taxable gain ($500 sale price – $0 adjusted basis = $500). He adds the $500 to his income on his Schedule C. He must pay both income tax and self-employment tax on his gain.

Maximum De Minimis Amount

Unless you have an applicable financial statement for your business (something few home businesses have—see below), you may use the de minimis safe harbor only for property whose cost does not exceed

$2,500 per invoice, or $2,500 per item as substantiated by the invoice. If the cost exceeds $2,500 per invoice (or item), no part of the cost may be deducted using the de minimis safe harbor. The de minimis limit was initially $500, but the IRS increased it to $2,500 effective January 1, 2016. If you have an applicable financial statement, then you may increase the per item or per invoice amount up to $5,000.

> **EXAMPLE:** Alice purchases the following items for her home-based consulting business from a local computer supply store:
> - a computer that cost $2,000
> - an office chair for $1,000, and
> - an office desk for $3,000.
>
> Alice's total bill is $6,000. However, she applies the de minimis safe harbor rule item by item as shown on the invoice. Each item is less than the $2,500 de minimis safe harbor limit except the desk. Thus, Alice may immediately deduct $3,000 of the total using the safe harbor. She can't use the safe harbor to deduct the $3,000 cost of the desk. Instead, she may deduct the desk in one year using Section 179 or depreciate it over five years.

Be sure to save all your receipts and invoices for property you deduct using the de minimis safe harbor.

Since the $2,500 de minimis limit is based on the cost of an item as shown on the invoice, you might be tempted to artificially break an item down into separate costs on the invoice, each of which is less than the limit. However, the IRS does not allow this. You cannot break into separate components property that you would normally buy as a single unit.

> **EXAMPLE:** Alice from the example above purchased an office desk for $3,000. She instructs the office supply store to separately bill her $250 for each of four desk drawers and $2,000 for the remainder of the desk. Since an office desk is normally purchased along with its drawers as a single unit, the IRS adds the cost of each component to determine that the actual cost is $3,000. Thus, the desk does not qualify for the safe harbor.

In determining whether the cost of an item exceeds the $2,500 threshold, you must include all additional costs included on the same invoice with the property—for example, delivery or installation fees. If the additional costs on a single invoice apply to several items, you must divide the costs among them in a reasonable way. IRS regulations give you three options: (1) equal division for each item, (2) specific identification (for example, if the installation costs apply only to one item), or (3) weighted average based on the property's relative cost.

Do You Have an Applicable Financial Statement?

If you have an applicable financial statement for your home business, you may increase your de minimis amount to $5,000 per item—twice more than the $2,500 limit for businesses without such statements. The most common type of applicable financial statement is a certified financial statement prepared by a CPA. These usually cost at least several thousand dollars, so few home businesses have them. A financial statement (other than a tax return) filed with the SEC or another state or federal agency (not including the IRS) can also qualify—for example, a Form 10-K or an annual statement to shareholders. Only larger corporations or businesses that are publicly traded usually file such statements.

Qualifying for the Safe Harbor

To qualify for the de minimis expensing safe harbor, a taxpayer must:
- establish before the first day of the tax year (January 1 for calendar year taxpayers) an accounting procedure requiring it to expense amounts paid for property either (1) costing less than a certain dollar amount, and/or (2) with an economic useful life of 12 months or less, and
- actually treat such amounts as currently deductible expenses on its books and records.

If you have an "applicable financial statement" and wish to qualify to use the $5,000 de minimis limit, your accounting procedure must be in writing and signed before January 1 of the tax year. If you don't have such a statement and qualify only for the $2,500 limit, you do not need to put your procedure in writing (although you still may do so). But it should still be in place before January 1 of the tax year. Here is an example of a written procedure for a taxpayer without an applicable financial statement:

De Minimis Safe Harbor Procedure

Effective January 1, 2016, XYZ hereby adopts the following policy regarding certain expenditures: Amounts paid to acquire or produce tangible personal property will be expensed, and not capitalized, in the year of purchase if (1) the property costs less than $2,500, or (2) the property has a useful life of 12 months or less.

Claiming the Safe Harbor

To take advantage of the de minimis safe harbor, you must file an election with your tax return each year, using the following format:

Section 1.263(a)-1(f) De Minimis Safe Harbor Election

Taxpayer's name:
Taxpayer's address:
Taxpayer's identification number:

The taxpayer is hereby making the de minimis safe harbor election under Section 1.263(a)-1(f).

The Materials and Supplies Deduction

Another deduction that took effect in 2014 is for materials and supplies. Items that fall within the definition of materials and supplies in IRS regulations may be currently deducted. However, many home businesses won't need (or be able) to use this deduction because these items can usually be deducted using the de minimis safe harbor.

"Materials and supplies" are tangible property used or consumed in your business operations that fall within any of the following categories:

- any item of tangible personal property that cost $200 or less
- any item of personal property with an economic useful life of 12 months or less (no cost limit), and
- components acquired to maintain or repair a unit of tangible property—that is, spare parts (no cost limit).

The cost of such items may be deducted in the year the item is used or consumed in your business—which may be later than the year purchased. To use this deduction, you are supposed to keep records of when such items are used or consumed in your business—something few small business owners do in practice. For this reason, this deduction may be useless for most small home businesses. Fortunately, they can use the de minimis safe harbor discussed above instead to deduct materials and supplies.

Incidental Materials and Supplies

Incidental materials and supplies are personal property items that are carried on hand and for which no record of consumption is kept or for which beginning and ending inventories are not taken. In other words, these are inexpensive items not worth keeping track of. Examples include pens, paper, staplers, toner, and trash baskets. Costs of incidental materials and supplies are deductible in the year they are paid for, not when the items are used or consumed in the business.

EXAMPLE: John, a home-based professional writer, purchases two packs of pens and three boxes of paper clips he plans to use for his writing activity over the next two years. The cost was minimal and he does not keep inventory of each pen or paper clip. These are incidental compared to his business and deductible the year he paid for them.

Interaction With De Minimis Safe Harbor

If you elect to use the de minimis safe harbor discussed above, and any materials and supplies also qualify for the safe harbor, you must deduct the amounts paid for them under the safe harbor in the tax year the amounts are paid or incurred. (IRS Reg. §§ 1.263(a)-1(f)(3)(ii).) Thus, if you use the de minimis safe harbor, you can largely ignore the materials and supplies deduction. This is to your advantage since the de minimis safe harbor has a $2,500 limit for most businesses, as opposed to the $200 materials and supplies limit for property with a useful life over one year. Moreover, the de minimis safe harbor permits you to deduct the cost of items the year they are purchased, instead of when they are actually used or consumed in your business.

General Rules for Deducting Long-Term Personal Property

The following general rules apply if you are deducting long-term personal property using bonus depreciation, Section 179 expensing, or regular depreciation. It doesn't matter which method you choose, these same basic rules apply. These rules don't apply to the de minimis safe harbor discussed above. Unlike the de minimis safe harbor, which for smaller businesses is limited to items costing no more than $2,500 apiece, these methods can be used for any asset, no matter what the cost (up to an annual $1 million limit for Section 179).

You get to decide which method to use, provided the property is eligible for that method. You don't have to use the same method for all of your business property. However, as discussed below, bonus depreciation must be used for all property in the same asset class. Bonus depreciation and Section 179 expensing enable you to deduct the full cost of personal property in a single year. Regular depreciation, on the other hand, forces you to spread your deduction out over several years. Because of inflation and the time value of money, it is usually better to get the largest possible deduction in the first year you own an asset.

What You Can Deduct

Long-term personal property consists of virtually any tangible property you buy for your business other than land, land improvements, buildings, and building components. For example, it includes computers and other electronic equipment, office furniture, and vehicles (subject to special rules covered below). Personal property also includes computer software you purchase (buy "off the shelf").

However, you can only depreciate or expense the cost of purchasing long-term business property that wears out, deteriorates, or gets used up over time. You cannot deduct:

- property that doesn't wear out, including land (whether undeveloped or with structures on it), stocks, securities, or gold
- property you use solely for personal purposes
- property purchased and disposed of in the same year
- inventory, or
- collectibles that appreciate in value over time, such as antiques and artwork.

If you use nondepreciable property in your business, you get no tax deduction while you own it. But if you sell it, you get to deduct its tax basis from the sales price to calculate your taxable profit. If the basis exceeds the sales price, you'll have a deductible loss on the property. If the price exceeds the basis, you'll have a taxable gain. (See "How Much You Can Deduct," below, for how to figure an asset's basis.)

> **EXAMPLE:** Amy bought a digital camera for her architecture business in January for $1,000 and sold it in December of the same year for $600. It was purchased and disposed of in the same year so it can't be depreciated or expensed. Instead, the property's basis (its original cost) is deducted from the sale price. This results in a loss of $400, which is a deductible business loss.

You also may not depreciate or expense property that you do not own. For example, you get no depreciation or expensing deduction for property you lease. The person who owns the property—the lessor—gets to depreciate it. (However, you may deduct your lease payments as current business expenses.) Leasing may be preferable to buying and depreciating equipment that wears out or becomes obsolete quickly. (See "Leasing Long-Term Assets," below.)

Mixed-Use Property

In order to deduct a long-term asset, you must have used the property in your business. You can't deduct an asset you use solely for personal purposes.

> **EXAMPLE:** Jill, a freelance writer, bought a computer for $3,000. She used it to play games, manage her checkbook, and surf the Internet for fun. In other words, she used it only for personal purposes. The computer is not deductible.

However, you need not use an asset 100% of the time for business to claim a deduction. You can use it for personal purposes part of the time. In this event, your deduction is reduced by the percentage of your personal use. This will, of course, reduce the amount of your deduction.

> **EXAMPLE:** Miranda buys a $3,000 computer for her real estate business. She uses the computer 75% of the time for business and 25% for personal use. Her deduction is reduced by 25%, so Miranda can deduct only $750 of the computer's $3,000 cost.

You can take a regular or bonus depreciation deduction even if you use an asset only 1% of the time for business, as long as it's not listed property. This is one advantage of depreciation over the Section 179 deduction, which is available only for property you use more than 50% of the time for business.

If you use property for both business and personal purposes, you must keep a diary or log with the dates, times, and reasons the property was used to distinguish business from personal use. Moreover, special rules apply if you use cars and other types of listed property less than 50% of the time for business.

Listed Property

The IRS imposes special rules on certain personal property items that can easily be used for personal as well as business purposes. These items, called "listed property," include cars and other passenger vehicles below 6,000 pounds; motorcycles, boats, and airplanes; and any other property generally used for entertainment, recreation, or amusement—for example, digital cameras. (Cellphones and computers used to be, but are no longer, listed property.)

As long as you use listed property more than 50% of the time for business, you may deduct its cost just like any other long-term business property under Section 179 or using bonus depreciation or regular depreciation. However, if you use listed property 50% or less of the time for business, you can only use the slowest method of regular depreciation: straight-line depreciation. (See "Depreciation Rules for Listed Property," below, for more on these special rules for deducting listed property.)

When Depreciation Begins

You begin to depreciate and/or expense your property when it is placed in service—that is, when it's ready and available for use in your business. As long as it is available for use, you don't have to actually use the property for business during the year to take depreciation.

EXAMPLE: Tom, a publicist, purchased a copy machine for his home office. He had the device ready for use in his office on December 31, 2020, but he didn't actually use it until January 2, 2021. Tom may take a depreciation deduction for the copier for 2020 because it was available for use that year.

CAUTION

You must actually be in business to take depreciation or expensing deductions. In other words, you cannot depreciate or expense an asset until your business is up and running. This is one important reason why it is a good idea to postpone large property purchases until your business has begun. (See Chapter 3 for a detailed discussion of tax deductions for business start-up expenses.)

How Much You Can Deduct

You are allowed to deduct your total investment in a long-term asset that you buy for your business, up to your business use percentage of the property. In tax lingo, your investment is called your basis or tax basis. Basis is a word you'll hear over and over again when the subject of depreciation comes up. Don't let it confuse you; it just means the amount of your total investment in the property.

Usually, your basis in long-term property is whatever you paid for it. This includes not only the purchase price, but also sales tax, delivery charges, installation, and testing fees, if any. You may deduct the entire cost, no matter how you paid for the property—in cash, with a credit card, or with a bank loan.

EXAMPLE: Jack purchases a 3D printer for his home business. Jack uses the printer 100% for business. He paid $20,000 cash, $1,800 in sales tax, and $500 for delivery and installation. His basis in the property is $22,300.

If you convert personal property to use in your home business, your depreciable basis is the lower of:

- what you originally paid for it (plus the amount of any improvements to the property) or,

- its fair market value at the time you convert it to business use.

Your basis will usually be its fair market value, as this is usually the lower number.

> **EXAMPLE:** Jack purchased a sofa for $1,000 that he used in his home solely for personal purposes. One year later, he starts a home business and places the sofa in his home office, which he uses exclusively for business. The sofa's fair market value when he placed it in his office was $500. This is his depreciable basis.

Whenever you use Section 179 expensing or bonus or regular depreciation, you must subtract the amount of your deduction from the property's basis—this is true regardless of whether you actually claimed any depreciation on your tax return. This new basis is called the adjusted basis because it reflects adjustments from your starting basis. When your adjusted basis is reduced to zero, you can no longer deduct any of the property's cost.

> **EXAMPLE:** Jack (from the above example) bought a 3D printer. His starting basis was $22,300. He expenses the entire cost that year using Section 179. The printer's adjusted basis is zero, and Jack gets no more deductions for the property.

Disposing of Long-Term Assets

Depreciable property doesn't last forever, and you probably don't want to use it forever anyway. Sooner or later, you'll get rid of such property. This can be done in a variety of ways—you can:

- sell the property
- trade it in when you buy new property, or
- abandon or destroy it.

Each method has tax consequences.

Sale of Long-Term Assets

If you sell long-term property, your gain or loss on the sale is determined by subtracting the property's adjusted basis from the sales price.

> **EXAMPLE:** Jill purchased a $10,000 computer system and uses it 100% for her Bitcoin mining business. She deducts the entire amount using Section 179. This leaves Jill with an adjusted basis of zero. Two years later, Jill sells the system for $5,000, resulting in a taxable gain of $5,000 ($5,000 – zero basis = $5,000).

The gain on the sale is taxed as ordinary income up to the amount of depreciation or Section 179 expensing that you claimed. This ordinary income does not go on your Schedule C, where it would be subject to the self-employment tax. Instead, it goes on IRS Form 4797, *Sales of Business Property*, because it is income from the sale of a business asset.

> **EXAMPLE:** Jill's entire $5,000 gain from selling her computer system is taxed as ordinary income, since this is less than the Section 179 expensing Jill claimed.

Any excess gain—that is, gain over the amount of depreciation or expensing claimed—is taxed at capital gains rates, which are usually lower than ordinary income tax rates.

You can't avoid this result by not taking a Section 179 or depreciation deduction to which you were entitled. The IRS will treat you as though you took the deduction anyway, even though you really didn't. Thus, you still have to pay tax on your "gain."

Trade-ins

Before 2018, if you traded in an old long-term asset for a new one, you could elect to do a tax-free exchange in which the tax basis of the old asset was subtracted from the cost of the new asset. With such an exchange, there would be no tax due on the sale of the trade-in. However, the Tax Cuts and Jobs Act eliminated this type of treatment for personal property. Today, if you trade in an old asset like a car for a new one, you must treat the trade-in transaction as a taxable sale. You subtract the old car's tax basis (original cost minus depreciation deductions) from what the dealer pays you for it and pay tax on any gain (or deduct any loss).

> **EXAMPLE:** Phil owns a pickup truck he uses exclusively for his contracting business. He trades in the truck for a new model that cost $20,000. He paid the dealer $15,000 cash and received $5,000 from the dealer for trading in the old pick-up. His old truck's adjusted basis was $4,000. Thus, he earned a $1,000 profit on the trade-in on which he must pay tax at ordinary income rates. His starting basis in the new truck is $20,000.

Abandonment

If you abandon long-term business property instead of selling it, you may deduct its adjusted basis as a business loss. Of course, if your adjusted basis in the property is zero, you get no deduction. You abandon property when you voluntarily and permanently give up possessing and using it with the intention of ending your ownership and without passing it on to anyone else. Loss from abandonment of business property is deductible as an ordinary loss, even if the property is a capital asset.

For more information on the tax implications of selling or otherwise disposing of business property, refer to IRS Publication 544, *Sales and Other Dispositions of Assets*.

Bonus Depreciation

Bonus depreciation enables you to deduct in a single year a specified percentage of a long-term asset's cost. For property placed into service starting September 28, 2017 through December 31, 2022, the percentage is a whopping 100%—in other words, you can deduct in one year the entire cost of property using bonus depreciation. This makes bonus depreciation the go-to method for deducting personal property during these five-plus years.

Unlike the de minimis safe harbor, bonus depreciation is not limited to items that cost $2,500 ($5,000 for businesses with financial statements). Nor is it limited to your annual net income, as is the case with Section 179 expensing discussed below. You can deduct any amount of eligible property using bonus depreciation, even if it results in your business's incurring a loss for tax purposes.

Bonus depreciation is optional—you don't have to take it if you don't want to. But if you want to get the largest depreciation deduction you can in the year you buy personal property for your business, you will want to take advantage of it whenever possible.

Property That Qualifies for Bonus Depreciation

You can use bonus depreciation to deduct any property you acquire by purchase that has a depreciation period of 20 years or less—this includes all types of tangible personal business property and off-the-shelf software (but not custom software). The property may be used or new, but you must not have used it before acquiring it. Thus, you can't convert property you previously used for personal use to business use and deduct the cost with bonus depreciation.

You can use bonus depreciation only for property that you purchase —not for leased property or property you inherit or receive as a gift. You also can't use it for property that you buy from a relative or a corporation or an organization that you control. Special rules apply to cars (see "Deducting Business Vehicles" below).

Bonus depreciation cannot be used for:
- land
- permanent structures attached to land (except for certain improvements, see below)
- inventory (see Chapter 10)
- intangible property, such as patents, copyrights, and trademarks, or
- property used outside the United States.

You can use bonus depreciation to deduct listed property only if you use the property at least 51% of the time for business use. For example, you may deduct a video camera with bonus depreciation only if you use it over 50% of the time for your business, not for personal use. If your business use falls below 51% during the asset's depreciation period (usually five or seven years) you have to give back the bonus depreciation you claimed the first year—a process called recapture (see below).

Calculating the Bonus Amount

You use bonus depreciation to figure out your depreciation deduction for the first year that you own an asset. You figure the deduction by multiplying the depreciable basis of the asset by the applicable bonus percentage. For property placed in service starting September 28, 2017 through December 31, 2022, the bonus percentage is 100%. You get the full 100% deduction no matter what month during the year you place the property into service. This differs from regular depreciation rules, where property bought later in the year may be subject to a smaller deduction for the first year.

> **EXAMPLE:** Stan purchases and places into service during 2020 a $10,000 computer system for his home-based Bitcoin mining business. He deducts the entire $10,000 cost that year with 100% bonus depreciation.

The amount you can deduct is initially based on the property's cost. The cost includes the amount you paid for the property, plus sales tax, delivery, and installation charges. It doesn't matter if you pay cash or finance the purchase with a credit card or bank loan. However, if you pay for property with both cash and a trade-in, the value of the trade-in is not deductible with bonus depreciation. You must depreciate the amount of the trade-in.

If you use property solely for business like in the above example, you can deduct 100% of the cost (subject to the other limitations discussed below). However, if you use property for both business and personal purposes, you must reduce your deduction by the percentage of the time that you use the property for personal purposes.

> **EXAMPLE:** Max buys a $4,000 computer. The year he buys it, he uses it for his consulting business 75% of the time, and for personal purposes 25% of the time. He may currently deduct 75% of the computer's cost (or $3,000) using bonus depreciation. The remaining $1,000 is not deductible because the 25% personal use of the computer is not a business expense.

Class-Wide Requirement

If you use bonus depreciation, you must use it for all assets that fall within the same class. You may not pick and choose the assets you want to apply it to within a class. For example, if you buy a car and take bonus depreciation, you must take bonus depreciation for any other property you buy that year within the same class. Cars are five-year property, so you must take bonus depreciation that year for any other five-year property—for example, computers and office equipment. (See the "Depreciation Periods" chart, below, for a list of the various classes of property.)

Opting Out of the Bonus

The bonus depreciation deduction is applied automatically to all taxpayers who qualify for it. However, the deduction is optional. You need not take it if you don't want to. You can elect not to take the deduction by attaching a note to your tax return. It may be advantageous to do this if you expect your income to go up substantially in future years, placing you in a higher tax bracket.

> CAUTION
> **When you opt out, you do so for the entire class of assets.** It's very important to understand that if you opt out of the bonus, you must do so for the entire class of assets, not just one asset within a class. This is the same rule that applies when you decide to take the bonus.

Bonus Depreciation Percentages

As the following chart shows, the bonus depreciation percentages vary over the years. The 100% bonus depreciation amount is scheduled to remain in effect for property placed into service through December 31, 2022. The bonus amount will then phase down each year in 20% increments.

Year Property Placed In Service	Bonus Depreciation Percentage
1/1/2015 through 9/27/2017 (new property only)	50%
9/28/2017 through 2022	100%
2023	80%
2024	60%
2025	40%
2026	20%
2027 and later	0%

Section 179 Deductions

Section 179 of the tax code is similar to bonus depreciation in that it allows you to deduct in one year the entire cost of personal property you use in your business (as well as certain real property improvements, see below). This is called first-year expensing or Section 179 expensing. (Expensing is an accounting term that means currently deducting a long-term asset.)

Section 179 may be used to deduct much the same property as bonus depreciation. However, during 2018 through 2022, Section 179 will likely not be used much by businesses because they can deduct 100% of the cost of the same property using bonus depreciation. Section 179 has several disadvantages that make it less desirable than bonus depreciation.

First, you can only use Section 179 for property you use over 50% of the time for business (this isn't the case with bonus depreciation, except for listed property). If your use of the property falls below 50% you have to give back your Section 179 deduction through recapture (see below). There is no such recapture with bonus depreciation except for listed property.

In addition, you can't use Section 179 to deduct in one year more than your net taxable business income for that year (not counting the Section 179 deduction but including your spouse's salary and business income). Amounts that are not deductible are carried forward and can be deducted in future years. Thus, Section 179 may never result in a loss whereas there is no such limitation on bonus depreciation. This limitation is particularly important to home business owners because many earn very small incomes. A study sponsored by the Small Business Administration found that 57% of all home businesses earned less than $10,000 in profits per year. Only 16% earned more than $10,000 in profit, while 27% incurred losses. (See *Homebased Business: The Hidden Economy*, by Joanne H. Pratt (Office of Advocacy, United States Small Business Administration).)

There is also an annual limit on the amount of property that can be deducted with Section 179. For 2020, the limit is $1,040,000. The dollar limit is phased out if the amount of qualifying property you place into service during the year exceeds $2,590,000. The annual deduction limit applies to all of your businesses combined, not to each business you own and run. If you're a partner in a partnership, member of a limited liability company (LLC), or shareholder in an S corporation, the limit applies both to the business entity and to each owner personally.

Unlike bonus depreciation, Section 179 expensing doesn't apply class-wide. Thus, you may pick and choose which assets you wish to deduct using Section 179 within the same asset class. This is a potential advantage. Section 179 deductions are not automatic. You must claim a Section 179 deduction on your tax return by completing IRS Form 4562, Part I, and checking a specific box. If you neglect to do this, you may lose your deduction.

Deducting Repairs and Improvements

The general rule is that repairs to business property are a currently deductible business operating expense, while improvements are a capital expense that must be depreciated over several years. However, there are exceptions to the rule. It's often possible to fully deduct the cost of improvements to personal property in one year using one of the following methods:

- 100% bonus depreciation (available 2018 through 2022)
- Section 179 expensing (for property used over 50% for business), or
- the de minimis safe harbor (for property that costs up to $2,500).

For example, you could use any of these methods to currently deduct the cost of buying and installing a new engine in a business vehicle—an expense that is an improvement.

However, repairs are still better than improvements for tax purposes. Since a repair is a business operating expense, you get to deduct the full amount in the year the repair expense is incurred and there will be no tax impact when you later sell the property. If you sell personal property used for business at a profit (more than its adjusted tax basis), it is taxed at low capital gains rates (15% or 20% if you owned the property over one year). In contrast, when you deduct an expense through regular depreciation, bonus depreciation, or Section 179 expensing and sell personal property at a profit, you must pay tax on your regular or bonus depreciation or Section 179 deductions at your ordinary income tax rates (as much as 37%). This is called recapture. Also, repairs don't have to be tracked on depreciation schedules or reported to the IRS on special tax forms, as is the case with depreciable improvements.

Under IRS repair regulations adopted in 2014, an expense is an improvement if it:

- makes an asset better than it was before (a "betterment" in tax jargon)
- restores it to operating condition, or
- adapts it to a new use.

Expenses that don't result in a betterment, restoration, or adaptation are currently deductible repairs. Unfortunately, there are no bright-line rules that explain exactly how much an asset must be altered to constitute an improvement. Instead, you have to look at all the facts and circumstances and make a judgment call to determine whether an expense results in a betterment, restoration, or adaptation of a business asset. For more guidance, see the detailed and extremely helpful FAQs the IRS has created at www.irs.gov/businesses/small-businesses-self-employed/tangible-property-final-regulations.

Additionally, IRS regulations permit you to fully deduct in one year as an operating expense the costs of routine maintenance to keep business property in ordinarily efficient operating condition. This "routine maintenance safe harbor" applies to:

- inspection, cleaning, and testing, and
- replacing damaged or worn parts with comparable and commercially available replacement parts.

Maintenance automatically qualifies for this treatment if, when you placed the asset into service, you reasonably expected to perform such maintenance more than once during its class life—that is, the time period over which it must be depreciated. (See the list of class lives in the "Depreciation Periods" chart later in this chapter.) There is no recapture involved when you use this safe harbor.

Regular Depreciation

The traditional method of getting back the money you spend on long-term business assets is to deduct the cost a little at a time over several years (exactly how many years is determined by the IRS). This process is called depreciation.

When to Use Regular Depreciation

With bonus depreciation, Section 179, and the de minimis safe harbor and materials and supplies deductions, you might not need to use regular depreciation for the foreseeable future. However, you may need to use regular depreciation to write off the cost of long-term assets that don't qualify for these methods. For example, you can't use any of those methods for:

- personal property items that you convert to business use
- structures, such as a building or building component
- items financed with a trade-in (the value of the trade-in must be depreciated)
- intangible assets, such as a patent, copyright, trademark, or business goodwill
- items purchased from a relative, or
- property inherited or received as a gift.

None of these limitations apply to regular depreciation.

Regular Depreciation Is Not Optional

Unlike bonus depreciation and the Section 179 deduction, regular depreciation is not optional. You *must* take a depreciation deduction if you qualify for it and you don't deduct the property under Section 179. If you fail to take it, the IRS will treat you as if you had taken it. This means that you could be subject to depreciation recapture when you sell the asset—even if you never took a depreciation deduction. This would increase your taxable income by the amount of the deduction you failed to take. So, if you don't expense a depreciable asset under Section 179 or claim bonus depreciation, be sure to take the proper depreciation deductions for it. If you realize later that you failed to take a depreciation deduction that you should have taken, you may file an amended tax return to claim any deductions that you should have taken in prior years.

Under some circumstances, it may be better to use depreciation and draw out your deduction over several years instead of getting your deductions all at once with the other methods. This may be the case where you have little or no business income in the current year and expect to have more in future years. In that case, you would be in a higher tax bracket in those later years, so taking your depreciation deduction then would result in more tax savings.

Depreciation Period

The depreciation period (also called the recovery period) is the time over which you must take your depreciation deductions for an asset.

The major depreciation periods are listed below. These periods are also called recovery classes; all property that comes within a period is said to belong to that class. For example, computers have a five-year depreciation period and thus fall within the five-year class, along with automobiles and office equipment.

The basic rule (called the "half-year convention") is that, no matter when you buy an asset, you treat it as being placed in service on July 1— the midpoint of the year. This means that you can take half a year of depreciation for the first year that you own an asset.

You are not allowed to use the half-year convention if more than 40% of the long-term personal property you buy during the year is placed in service during the last three months of the year. The 40% figure is determined by adding together the basis of all the depreciable property you bought during the year and comparing that to the basis of all of the property you bought during the fourth quarter.

If you exceed the 40% ceiling, you must use the midquarter convention. You must group all of the property that you purchased during the year by quarter (depending on when you bought it) and treat it as if you had placed it in service at the midpoint of that quarter.

It's usually best to avoid having to use the midquarter convention, which means you'll want to buy more than 60% of your total depreciable assets before September 30 of the year. Assets you currently deduct using

Section 179 do not count toward the 40% limitation, so you can avoid the midquarter convention by using Section 179 to deduct most or all of your purchases in the last three months of the year.

Depreciation Methods

Tax preparation software can calculate depreciation for you, but you must choose which depreciation method to use. Most tangible property is depreciated using the Modified Accelerated Cost Recovery System, or MACRS. (A slightly different system, called ADS, applies to certain listed property; see "Depreciation Rules for Listed Property," below.)

You can ordinarily use three different methods to calculate the depreciation deduction under MACRS: straight-line depreciation or one of two accelerated depreciation methods. Once you choose your method, you're stuck with it for the entire life of the asset.

In addition, you must use the same method for all property of the same class that you purchase during the year. For example, if you use the straight-line method to depreciate a computer, you must use that method to depreciate any other property in the same class as computers. Computers fall within the five-year class, so you must use the straight-line method for all other five-year property you buy during the year, such as office equipment. If you're interested in learning about them all, refer to IRS Publication 946, *How to Depreciate Property*.

Straight-Line Method

Using the straight-line depreciation method, you deduct an equal amount each year over the useful life of an asset. However, if the midyear convention applies (as it often does), you deduct only a half-year's worth of depreciation in the first year. You make up for this by taking an extra one-half year of depreciation at the end. You can use the straight-line method to depreciate any type of depreciable property. For example, if you depreciate an item with a five-year recovery period that cost $10,000, you'd deduct $1,000 the first year, $2,000 each year for the next four years, and $1,000 the last year.

Depreciation Periods	
Depreciation Period	**Type of Property**
3 years	Computer software
	Tractor units for over-the-road use
	Any race horse over 2 years old when placed in service
	Any other horse over 12 years old when placed in service
5 years	Automobiles, taxis, buses, and trucks
	Computers and peripheral equipment
	Office machinery (such as typewriters, calculators, and copiers)
	Any property used in research and experimentation
	Breeding cattle and dairy cattle
	Appliances, carpets, furniture, and so on used in a residential rental real estate activity
7 years	Office furniture and fixtures (such as desks, files, and safes)
	Agricultural machinery and equipment
	Any property that does not have a class life and has not been designated by law as being in any other class
10 years	Vessels, barges, tugs, and similar water transportation equipment
	Any single-purpose agricultural or horticultural structure
	Any tree or vine bearing fruits or nuts
15 years	Improvements made directly to land or added to it (such as shrubbery, fences, roads, and bridges)
20 years	Farm buildings (other than single-purpose agricultural or horticultural structures)
27.5 years	Residential rental property—for example, an apartment building
39 years	Nonresidential real property, such as a home office, office building, store, or warehouse

Accelerated Depreciation Methods

There is nothing wrong with straight-line depreciation, but the tax law provides an alternative that most businesses prefer: accelerated depreciation. As the name implies, this method provides faster depreciation than the straight-line method. It does not increase your total depreciation deduction, but it permits you to take larger deductions in the first few years after you buy an asset. You make up for this by taking smaller deductions in later years.

The fastest and most commonly used form of accelerated depreciation is the double-declining balance method. This is a confusing name, but all it means is that you get double the deduction that you would get for the first full year under the straight-line method. You then get less in later years. For example, if you depreciate an item with a five-year recovery period that cost $10,000, using the double-declining balance method you'd deduct $2,000 the first year, $3,200 the second year, $1,920 the third year, $1,152 the fourth and fifth year, and $576 the last year. You may use this method to depreciate virtually all tangible personal property you buy for your business, except for listed property you use less than half the time for business (see "Depreciation Rules for Listed Property," below).

Depreciation Rules for Listed Property

The IRS imposes special record-keeping rules on listed property—items that can easily be used for personal as well as business purposes. (See "Listed Property" in Chapter 15.) If you use listed property for business more than 50% of the time, you may deduct its cost just like any other long-term business property (under Section 179 or using bonus or regular depreciation rules).

However, if you use listed property 50% or less for business, you may not deduct the cost under Section 179 or use bonus depreciation or accelerated depreciation. Instead, you must use the slowest method of depreciation: straight-line depreciation. In addition, you are not allowed to use the normal depreciation periods allowed under the MACRS depreciation system. Instead, you must use the depreciation periods provided for by the Alternative Depreciation System (ADS for short). These are generally longer than the ordinary MACRS periods. However, you may still depreciate cars and trucks over five years. The main ADS depreciation periods for listed property are provided in the chart below.

ADS Depreciation Periods	
Property	**Depreciation Period**
Cars and light trucks	5 years
Communication equipment	10 years
Personal property with no class life	12 years

If you start out using accelerated depreciation and in a later year your business use drops to 50% or less, you have to switch to the straight-line method and ADS period for that year and subsequent years. In addition, you are subject to depreciation recapture for the prior years—that is, you must calculate how much more depreciation you got in the prior years by using accelerated depreciation and count that amount as ordinary taxable income for the current year. This will, of course, increase your tax bill for the year.

Real Property

You can't use bonus depreciation or Section 179 expensing for real property. Instead, you are limited to using regular depreciation. Moreover, when you depreciate real property, you only deduct the cost of the buildings or other structures on it. Land cannot be depreciated because it never wears out.

As you might expect, the depreciation periods for buildings are quite long (after all, buildings usually last a long time). The depreciation period for nonresidential buildings is 39 years. Nonresidential buildings include office buildings, stores, workshops, and factories. Residential real property—an apartment building, for example—is depreciated over 27.5 years. For detailed guidance on how to depreciate residential real property, refer to *Every Landlord's Tax Deduction Guide*, by Stephen Fishman (Nolo).

You must use the straight-line method to depreciate real property. This means you'll only be able to deduct a small fraction of its value each year—$1/39$ of its value annually if the 39-year period applies (less the first and last year depending on the month of the year the property was placed in service).

The only depreciable real property most home-based business owners have is a home office. If you own your home and take the home office deduction, you are entitled to depreciate the business portion of the home. For example, if you use 10% of your home for your business, you may depreciate 10% of the home's original cost (excluding the cost of the land) plus any improvements made to the home after it was purchased. In the event your home has gone down in value since you bought it, you must use its fair market value on the date you began using your home office as your tax basis. You depreciate a home office over 39 years— the term used for nonresidential property. (A home office is non-residential property because you don't live in that portion of your home.) (See Chapter 6 for a detailed discussion of the home office deduction.)

Deducting Business Vehicles

If you use a car, truck, van, or other vehicle in your business, you can deduct your costs using the standard mileage rate (in which you deduct a set amount for each business mile), or the actual expense rate (in which you deduct what you actually spend on business driving). If you use the standard mileage rate to calculate your vehicle deductions, you don't separately depreciate the vehicle. Your depreciation deduction is included in the standard mileage rate and you need not be concerned with the rest of this section. However, if you elect to use the actual expense method instead of the standard mileage rate, you must separately depreciate the vehicle.

Depreciation for a business vehicle works exactly the same way as for any other personal property used in a business, subject to some special rules that limit your annual deductions. However, the Tax Cuts and Jobs Act greatly increased the annual maximum depreciation deductions for vehicles starting in 2018.

Is Your Vehicle a Passenger Automobile?

First, you must figure out whether your vehicle is a passenger automobile as defined by the IRS. A passenger automobile is any four-wheeled vehicle made primarily for use on public streets and highways that has an unloaded gross weight of 6,000 pounds or less. The vehicle weight includes any part or item physically attached to the automobile or usually included in the purchase price of an automobile. This definition includes virtually all automobiles.

However, if your vehicle is a truck, an SUV, or a van, or has a truck base (as do most SUVs), it is a passenger automobile only if it has a gross loaded vehicle weight of 6,000 pounds or less. The gross loaded weight is based on how much the manufacturer says the vehicle can carry and is different from unloaded weight—that is, the vehicle's weight without any passengers or cargo.

You can find out your vehicle's gross loaded and unloaded weight by looking at the metal plate in the driver's side doorjamb, looking at your owner's manual, checking the manufacturer's website or sales brochure, or asking an auto dealer. The gross loaded weight is usually called the Gross Vehicle Weight Rating (GVWR for short). The gross unloaded weight is often called the curb weight.

Vehicles that would otherwise come within the passenger automobile definition are excluded if they are not likely to be used more than a minimal amount for personal purposes—for example, moving vans, construction vehicles, ambulances, hearses, tractors, and taxis or other vehicles used in a transportation business. Also excluded are trucks and vans that have been specially modified so they are not likely to be used more than a minimal amount for personal purposes—for example, by installation of permanent shelving, or painting of the vehicle to display advertising or a company's name. The restrictions on depreciation discussed in this section don't apply to these vehicles.

Annual Depreciation Limits for Passenger Automobiles

Depreciating a passenger automobile is unique in one very important way: The annual depreciation deduction for automobiles is subject to a maximum dollar limit. The Tax Cuts and Jobs Act greatly increased the annual limits for passenger vehicles placed into service during 2018 and later. The amounts are shown in the following chart and they apply to all passenger vehicles, including automobiles, trucks, and vans that come within the definition. The chart shows that if you place a passenger vehicle into service in your business in 2020, you may take a maximum depreciation deduction of $10,100. The second year, you may deduct a whopping $16,100. That's $26,200 in depreciation deductions in the first two years—$34,200 if bonus depreciation is also claimed. These are by far the highest annual limits for passenger vehicle depreciation that have ever been allowed. In contrast, under prior law, only $3,160 could be deducted the first year and $5,100 the second year for passenger automobiles placed into service during 2017. The annual limits are now so high that only vehicles placed into service during 2020 that cost $50,000 or more are impacted.

Depreciation Limits for Passenger Vehicles (must be reduced by percentage of personal use)	
Year Placed in Service	2020
1st tax year	$10,100 ($18,100 if $8,000 bonus depreciation used)
2nd tax year	$16,100
3rd tax year	$9,700
4th and later years	$5,760

This chart assumes 100% business use of the vehicle. If you use the vehicle for personal use as well as business use, the limits are reduced by the percentage of personal use. For example, if you use the vehicle 40% of the time for personal use, your annual deductions are reduced by 40%. Moreover, your actual depreciation deduction, up to the annual limit, depends on the cost of your car and how much you drive for business.

Bonus depreciation may be used to deduct a substantial amount of an asset's cost the first year it is placed in service. For assets other than passenger vehicles, the bonus amount is 100% during 2018 through 2022. Bonus depreciation may be applied to vehicles, but the bonus amount is fixed at $8,000, no matter how much the vehicle costs. Thus, by using bonus depreciation, you can depreciate a maximum of $18,100 for a passenger vehicle the first year it is placed in service during 2020 instead of $10,100. However, you may use bonus depreciation for used or new vehicles you use more than 50% of the time for business purposes.

There are three regular depreciation methods that may be used for vehicles: two types of accelerated depreciation that provide larger deductions in the first two years, and straight-line depreciation. No matter which method you use, your deduction will be subject to the annual limits set forth above.

When you claim bonus depreciation, Section 179 expensing, and/or accelerated depreciation for a vehicle, you must use the vehicle at least 50% of the time for business during the entire six-year recovery period. If your business use of a vehicle falls below 50% in the second through sixth years, you'll be subject to recapture. This requires you to recompute your depreciation deductions for the prior years using the straight-line method and add to your ordinary income the amount of depreciation you took in prior years that exceeded that amount.

Heavy Deductions for Heavy Metal: Bonus Depreciation for SUVs and Other Weighty Vehicles

The depreciation limits discussed above apply only to passenger automobiles—that is, vehicles with a gross loaded weight of less than 6,000 pounds. (See "Is Your Vehicle a Passenger Automobile?" above.) Vehicles that weigh more than this are not subject to the limits. This means that using bonus depreciation and/or Section 179, you may be able to deduct all or most of the cost of such a vehicle in a single year— a potentially enormous deduction for businesspeople who purchase heavy SUVs and similar vehicles for their business.

So long as the vehicle is used over 50% of the time for business, you can claim 100% bonus depreciation during 2018 through 2022, no matter how much this amounts to. This means you can deduct 100% of the cost in one year if you use the vehicle 100% for business. However, there is a $25,900 limit on your Section 179 deduction. The limit applies to any four-wheeled vehicle primarily designed or used to carry passengers over public streets, roads, or highways that has a gross vehicle weight of 6,000 to 14,000 pounds. With bonus depreciation set at 100% during 2018 through 2022, there would appear to be little reason to use Section 179 for this purpose.

Tax Reporting and Record Keeping

You must report depreciation and Section 179 deductions on IRS Form 4562, *Depreciation and Amortization*. If you have more than one business for which you're claiming depreciation, you must use a separate Form 4562 for each business. If you're a sole proprietor, you carry over the amount of your depreciation and Section 179 deductions to your Schedule C and subtract them from your gross business income along with your other business expenses.

> **TIP**
>
> **Let your computer handle the fine print.** Form 4562 is one of the most complex and confusing IRS forms. If you want to complete it yourself, do yourself a favor and use tax preparation software.

You need to keep accurate records for each asset you depreciate or expense under Section 179, showing:

- a description of the asset
- when and how you purchased the property
- the date it was placed in service
- its original cost
- the percentage of time you use it for business
- whether and how much you deducted under Section 179
- the amount of depreciation you took for the asset in prior years, if any
- the asset's depreciable basis
- the depreciation method used
- the length of the depreciation period, and
- the amount of depreciation you deducted for the year.

If you use tax preparation software, it should create a worksheet containing this information. Be sure to check this carefully and save it.

You can also use an accounting program, such as *QuickBooks,* to keep track of your depreciating assets. (Simple checkbook programs like *Quicken* are not designed to track depreciation.) You may also use a spreadsheet program to create your own depreciation worksheet. Spreadsheet templates are available for this purpose. Of course, you can also do the job by hand. The instructions to IRS Form 4562 contain a worksheet you can use.

For listed property, you'll also have to keep records showing how much time you spend using it for business and personal purposes. You should also keep proof of the amount you paid for the asset—receipts, canceled checks, and purchase documents. You need not file these records with your tax return, but you must have them available to back up your deductions if you're audited.

Leasing Long-Term Assets

When you're acquiring a long-term asset for your business, you should consider whether it makes more sense to lease the item rather than purchase it. Almost everything a business needs can be leased—computers, office furniture, equipment. And leasing can be an attractive alternative to buying. However, when making your decision, it's important to understand the tax consequences of leasing.

So which is better, leasing or buying? It depends. Leasing equipment and other long-term assets can be a better option for small business owners who have limited capital or who need equipment that must be upgraded every few years. Purchasing equipment can be a better option for businesses with ample capital or for equipment that has a long usable life. Each business's situation is unique, and the decision to buy or lease must be made on a case-by-case basis. The following chart summarizes the major tax and nontax differences between leasing and buying equipment.

	Leasing	Buying
Tax Treatment	Lease payments are a currently deductible business operating expense. No depreciation or Section 179 deductions.	Up to $1,040,000 in equipment purchases can be deducted in one year under Section 179. 100% can be deducted through 2022 using bonus depreciation. Otherwise, cost is depreciated over several years (usually five to seven). Interest on loans to buy equipment is currently deductible.
Initial Cash Outlay	Small. No down payment is required; a deposit is ordinarily required.	Large. At least a 20% down payment is usually required. A bank loan may be required to finance the remaining cost.
Ownership	You own nothing at end of lease term.	You own the equipment.
Costs of Equipment Obsolescence	Lessor bears costs because it owns equipment. Lessee may lease new equipment when lease expires.	Buyer bears costs because buyer owns the equipment, which may have little resale value.

Before deciding whether to purchase or lease an expensive item, it's a good idea to determine the total actual costs of each option. This depends on many factors, including:

- the cost of the lease
- the purchase price for the item
- the item's useful life
- the interest rate on a loan to purchase the item
- the item's residual value—how much it would be worth at the end of the lease term
- whether you will purchase the item at the end of the lease and how much this would cost
- how much it would cost to dispose of the item
- your income tax bracket

- whether the item qualifies for 100% bonus depreciation or one-year Section 179 expensing or must be depreciated using regular depreciation, and
- if the item must be depreciated, the length of the depreciation period.

There are several lease-versus-buy calculators on the Internet that you can use to compare the costs of leasing versus buying. Commercial software and computer spreadsheets can also be used for this purpose.

The Home Office Deduction

The home office deduction allows you to deduct many of the costs associated with running a business from your home. For many home business owners, this is one of their largest tax deductions.

Qualifying for the Home Office Deduction

The federal government helps out home business owners by letting them deduct their home office expenses from their taxable income. This is true whether you own your home or apartment or are a renter. Although this tax deduction is commonly called the home office deduction, it applies not only to space devoted to office work, but also to a workshop, lab, studio, or any other home workspace that you use for your business.

> EXAMPLE: Rich, a professional musician and freelance writer, uses the basement of his San Francisco rental home as his writing office and recording studio. He can deduct his home office expenses, including a portion of his rent, from his business income. This saves him over $2,000 per year on his income and self-employment taxes.

If you've heard stories about how difficult it is to qualify for the home office deduction, you can breathe more easily. Changes in the tax law have made it easier for businesspeople to qualify for the deduction. So even if you haven't qualified for the deduction in the past, you may be entitled to take it now.

Some people believe that taking the home office deduction invites an IRS audit. The IRS denies this. But even if taking the deduction increases your audit chances, the risk of an audit is still low (see Chapter 17). Moreover, you have nothing to fear from an audit if you're entitled to take the deduction and you keep good records to prove it. Unfortunately, because of these fears, only about one third of all taxpayers who qualify for the home office deduction actually take it—as many as 5 million taxpayers who could take the deduction, don't. In an apparent effort to encourage small business owners to take the deduction, the IRS created a new simplified method of claiming the deduction. (See "Simplified Home Office Deduction Method," below.)

However, if you plan on taking the deduction, you need to learn how to do it properly. There are strict requirements you must meet in order to qualify for the home office deduction. You are entitled to the home office deduction if you:

- are in business
- use your home office exclusively for business (unless you store inventory or run a day care center in your home—see "Additional Requirements," below), and
- use your home office for business on a regular basis.

These are the three threshold requirements that everyone must meet. If you get past this first hurdle, then you must also meet *any one* of the following requirements:

- Your home office is your principal place of business.
- You regularly and exclusively use your home office for administrative or management activities for your business and have no other fixed location where you perform such activities.
- You meet clients or customers at home.
- You use a separate structure on your property exclusively for business purposes.
- You store inventory or product samples at home.
- You run a day care center at home.

These rules apply whether you are a sole proprietor, a partner in a partnership, a limited liability company (LLC) owner, or an S corporation owner. If you're one of the few home businesspeople who has formed a regular C corporation that you own and operate, and you work as its employee, however, you must meet some additional requirements (see "Corporation Employees," below).

Requirements for Home Office Deduction

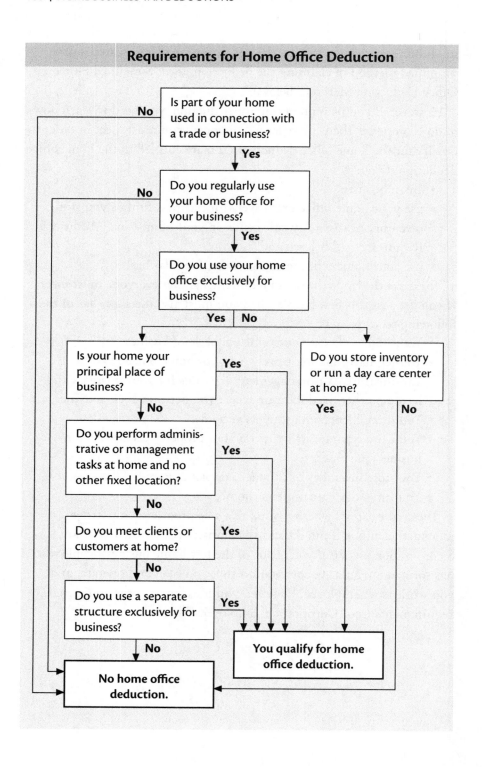

Threshold Requirements: Regular and Exclusive Business Use

To take the home office deduction, you must have a home office—that is, an office or other workplace in your home that you use regularly and exclusively for business. Your home may be a house, an apartment, a condominium, a mobile home, or even a boat. You can also take the deduction for separate structures on your property that you use for business, such as an unattached garage, workshop, studio, barn, or greenhouse.

You Must Be in Business

You must be in business to take the home office deduction. You can't take the deduction for a hobby or another nonbusiness activity that you conduct out of your home. Nor can you take it if you perform personal investment activities at home—for example, researching the stock market. (See Chapter 2 for information on what constitutes a business for tax purposes.)

You don't have to work full time in a business to qualify for the home office deduction. If you satisfy the requirements, you can take the deduction for a side business that you run from a home office. However, you must use your home office regularly, and the total amount you deduct cannot exceed your profit from the business. (See "What Expenses Can You Deduct?" later in this chapter, for more on the profit limitation.)

> EXAMPLE: Barbara works full time as an editor for a publishing company. She also spends about 15 hours a week writing and publishing freelance articles. She does all the work on the articles from an office in her apartment. Barbara may take the home office deduction, but she can't deduct more than she earns from her freelancing business.

If you have more than one business, each business must qualify separately for the home office deduction. Depending on where you do your work, it's possible that one of your businesses will qualify while the other does not.

> **EXAMPLE:** Jim has two businesses: He runs a bookkeeping service and also works as a professional magician, performing at birthdays, conventions, and similar events. He performs all of his bookkeeping work at home, so he can take a home office deduction for his bookkeeping business. However, because he does not work on his magic business at home, he gets no home office deduction for that income.

This rule can be important because of the profit limit on the amount of the home office deduction—that is, your deduction may not exceed the net profit you earn from your home office business or businesses. You'll want to make sure that your most profitable enterprises qualify for the deduction.

You Must Use Your Home Office Exclusively for Business

You can't take the home office deduction unless you use part of your home exclusively for your business. In other words, you must use your home office *only for your business.* The more space you devote exclusively to your business, the more your home office deduction will be worth. (See "Calculating the Home Office Deduction," below.) This requirement doesn't apply if you store inventory at home or run a home day care center. (See "Additional Requirements," below.)

If you use part of your home—such as a room or studio—as your business office, but you also use that space for personal purposes, you won't qualify for the home office deduction.

> **EXAMPLE:** Johnny, a home-based professional fundraiser, has a den at home furnished with a desk, chair, bookshelf, filing cabinet, and a bed for visiting guests. He uses the desk and chair for both business and personal reasons. The bookshelf contains both personal and business books, the filing cabinet contains both personal and business files, and the bed is used only for personal reasons. Johnny can't claim a business deduction for the den because he does not use it, or any part of it, exclusively for business purposes.

The easiest way to meet the exclusive use test is to devote an entire room in your home to your business—for example, by using an extra bedroom as your office. However, not everybody has a room to spare—

and the IRS recognizes this. You can still claim the deduction even if you use just part of a room as your office, as long as you devote that portion of the room exclusively to your business.

How Big (or Small) Can Your Home Office Be?

Your home office can be as big or small as you want or need. You are not required to use as small a space as possible. If you like plenty of office space, you can spread out and even use more than one room. But remember, you may use your home office space only for business. You aren't even supposed to use it for personal business, such as writing personal checks.

Although the IRS probably won't be inspecting your home office, your deduction must still make sense in the event you are audited. If you live in a one-bedroom apartment and claim the entire bedroom as a home office, you'll have to have an answer ready when the IRS asks where you sleep.

In one case, for example, a psychologist who lived in San Francisco claimed a home office deduction for one-quarter of her apartment. However, the entire apartment was a 400-square-foot studio, consisting of an open area (approximately 13 feet by 15 feet) furnished with a desk and a couch, and a small dining area and kitchen (each approximately seven feet by eight feet). Given the layout of this tiny apartment, neither the IRS nor the tax court bought the psychologist's claim that she used 100 square feet exclusively for her psychology practice. (*Mullin v. Comm'r.*, TC Memo 2001-121.) On the other hand, Lauren Miller, a public relations professional with a 700-square-foot studio apartment in Manhattan, did qualify for the home office deduction. Miller's apartment was divided into three equal sections: (1) an entryway, a bathroom, and a kitchen area; (2) office space, including a desk, two shelving units, a bookcase, and a sofa; and (3) a bedroom area including a platform bed and dressers. Miller admitted that she had to pass through the office space to get to the bedroom area. Nevertheless, the Tax Court found that the office area of her apartment satisfied the exclusivity requirement for the home office deduction. It held that "her personal use of the space was de minimis and wholly attributable to the practicalities of living in a studio apartment of such modest dimensions." (*Miller v. Comm'r.*, T.C. Summary Opinion 2014-74.)

> **EXAMPLE:** Paul, a software engineer, keeps his desk, chair, bookshelf, computer, and filing cabinet in one part of his den and uses them exclusively for business. The remainder of the room—one-third of the space—is used to store a bed for houseguests. Paul can take a home office deduction for the two-thirds of the room that he uses exclusively as an office.

If you use the same room (or rooms) for your office and for other purposes, you'll have to arrange your furniture and belongings so that a portion of the room is devoted exclusively to your business. Place only your business furniture and other business items in the office portion of the room. Business furniture includes anything that you use for your business, such as standard office furniture like a desk and chair. Depending on your business, it could include other items as well—for example, a psychologist might need a couch, an artist might need work tables and easels, and a consultant might need a seating area to meet with clients. One court held that a financial planner was entitled to have a television in his home office because he used it to keep up on financial news. Be careful what you put in this space, however. In another case, the IRS disallowed the deduction for a doctor because he had a television in the part of his living room that he claimed as his home office. The court wouldn't buy the doctor's claim that he used the TV only to watch medical programs.

The IRS does not require you to physically separate the space you use for business from the rest of the room. However, doing so will help you satisfy the exclusive use test. For example, if you use part of your living room as an office, you could separate it from the rest of the room with folding screens or bookcases.

Although you must use your home office exclusively for business, you and other family members or visitors may walk through it to get to other rooms in your residence.

As a practical matter, the IRS doesn't have spies checking to see whether you're using your home office just for business. However, complying with the rules from the beginning means you won't have to worry if you are audited.

When the IRS Can Enter Your Home

IRS auditors may not enter your home unless you or another lawful occupant gives them permission. The only exception is if the IRS obtains a court order to enter your home, which is very rare. In the absence of such a court order, an IRS revenue officer must ask permission to come to your home to verify your home office deduction. You don't have to grant permission for the visit—but if you don't, the officer will probably disallow your deduction.

You Must Use Your Home Office Regularly

It's not enough to use a part of your home exclusively for business; you must also use it regularly. For example, you can't place a desk in a corner of a room and claim the home office deduction if you almost never use the desk for your business.

Unfortunately, the IRS doesn't offer a clear definition of regular use. The agency has stated only that you must use a portion of your home for business on a continuing basis—not just for occasional or incidental business. One court has held that 12 hours of use a week is sufficient. (*Green v. Comm'r.*, 79 TC 428 (1982).) You might be able to qualify with less use—for example, an hour a day—but no one knows for sure.

Additional Requirements

Using a home office exclusively and regularly for business is not enough to qualify for the home office deduction: You also must satisfy at least one of the additional tests described below.

Your Home Is Your Principal Place of Business

The most common way to satisfy the additional home office deduction requirement is to show that you use your home as your principal place of business. How you accomplish this depends on where you do most of your work and what type of work you do at home.

If you work only at home. If, like many home business owners, you do all or almost all of your work in your home office, your home is clearly your principal place of business, and you'll have no trouble qualifying for the home office deduction. This would be the case, for example, for a writer who writes only at home or a salesperson who sells by phone and makes sales calls from home.

If you work in multiple locations. If you work in more than one location, your home office still qualifies as your principal place of business if you perform your most important business activities—those activities that most directly generate your income—at home.

> EXAMPLE: Charles is a self-employed author who uses a home office to write. He spends 30 to 35 hours per week in his home office writing and another ten to 15 hours a week at other locations conducting research, meeting with publishers, and attending promotional events. The essence of Charles's business is writing—this is how he generates his income. Therefore, his home qualifies as his principal place of business because that's where he writes.

If you perform equally important business activities in several locations, your principal place of business is where you spend more than half of your time. If there is no such location, you don't have a principal place of business.

> EXAMPLE: Sue sells costume jewelry over eBay from her home office, at crafts fairs, and through consignments to craft shops. She spends 25 hours per week in her home office and 15 hours at fairs and crafts shops. Her home office qualifies as her principal place of business.

You Conduct Administrative or Management Activities From Home

Of course, many businesspeople spend the bulk of their time working away from home. This is the case, for example, for:

- building contractors who work primarily on building sites
- doctors who work primarily in hospitals

- traveling salespeople who visit clients at their places of business, and
- housepainters, gardeners, and home repair people who work primarily in their customers' homes.

Fortunately, legal changes that took effect in 1999 make it possible for these people to qualify for the home office deduction. Under the rules, your home office qualifies as your principal place of business, even if you work primarily outside your home, if you:

- use the office to conduct administrative or management activities for your business, and
- use no other fixed location where you conduct substantial administrative or management activities.

Administrative or management activities include, but are not limited to:

- billing clients or patients
- keeping books and records
- ordering supplies
- setting up appointments, and
- writing reports.

This means that you can qualify for the home office deduction even if your home office is not where you generate most of your business income. It's sufficient that you regularly use your office to administer or manage your business—for example, to keep your books, schedule appointments, do research, write reports, forward orders, or order supplies. As long as you have no other fixed location where you regularly do these things—for example, an outside office—you'll get the deduction.

Because of these rules, almost any home business owner can qualify for the home office deduction. All you have to do is set up a home office that you regularly use to manage or administer your business. Even people who spend most of their work time away from home can usually find plenty of business-related work to do in a home office.

> **EXAMPLE:** Sally, a self-employed handyperson, performs home repair work for clients in their homes. She also has a home office that she uses regularly and exclusively to keep her books, arrange appointments, and order supplies. Sally is entitled to a home office deduction.

Under these rules, you may have an outside office or workplace and still qualify for the home office deduction as long as you use your home office to perform administrative or management tasks and you don't perform substantial administrative tasks at your outside office.

> **EXAMPLE:** Bill, a self-employed goldsmith, maintains a workshop in an industrial park where he performs his goldsmithing. He also has a home office where he takes care of all the administrative functions for his business, including taking orders and record keeping. Bill may take the home office deduction.

You may occasionally conduct minimal administrative or management activities at your outside office (or another fixed location). You may also perform some administrative tasks in a place other than a fixed location, such as your car, hotel room, or clients' offices (a client's office is a fixed location only for the client, not for you).

> **EXAMPLE:** Millie sells Bibles door-to-door. She stores order forms and keeps track of appointments in her car. She regularly uses her home office to forward orders and perform other administrative tasks. Millie is entitled to take a home office deduction.

All the administrative or management activities for your business don't have to be done at home to qualify for the home office deduction. Your home office can qualify for the deduction even if you have others conduct your administrative or management activities at locations other than your home—for example, an outside company does your billing from its place of business.

Moreover, you can qualify for the deduction even if you have suitable space to conduct administrative or management activities outside your home, but choose to use your home office for those activities instead.

> **EXAMPLE:** Paul, a self-employed anesthesiologist, spends most of his time administering anesthesia and postoperative care in three local hospitals. One of the hospitals provides him with a small shared office

where he could conduct administrative or management activities, but rarely does. Instead, he uses a room in his home that he has converted to an office. He uses this room exclusively and regularly to contact patients, surgeons, and hospitals regarding scheduling; prepare for treatments and presentations; maintain billing records and patient logs; satisfy continuing medical education requirements; and read medical journals and books. Paul qualifies for the home office deduction even though he could use the office provided by the hospital.

You Meet Clients or Customers at Home

Even if your home office is not your principal place of business, you may deduct your expenses for any part of your home that you use exclusively to meet with clients, customers, or patients. You must physically meet with others in this home location; phoning them from there is not sufficient. And the meetings must be a regular part of your business; occasional meetings don't qualify.

It's not entirely clear how often you must meet clients at home for those meetings to be considered regular. However, the IRS has indicated that meeting clients one or two days a week is sufficient. Exclusive use means you use the space where you meet clients only for business. You are free to use the space for business purposes other than meeting clients—for example, doing your business bookkeeping or other paperwork. But you cannot use the space for personal purposes, such as watching television.

> **EXAMPLE:** June, an attorney, works three days a week in her city office and two days in her home office, which she uses only for business. She meets clients at her home office at least once a week. Because she regularly meets clients at her home office, she qualifies for the home office deduction even though her city office is her principal place of business.

If you want to qualify under this part of the rule, encourage clients or customers to visit you at home and keep a log or an appointment book showing all of their visits.

You Use a Separate Structure for Business

You can also deduct expenses for a separate freestanding structure, such as a studio, garage, or barn, if you use it exclusively and regularly for your business. The structure does not have to be your principal place of business, and you do not have to meet patients, clients, or customers there.

Exclusive use means that you use the structure only for business—for example, you can't use it to store gardening equipment or as a guesthouse. Regular use is not precisely defined, but it's probably sufficient to use the structure ten or 15 hours a week.

> EXAMPLE: Deborah is a freelance graphic designer. She has her main office in a downtown office building, but also works every weekend in a small studio in her backyard. Because she uses the studio regularly and exclusively for her design work, she qualifies for the home office deduction.

You Store Inventory or Product Samples at Home

You can also take the home office deduction if you are in the business of selling retail or wholesale products and you store inventory or product samples at home. To qualify, you can't have an office or other business location outside your home. And you must store your inventory in a particular place in your home—for example, a garage, closet, or bedroom. You can't move your inventory from one room to the other. You don't have to use the storage space exclusively to store your inventory to take the deduction—you just have to regularly use it for that purpose.

> EXAMPLE: Lisa sells costume jewelry door to door. She rents a home and regularly uses half of her attached garage to store her jewelry inventory; she also parks her Harley-Davidson motorcycle there. Lisa can deduct the expenses for the storage space even though she does not use her entire garage exclusively to store inventory.

You Operate a Day Care Center at Home

You're also entitled to a home office deduction if you operate a day care center at home. This is a place where you care for children, people who are at least 65 years old, or people who are physically or mentally unable to care for themselves. Your day care must be licensed by the appropriate licensing agency, unless it's exempt. You must regularly use part of your home for day care, but your day care use need not be exclusive—for example, you could use your living room for day care during the day and for personal reasons at night.

Corporation Employees

If you form a corporation to own and operate your business, you'll probably work as its employee. Prior to 2018, employees could claim a home office deduction if they satisfied the requirements discussed above and maintained the home office for the convenience of the employer. In this event, they could claim the home office deduction as a personal miscellaneous itemized deduction on Schedule A. However, starting in 2018 and lasting through 2025, this deduction is no longer available for employees.

If you work as an employee of your own corporation (or a corporation owned by someone else), you should seek to have your home office expenses reimbursed by your employer. These expenses would include all the applicable amounts covered in "Calculating the Home Office Deduction," below. The corporation can then deduct this amount as an ordinary business expense for office space. If you satisfy the requirements discussed below, the reimbursement will not be taxable to you personally.

> **EXAMPLE:** Jill operates her consulting business as a corporation. She incurs $10,000 in home expenses during the year. She submits an expense report to her corporation for $10,000 in home office expenses. The corporation deducts the $10,000 as an office space expense. Jill, the employee-owner, has no taxable income for her employee expense reimbursement.

To avoid paying tax on your reimbursement, all of the following must be true:

- You satisfy all the requirements for the home office deduction discussed above in "Qualifying for the Home Office Deduction."
- You maintain the home office for the convenience of your employer.
- You keep careful track of your home office expenses and can prove them with receipts or other records.
- Your corporation formally approves reimbursement of your home office expenses and the approval is documented in its corporate minutes.
- You have an "accountable reimbursement plan"—a written agreement in which the corporation agrees to reimburse you if you provide proper substantiation for your expenses.
- You provide your corporation with a complete and accurate expense report. A good way to accomplish the reimbursement is to complete IRS Form 8829, *Expenses for Business Use of Your Home*, and attach it to your expense report.

The convenience of the employer requirement can be difficult to meet. An employee's home office is deemed to be for an employer's convenience only if it is:

- a condition of employment
- necessary for the employer's business to properly function, or
- needed to allow the employee to properly perform his or her duties.

When you own the business that employs you, you ordinarily won't be able to successfully claim that a home office is a condition of your employment—after all, as the owner of the business, you're the person who sets the conditions for employees, including yourself. If there is no other office where you do your work, however, you should be able to establish that your home office is necessary for your business to properly function and/or for you to perform your employee duties.

It will be more difficult to establish convenience if you have separate corporate offices. Nevertheless, business owners in this situation have successfully argued that their home offices were necessary—for example, because their corporate offices were not open or not usable during evenings, weekends, or other nonbusiness hours, or were too far from home to use during off-hours. The necessity test would clearly be satisfied if you worked at home during 2020 because your outside office was closed due to the coronavirus (COVID-19) pandemic.

Calculating the Home Office Deduction

This is the fun part—figuring out how much the home office deduction will save you in taxes. There are now two ways you can calculate the home office deduction. You can use the standard method discussed below. Alternatively, you may use a simplified method. (See "Simplified Home Office Deduction Method," below.)

How Much of Your Home Is Used for Business?

To calculate your home office deduction, you need to determine what percentage of your home you use for business. The law says you can use "any reasonable method" to do this. Obviously, you want to use the method that will give you the largest home office deduction. To do this, you want to maximize the percentage of your home that you claim as your office. There is no single way to do this for every home office. Try both methods described below, the square footage and the room methods, and use the one that gives you the larger deduction.

Some tax experts advise not to claim more than 20% to 25% of your home as an office unless you store inventory at home. However, home business owners have successfully claimed much more. In one case, for example, an interior decorator claimed 74% of his apartment (850 of 1,150 square feet) as a home office. He was audited by the IRS, but the Service did not object to the amount of space he claimed for his office. (*Visin v. Comm'r.*, TC Memo 2003-246.) And a professional violinist successfully claimed a home office deduction for her entire living room, which took up 40% of her one-bedroom apartment. She used the room solely for violin practice. (*Popov v. Comm'r.*, 246 F.3d 1190 (9th Cir. 2002).) It is probably true, though, that the larger your home office deduction, the greater your chances of being audited.

Renting Your Home Office to Your Corporation

If you've incorporated your business as a C corporation and you can't meet the convenience of the employer test or the other requirements for the home office deduction, you have another option: Forget about the home office deduction and rent your home office to your C corporation. You won't save any income tax this way, but you can still save on Social Security and Medicare taxes.

Here's how it works:

- You rent your home office to your C corporation for a fair market rental.
- Your C corporation deducts the rent as a business expense on its tax return (Form 1120).
- You report the rent you receive as ordinary income on your personal tax return, and pay income tax on it.

Ordinarily, a landlord may deduct his or her rental expenses, such as mortgage interest, depreciation, and utilities. However, a special tax rule prohibits an employee who rents part of his or her home to his or her employer from deducting such expenses. (I.R.C. § 280A(c)(6).) So, you can forget about taking any deductions for your rental expenses to reduce your income taxes.

However, you still save on Social Security and Medicare taxes because the rental income you receive is not subject to these taxes. For the rent to be deductible by the corporation, however, there must be a legitimate business reason for this rental arrangement. This would be the case if your home office was your only office, or if you could otherwise show a legitimate need for it.

EXAMPLE: Rod, an accountant who works out of his home, formed a C corporation. Rod does not qualify for the home office deduction because he does not use his office exclusively for his accounting business. He charges his corporation $10,000 per year for the use he makes of his office for his accounting business. Rod gets no home office deduction, but his corporation deducts the rent on its own tax return. He reports the $10,000 on his personal tax return as rental income, but takes no deductions for rental expenses, such as depreciation and utilities. Rod saves nothing on his income taxes, but he and his corporation need not pay Social Security and Medicare taxes on the $10,000 rental payment. This saves Rod $1,530 in taxes that he would have had to pay if the $10,000 were paid to him as employee salary.

> ## Renting Your Home Office to Your Corporation (continued)
>
> This strategy only works for C corporations because they are not subject to the home office deduction rules (although their employees are). It won't work with an S corporation because the home office rules apply to pass-through entities. As a result, an S corporation can't deduct rent paid for a home office that doesn't satisfy all the rules discussed above.
>
> You need to be careful not to charge your corporation too much rent. Amounts the IRS deems excessive may be recharacterized as constructive dividends that are not deductible by the corporation. They will, therefore, be subject to corporate income tax at a 21% rate. To avoid this, the rent you charge your corporation should be the same as what you would charge a stranger.

CAUTION

The day care center deduction amount is calculated differently. If you operate a day care center at home but you don't devote a portion of your home exclusively to day care, your home office deduction is calculated differently than described here. You need to compare the time you use the space for day care with the time you use it for personal purposes—for example, if you use 50% of your house as a day care center for 25% of the hours in a year, you can claim a deduction for 12.5% of your housing costs (50% × 25% = 12.5%). See IRS Publication 587, *Business Use of Your Home*, for more information.

Square Footage Method

The most precise method of measuring your office space is to divide the square footage of your home office by the total square footage of your home. For example, if your home is 1,600 square feet and you use 400 square feet for your home office, 25% of the total area is used for business. Of course, you must know the square footage of your entire home and your office to make this calculation. Your home's total square footage may be listed on real estate documents or plans; otherwise, you'll have to measure your office space yourself. You don't need to use a tape measure; you can just pace off the measurements.

You are allowed to subtract the square footage of common areas—such as hallways, entries, stairs, and landings—from the total area that you are measuring. You can also exclude attics and garages from your total space if you don't use them for business purposes. You aren't required to measure this way, but doing so will give you a larger deduction because your overall percentage of business use will be higher.

When Is an Office Part of a Home?

Kenneth Burkhart, a professional photographer, purchased a two-story building with a full basement. The building was originally constructed and used as a three-flat apartment building with a separate apartment in the basement and on each of the two upper floors. Burkhart converted the upper two floors into a single residence for his use and converted the basement into a studio and darkroom for his photography business.

Was the studio part of his residence or a separate apartment? This was not an idle question. The home office deduction rules apply only to offices or other workspaces that are part of a business owner's "dwelling."

Courts faced with this issue look at whether the area used for business is physically and functionally part of the business owner's residence. In this case, the court noted that Burkhart had removed the basement's outside entrance, kitchen, bathroom, and sleeping area. Because the basement could only be reached from the upper floors of the building, the court reasoned that the upper floors and the basement had become a single "house," similar to millions of other family homes with two upper floors and a basement. Thus, Burkhart's studio was part of his dwelling and was subject to the home office deduction rules. (*Burkhart v. Comm'r.*, TC Memo 1989-417.)

Room Method

Another way to measure is the room method. You can use this method only if all of the rooms in your home are about the same size. Using this method, you divide the number of rooms used for business by the total number of rooms in the home. Don't include bathrooms, closets, or

Square Footage Method (Total Area)

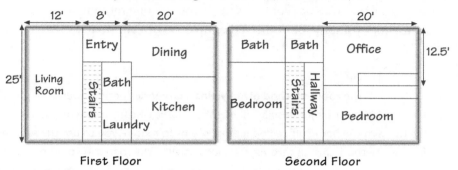

First Floor

Second Floor

Square Footage Method (Excluding Common Areas)

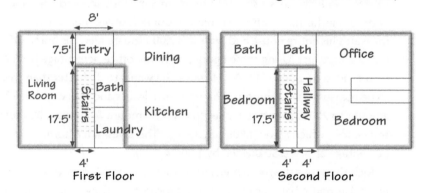

First Floor

Second Floor

Room Method

First Floor

Second Floor

other storage areas. You may also leave out garages and attics if you don't use them for business. For example, if you use one room in a five-room house for business, your office takes up 20% of your home.

> **TIP**
>
> **The room method often yields a larger deduction.** Even though IRS Form 8829, *Expenses for Business Use of Your Home* (the form sole proprietors file to claim the home office deduction), seems to require you to use the square footage method, this isn't the case. As long as all of the rooms in your home are about the same size, you can use the room method. Using the room method will often result in a larger deduction.

> **EXAMPLE:** Rich rents a six-room house in San Francisco and uses one bedroom as his home office. Using the square footage method, Rich measures his entire house and finds it is 2,000 square feet. His home office is 250 square feet. Using these figures, his home office percentage is 12.5% (250 divided by 2,000 = 12.5%). However, he wants to do better than this, so he measures his common areas, such as hallways and stairways, which amount to 200 square feet. He subtracts this amount from the 2,000 total square feet, which leaves 1,800 square feet. This gives him a home office percentage of 14% (250 divided by 1,800 = 14%).
>
> Rich then tries the room method to see whether this provides a better result. His house has six rooms—three bedrooms, a living room, a dining room, and a kitchen. He doesn't count the bathroom, garage, or attic. Because he uses one entire room as his home office, he divides one by six, leaving 16.7% as his home office percentage. Rich uses this amount to figure his home office deduction.

What Expenses Can You Deduct?

The home office deduction is not one deduction, but many. Most costs associated with maintaining and running your home office are deductible. However, because your office is in your home, some of the money you spend also benefits you personally. For example, your utility bill pays to heat your home office, but it also keeps the rest of your living space warm.

The IRS deals with this issue by dividing home office expenses into two categories: direct expenses, which benefit only your home office; and indirect expenses, which benefit both your office and the rest of your home.

Direct Expenses

You have a direct home office expense when you pay for something just for the home office portion of your home. This includes, for example, the cost of painting your home office, carpeting it, or hiring someone to clean it. The entire amount of a direct home office expense is deductible.

> EXAMPLE: Jean pays a housepainter $400 to paint her home office. She may deduct this entire amount as a home office deduction.

Virtually anything you buy for your office that wears out, becomes obsolete, or gets used up is deductible. However, you may have to depreciate permanent improvements to your home office over 39 years, rather than deduct them in the year when you pay for them. Permanent improvements are changes that go beyond simple repairs, such as adding a new room to your home to serve as your office. (See Chapter 5 for more information.)

Indirect Expenses

An indirect expense is a payment for something that benefits your *entire home*, including both the home office portion and your personal space. You may deduct only a portion of this expense—the home office percentage of the total.

> EXAMPLE: Instead of just painting her home office, Jean decides to paint her entire home for $1,600. She uses 25% of her home as an office, so she may deduct 25% of the cost, or $400.

Most of your home office expenses will be indirect expenses, including:
- **Rent.** If you rent your home or apartment, you can use the home office deduction to deduct part of your rent—a substantial expense that is ordinarily not deductible. Your tax savings will be particularly great if you live in a high-rent area.

> **EXAMPLE:** Sam uses 20% of his Manhattan studio apartment as a home office for his consulting business. He pays $3,000 per month in rent, and may therefore deduct $600 of his rent per month ($7,200 per year) as a home office expense. This saves him over $2,500 in federal, state, and self-employment taxes.

- **Mortgage interest and property taxes.** Whether or not you have a home office, you may be able to deduct your monthly mortgage interest and property tax payments as a personal itemized income tax deduction on your Schedule A, *Itemized Deductions* (the tax form where you list your personal income tax deductions). However, the Tax Cuts and Jobs Act has lessened the value of this deduction and made it impossible for many taxpayers to take it at all. You can take a personal deduction for mortgage interest and property tax only if you itemize your personal expenses on your return. You should do this only if your mortgage interest, property taxes, and other personal deductions exceed the standard deduction. The Tax Cuts and Jobs Act almost doubled the standard deduction. As a result, only about 10% of all taxpayers are able to itemize, compared with 30% in past years. In addition, starting in 2018 and continuing through 2025, the itemized deduction for property taxes is limited to $10,000 per year. Also, for homes purchased in 2018 through 2025, the deduction for home mortgage interest is limited to acquisition loans for a main and second home totaling a maximum of $750,000. The amount is $1 million for homes purchased before 2018.

   If you have a home office, you have the option of deducting the home office percentage of your mortgage interest and property tax payments as part of your home office deduction. If you do this, you do not deduct this amount on your Schedule A (you can't deduct the same item twice). This means you can deduct this amount without itemizing. If you do itemize, these amounts don't count toward the limits on deducting property tax and home mortgage interest as a personal itemized deduction.

> **EXAMPLE:** Ed pays $12,000 per year in property tax on his home. He uses 25% of the home as an office for his business. This enables him to deduct $3,000 of his property tax (25%) as part of his home office deduction. He deducts the remaining $9,000 as a personal itemized deduction on his Schedule A. Had he not had a home office, he could have deducted only $10,000 of his $12,000 in property tax as a personal itemized deduction.

Another advantage of deducting the home office percentage of your monthly mortgage interest and real estate tax payments as part of your home office deduction is that it is a business deduction, not a personal deduction; as such, it reduces the amount of your business income subject to self-employment taxes, as well as reducing your income taxes. The self-employment tax is 15.3%, so you save $153 in self-employment taxes for every $1,000 in mortgage interest and property taxes you deduct as part of your home office deduction.

> **EXAMPLE:** Suzy, a self-employed medical record transcriber, uses 20% of her three-bedroom Tulsa home as a home office. She pays $10,000 per year in mortgage interest and property taxes. When she does her taxes for the year, she may deduct $2,000 of her interest and taxes as part of her home office deduction (20% of $10,000). She adds this amount to her other home office expenses and decreases her business income for both income tax and self-employment tax purposes. The extra $2,000 business deduction saves her $306 in self-employment tax (15.3% × $2,000). She may deduct the remaining $8,000 of mortgage interest and property tax as a personal deduction on her Schedule A.

- **Depreciation.** If you own your home, you're also entitled to a depreciation deduction for the office portion of your home. Home offices are depreciated over 39 years, so you may deduct 1/39 of the office's tax basis each year (except the first and last year; the first year deduction is based on the month you began to use the office). Your home office's tax basis is the home office percentage of the adjusted basis of your entire home. Your home's adjusted basis is its original cost plus the cost of any improvements you made before you established your home office. However, if your home has declined in value since you bought it, you use that value instead of unadjusted basis.

> **EXAMPLE:** Stan purchased a home five years ago for $500,000, and its fair market value is now $700,000. He figures his land is worth 20% of the home's cost, so his adjusted basis is $400,000. He starts to use 10% of the home as the office for his consulting business in April of 2018. His office's basis is $40,000 (10% x $400,000 = $40,000). His 2018 depreciation deduction is $641. His deduction in 2019 and the following 36 years will be $1,025.

See Chapter 5 for a detailed discussion of depreciation. If you take this deduction, it can help you qualify for the pass-through tax deduction as well. At higher income levels ($163,300 for singles and $326,600 for marrieds filing jointly) this deduction is based wholly or partly on the value of the depreciable long-term property used in your business, which can include a homeowner's home office. (See Chapter 7.)

- **Utilities.** You may deduct your home office percentage of your utility bills for your entire home, including electricity, gas, water, heating oil, and trash removal. If you use a disproportionately large amount of electricity for your home office, you may be able to deduct more.

> **EXAMPLE:** Sheila, a pottery maker, works out of a home workshop that takes up 25% of the space in her home. Her work requires a substantial amount of electricity. About 50% of her monthly electricity bill is for her home workshop. She may deduct 50% of her electricity costs as a home office expense, instead of just 25%. However, to prove that she isn't deducting too much, she should keep electricity bills for her home before she began using the workshop, or for periods when she doesn't use the workshop, to show that her bills for these months are about 50% lower than the bills for her working months.

You Can Deduct Business Expenses Even If You Don't Qualify for the Home Office Deduction

Many business owners believe that they can't deduct any expenses they incur while working at home unless they qualify for the home office deduction. This is a myth that has cost many taxpayers valuable deductions. Even if you don't qualify for or take the home office deduction, you can still take tax deductions for expenses you incur while doing business at home. These are expenses that arise from the fact that you are doing business, not from your use of the home itself.

These include:

- **Telephone expenses:** You can't deduct the basic cost of a single telephone line into your home, but you can deduct the cost of long-distance business calls and special phone services that you use for your business (such as call waiting or message center). You can also deduct the entire cost of a second phone line that you use just for business, including a smartphone.

- **Business equipment and furniture:** The cost of office furniture, copiers, fax machines, and other personal property you use for your business and keep at home is deductible, whether or not you qualify for the home office deduction. If you purchase these items specifically for your home business, you can deduct them using the de minimis safe harbor if they cost less than $2,500, deduct them with 100% bonus depreciation (in effect 2018 through 2022), expense them (deduct them in one year) under Section 179, or depreciate them over several years. If you convert personal property you already own to business use, you may depreciate the fair market value. If you're a sole proprietor or owner of a one-person LLC, you deduct these costs directly on Schedule C, *Profit or Loss From Business*. You don't have to list them on the special tax form used for the home office deduction. If you use the property for both business and personal reasons, the IRS requires you to keep records showing when the item was used for business or personal reasons—for example, a diary or log with the dates, times, and reasons the item was used. See Chapter 5 for a detailed discussion of these rules.

- **Supplies:** Supplies for your business are currently deductible if you elect to use the de minimis safe harbor or the materials and supplies deduction.

- **Insurance.** Both homeowners' and renters' insurance are partly deductible as indirect home office expenses. However, special insurance coverage you buy just for your home office—for example, insurance for your computer or other business equipment—is fully deductible as a direct expense.

- **Home maintenance.** You can deduct the home office percentage of home maintenance expenses that benefit your entire home, such as housecleaning of your entire house, roof and furnace repairs, and exterior painting. These costs are deductible whether you hire someone or do them yourself. If you do the work yourself, however, you can only deduct the cost of materials, not the cost of your own labor. Termite inspection, pest extermination fees, and snow removal costs are also deductible. However, the IRS won't let you deduct lawn care unless you regularly use your home to meet clients or customers. Home maintenance costs that don't benefit your home office—for example, painting your kitchen—are not deductible at all.

- **Casualty losses.** Casualty losses are damage to your home caused by such things as fire, floods, or theft. Casualty losses that affect your entire house—for example, a leak that floods your entire home—are deductible as a home office expense in the amount of your home office percentage. Casualty losses that affect only your home office—for example, a leak that floods only the home office area of the house—are fully deductible direct expenses. Casualty losses that don't affect your home office—for example, if only your kitchen floods—are not deductible as a home office expense. There is a personal deduction for casualty losses to the nonoffice portions of a home, but from 2018 through 2025 it is limited to losses that occur in a presidentially declared disaster area. (See Chapter 14 for a detailed discussion of casualty losses.)

- **Condominium association fees.** These fees (often substantial) are partly deductible as an indirect expense if you have a home office.

- **Security system costs.** Security system costs are partly deductible as an indirect expense if your security system protects your entire home. If you have a security system that protects only your home office, the cost is a fully deductible direct expense.

- **Supplies and materials.** Office supplies and materials you use for your home business are not part of the home office deduction. They are deductible whether or not you qualify for the home office deduction.

Mileage Deductions for Leaving the House

If your home office is your principal place of business, you can deduct the cost of traveling from your home to other work locations for your business. For example, you can deduct the cost of driving to perform work at a client's or customer's office. The value of this deduction often exceeds the value of the home office deduction itself. If you don't have a tax deductible home office, these costs are not deductible. See Chapter 8 for a detailed discussion of the business mileage deduction.

Profit Limit on Deductions

Gilbert Parker worked full time for a large accounting firm, but in his spare time he was writing a book. Parker set aside a portion of his home as an office he used exclusively for writing. Like many beginning authors, he earned no money from writing. But he thought that he could at least get a tax deduction for his writing efforts by deducting his home office expenses, totaling $6,571, $4,904, and $5,444 over three years. He used these deductions to reduce the income tax he had to pay on his salary from his day job. However, both the IRS and the tax court held he could not deduct these expenses. Although he had a legitimate home office, Parker wasn't entitled to a home office deduction because he earned no money from writing. (*Parker v. Comm'r.*, TC Memo 1984-233.)

Gilbert Parker ran afoul of the most significant limitation on the home office deduction: You cannot deduct more than the net profit you earn from your home office. If you run a successful business out of your home office, this won't pose a problem. But if your business earns very little or loses money, the limitation could prevent you from deducting part or even all of your home office expenses in the current year.

If your deductions exceed your profits, you can deduct the excess in the following year and in each succeeding year until you deduct the entire amount. There is no limit on how far into the future you can deduct these expenses; you can claim them even if you are no longer living in the home where they were incurred.

So, whether or not your business is making money, you should keep track of your home office expenses and claim the deduction on your tax return. You do this by filing IRS Form 8829, *Expenses for Business Use of Your Home* (see "IRS Reporting Requirements," below). When you complete the form by plugging in the figures for your business income and home office expenses, it will show you how much you can deduct in the current year and how much you must carry over to the next year.

The profit limitation applies only to the home office deduction. It does not apply to business expenses that you can deduct under other provisions of the tax code.

For these purposes, your profit is the gross income you earn from your business minus your business deductions other than your home office deduction. You must also subtract the home office portion of your mortgage interest, real estate taxes, and casualty losses.

Tax preparation software can calculate your profit for home office deduction purposes, but it's a good idea to understand how it works. First, start with your gross income from your business—if you sell goods, this is the total sales of your business minus the cost of goods sold; if you sell services, it's all the money you earn. You must list this amount on Line 7 of your Schedule C. Next, figure out how much money you earn from using your home office. If you do all of your work at home, this will be 100% of your business income. But if you work in several locations, you must determine the portion of your gross income that comes from working in your home office. To do this, consider how much time you spend working in your home office and the type of work you do at home.

Then, subtract from this amount:

- the business percentage of your mortgage interest and real estate taxes (you'll have these expenses only if you own your home), plus any casualty losses, and

- all of your business expenses that are not part of the home office deduction; these are all the deductions listed in Part II of your Schedule C—for example, car expenses, travel, insurance, depreciation of business equipment, business phone, supplies, or salaries. You must deduct these separately from the home office deduction, even if you incurred them while doing business at home.

The remainder is your net profit—the most you can deduct for using your home office.

Types of Home Expenses		
Expense	**Description**	**Deductibility**
Direct	Things you buy only for your home office	Deductible in full
Indirect	Things you buy to keep your entire home up and running	Deductible based on the percentage of your home used as a business office
Unrelated	Things you buy only for parts of your home that are not used for business	Not deductible

EXAMPLE: Sam runs a part-time consulting business out of his home office, which occupies 20% of his home. In one year, his gross income from the business was $6,000 and he had $2,000 in expenses separate from his home office deduction. He paid $15,000 in mortgage interest and real estate taxes for the year. His home office deduction for the year is limited to $1,000. He calculates this as follows:

Gross income from business:	$ 6,000
Minus deductible mortgage interest and real estate taxes ($15,000 × 20% = $3,000)	– 3,000
Minus business expenses not related to use of home (100%)	– 2,000
Deduction limit:	$ 1,000

Sam Creates a Home Office

Sam starts a part-time home business to help people repair bad credit. He converts one of the bedrooms of his two-bedroom condominium into a home office. He goes on something of a shopping spree, purchasing the following items:

- carpeting for his office and living room
- a separate telephone for the office
- office supplies, such as stapler and paper
- a new desk for his office, and
- a new computer for his office (and one for his family).

He also moves a fancy chair he already owns to his office and uses it solely for his business. In the meantime, Sam's wife has their kitchen repainted and hires a maid to clean the entire condo twice a month. Sam and his wife pay $2,000 each month on mortgage interest, real estate taxes, and homeowners' insurance.

The chart below shows which of these expenses are direct and indirect home office expenses, business operating expenses that are deductible whether or not Sam qualifies for the home office deduction, long-term asset expenses that are also deductible without regard to the home office deduction, and expenses that are not deductible.

Direct Home Office Expenses (100% Deductible)	Indirect Home Office Expense (Deductible in Amount of Home Office Percentage)	Business Operating Expenses	Long-Term Asset Expenses	Not Deductible
Carpet for home office	Mortgage interest and real estate taxes	Office supplies	Office desk	Carpet for living room
	Utilities (electricity and heat)	Business telephone	Office chair	Computer for family
	Maid service		Computer for business	
	Homeowners' insurance			

You then subtract from your annual limit the following amounts in the following order:

- home-related expenses that are due to use of the home office (such as maintenance, insurance, and utility expenses allocable to the home office), and
- depreciation expenses allocable to the home office.

These items are not deductible to the extent they exceed the annual home office deduction limit. In this event, they must be carried over to the following year (and will be subject to the limit for that year).

> **EXAMPLE:** Assume that Sam from the example above has $800 in maintenance, utilities, and insurance expenses allocable to his home office; and $1,600 in depreciation. He first deducts the $800 expense from his $1,000 annual limit, leaving him with $200. He can then only deduct $200 of his $1,600 depreciation expense this year. He must carry over the remaining $1,400 to future years. He may deduct all of the business part of his deductible mortgage interest and real estate taxes ($3,000). He also can deduct all of his business expenses not related to the use of his home ($2,000).

Special Concerns for Homeowners

If you've taken the home office deduction, are there any tax consequences if you sell your home for a profit? Yes, but they don't outweigh the benefit of the home office deduction.

If your home office was located within your home, you do not need to allocate the gain (profit) on the sale of the property between the business part of the property and the part used as a home. This means that your entire profit qualifies for the special home sale tax exclusion.

Under this exclusion, a substantial amount of the profit you make on the sale of your home is not taxable: up to $250,000 of the profit for single taxpayers and $500,000 for married taxpayers filing jointly. You qualify for the exclusion if you lived in your home for at least two out of five years before you sell it. (See IRS Publication 523, *Selling Your Home*.)

> **EXAMPLE:** Richard, a single taxpayer, lived in his home for ten years and had a home office in a bedroom, amounting to 20% of the home. He sells the home for $100,000 profit. Because the office was within the walls of his home, his entire profit qualifies for the $250,000 exclusion and Richard owes no tax on it.

On the other hand, if your home office was not located inside your home—for example, it was in an unattached garage, cottage, or guest house—you must allocate your profit between the living and office portions of the home and pay taxes on the profits that you allocate to your office.

> **EXAMPLE:** Assume that Richard from the above example has his home office in an unattached garage, amounting to 20% of his total home. Since his home office was not within the walls of his home, he must allocate his $100,000 profit between the main home and office. He owes tax on the $20,000 of capital gains attributable to his office (20% x $100,000 = $20,000).

To avoid this, you should eliminate the office outside the walls of your home and move it inside your home at least two years before you sell it.

However, you will have to pay a capital gains tax on the depreciation deductions you took after May 6, 1997 for your home office. This is the deduction you are allowed for the yearly decline in value due to wear and tear of the portion of the building that contains your home office. (See Chapter 5 for more information on depreciation deductions.) These recaptured deductions are taxed at a 25% rate (unless your income tax bracket is lower than 25%).

> **EXAMPLE:** Sally bought a $200,000 home six years ago and used one of her bedrooms as her home office. She sold her home this year for $300,000, realizing a $100,000 gain (profit). Her depreciation deductions for her home office for the last six years totaled $2,000. She must pay a tax of 25% of $2,000, or $500.

Having to pay a 25% tax on the depreciation deductions you took in the years before you sold your house is actually not a bad deal. This is probably no more—and is often less—tax than you would have had to pay if you hadn't taken the deductions in the first place and instead paid tax on your additional taxable income at ordinary income tax rates.

You can avoid depreciation recapture if you use the new simplified method of calculating the home office deduction (see "Simplified Home Office Deduction Method," below). When you use this method, you deduct $5 per square foot of your home office and your depreciation deduction for the home office is deemed to be zero for the year. Thus, you have no depreciation recapture when you sell your home. Also, the adjusted basis of your home does not change.

Simplified Home Office Deduction Method

Lots of people who qualify for the home office deduction don't take it because they don't think it's worth the trouble or they are afraid it will result in an IRS audit. In a rare move to simplify life for taxpayers, in 2013 the IRS created a simplified optional home office deduction method.

It's important to understand that all the regular rules for qualifying for the home office deduction still apply if you use the optional simplified method—that is, you must use a portion of your home regularly and exclusively for business. In addition, the simple method cannot be used by an employee with a home office if the employee receives advances, allowances, or reimbursements for home office expenses from his or her employer.

How the Simple Method Works

The simple method really is simple: You deduct $5 for every square foot of your home office. Thus, all you need to do is measure the square footage of your home office. For example, if your home office is 200 square feet, you'll get a $1,000 home office deduction. That's all there is to it.

You don't need to figure out what percentage of your home your office occupies. You also don't need to keep records of your direct or indirect home office expenses, such as utilities, rent, mortgage payments, real estate taxes, or casualty losses. These expenses aren't deductible when you use the simplified method. Another big plus: You don't have to complete Form 8829.

Homeowners using the new option cannot claim a depreciation deduction for their home office. However, they can claim allowable mortgage interest, real estate taxes, and deductible casualty losses on the home as itemized deductions on Schedule A. These deductions need not be allocated between personal and business use, as is required under the regular method. Business expenses unrelated to the home, such as advertising, supplies, and wages paid to employees are still fully deductible.

When you use the simplified method, your home office deduction is capped at $1,500 per year. You'll reach the cap if your home office is 300 square feet. Thus, for example, if your home office is 400 square feet, you'll still be limited to a $1,500 home office deduction if you use the simplified method. You can't carry over any part of the deduction to future years.

As with the regular home office deduction, your total annual deduction using the simplified method is limited to the gross income you earned from the business use of your home during the year. Moreover, if you use the simplified method, you can't carry over any excess to a future tax year—something you can do when you use the regular method. Nor can you deduct amounts carried over from past years that you couldn't deduct using the regular method. For this reason, you should never use the simplified method if the profit from your business for the year is less than the amount of your simplified home office deduction.

You may choose either the simplified method or the regular method for any year. You choose your method by using it on your timely filed, original federal income tax return for the year. Once you have chosen a method for a tax year, you cannot later change to the other method for that same year. If you use the simplified method for one year and use the regular method for any subsequent year, you must calculate the depreciation deduction for the subsequent year using the appropriate optional depreciation table. This is true regardless of whether you used an optional depreciation table for the first year the property was used in business.

Comparison of Regular and Simplified Home Office Deduction Methods

Simplified Method	Regular Method
Deduction for home office use of a portion of a residence only if that portion is exclusively used on a regular basis for business purposes	Same
Allowable square footage of home used for business (not to exceed 300 square feet)	Percentage of home used for business
Standard $5 per square foot used to determine home business deduction	Actual expenses determined and records maintained
Home-related itemized deductions claimed in full on Schedule A	Home-related itemized deductions apportioned between Schedule A and business schedule (Schedule C or Schedule F)
No depreciation deduction	Depreciation deduction for portion of home used for business
No recapture of depreciation upon sale of home	Recapture of depreciation on gain upon sale of home
Deduction not to exceed gross income from business use of home less business expenses	Same
Amount in excess of gross income limitation not to be carried over	Amount in excess of gross income limitation carryover allowable
Loss carryover from use of regular method in prior year not to be claimed	Loss carryover from use of regular method in prior year allowable if gross income test is met in current year

Is the Simplified Method a Good Deal?

Is it a good idea to use the new simplified home office deduction? Only if the deduction you could obtain using the regular method isn't much more than $1,500. Many people with home offices, particularly those who rent their homes, can qualify for a home office deduction much larger than $1,500. For example, a person with a 100-square-foot home office in a 1,000-square-foot apartment who pays $1,000 per month in rent and utilities would qualify for a $500 deduction using the simplified method (100 sq. ft. x $5 = $500), and at least a $1,200 deduction using the regular method (10% x $12,000 = $1,200). On the other hand, the simplified method may work out better for homeowners because they have no rent to deduct using the home office deduction and can still deduct mortgage interest and real estate taxes as itemized personal deductions on Schedule A (but the personal deduction for property tax is limited to $10,000 per year from 2018 through 2025). Moreover, using the simplified method eliminates having to pay tax on recaptured depreciation deductions for your home office when you sell your home. If you don't plan to live in your home for very long, this can be a substantial benefit. You may also come out ahead with the simplified method if your home office is quite small. For example, one home business owner who works out of a 127-square-foot office converted from a bedroom calculated that he would receive a $635 ($5 x 127) deduction with the simplified method; but only a $302 deduction using the regular method.

If you're thinking about using the simplified method, you should figure your deduction using both methods and use the one that gives you the larger deduction. The regular method does require more record keeping than the optional method, but you probably keep these types of records anyway. Doing the required calculations and filling out the form can be challenging, but will be much easier if you use tax preparation software.

IRS Reporting Requirements

If, like the vast majority of home business owners, you are a sole proprietor or owner of a one-person LLC, you deduct your business operating expenses by listing them on IRS Schedule C, *Profit or Loss From Business*. You must list your home office deduction on Schedule C, but you also have to file a special tax form to show how you calculated the home office deduction: Form 8829, *Expenses for Business Use of Your Home*. This form tells the IRS that you're taking the deduction and shows how you calculated it. You should file this form even if you can't currently deduct your home office expenses because your business has no profits. By filing, you can apply the deduction to a future year in which you earn a profit. For detailed guidance on how to fill out Form 8829, see IRS Publication 587, *Business Use of Your Home*.

If you organize your business as a partnership, a multimember LLC, or an S corporation, you don't have to file Form 8829. Instead, you deduct your unreimbursed home office expenses (and any other unreimbursed business expenses) on IRS Schedule E (Part II) and attach it to your personal tax return. However, these expenses are deductible only if you have a written partnership or an LLC agreement that requires you to pay these expenses. You must attach a separate schedule to Schedule E listing the home office and other business expenses you're deducting. Any home office expense for which your partnership or LLC reimbursed you must be listed on the partnership or LLC tax return, IRS Form 1065, *U.S. Return of Partnership Income*. These deductions pass through to you along with other partnership deductions.

Audit-Proofing Your Home Office Deduction

If you are audited by the IRS and your home office deduction is questioned, you want to be able to prove that you:
- qualify for the deduction, and
- have correctly reported the amount of your home office expenses.

If you can do both those things, you should be home free.

Prove That You Are Following the Rules

Here are some ways to convince the IRS that you qualify for the home office deduction:

- Take a picture of your home office and draw up a diagram showing your home office as a portion of your home. Do not send the photo or diagram to the IRS. Just keep it in your files to use in case you're audited.
- Have all of your business mail sent to your home office.
- Use your home office address on all of your business cards, stationery, and advertising.
- Obtain a separate phone line for your business and keep that phone in your home office.
- Encourage clients or customers to regularly visit your home office, and keep a log of their visits.
- To make the most of the time you spend in your home office, communicate with clients by phone, fax, or email instead of going to their offices. Use a mail or messenger service to deliver your work to customers.
- Keep a log of the time you spend working in your home office. This doesn't have to be fancy; notes on your calendar will do.

Keep Good Expense Records

Be sure to keep copies of your bills and receipts for home office expenses, including:

- IRS Form 1098, *Mortgage Interest Statement* (sent by whoever holds your mortgage), showing the interest you paid on your mortgage for the year
- property tax bills and your canceled checks as proof of payment
- utility bills, insurance bills, and receipts for payments for repairs to your office area, along with your canceled checks paying for these items, and
- a copy of your lease and your canceled rent checks, if you're a renter.

The Pass-Through Tax Deduction

The Tax Cuts and Jobs Act established a new income tax deduction for owners of pass-through businesses, which includes the vast majority of home-based businesses. This is commonly referred to as the pass-through deduction or qualified business income (QBI) deduction. Pass-through owners who qualify can deduct up to 20% of their net business income from their income taxes, reducing their effective income tax rate by 20%. The deduction was intended to avoid placing pass-through owners at a disadvantage compared with regular C corporations, whose tax rate was lowered to a flat rate of 21% by the Tax Cuts and Jobs Act.

This deduction began in 2018 and is scheduled to last through 2025, unless it is extended (or earlier terminated) by Congress. Here are the basic requirements you must satisfy to qualify for this complex deduction.

You Must Have a Pass-Through Business

You must have a pass-through business to qualify for this deduction. A pass-through business is any business that is owned and operated through a pass-through business entity. This includes any business that is:

- a sole proprietorship (a one-owner business in which the owner personally owns all the business assets; technically, a proprietorship is not a "pass-through entity" but it still qualifies for the deduction)
- a partnership
- an S corporation
- a limited liability company (LLC), or
- a limited liability partnership (LLP).

For tax purposes, what distinguishes these types of businesses is that they pay no taxes themselves. Instead, the profits (or losses) from these businesses are passed through the business and the owners pay tax on the money on their individual tax returns at their individual tax rates. The vast majority of smaller businesses are pass-through entities. Indeed, over 86% of all businesses without employees are sole proprietorships.

Regular "C" corporations do not qualify for this deduction; however, starting in 2018 they do qualify for a flat 21% corporate tax rate.

Employees may not take this deduction from their employment income. Moreover, employees cannot get the deduction simply by having their employers reclassify them as independent contractors. IRS regulations provide that if a worker is reclassified as a contractor, but continues to perform the same work directly or indirectly for the hiring firm that he or she did as an employee, the IRS will presume that worker doesn't qualify for the pass-through deduction for the next three years. This presumption can be overcome only by convincing the IRS that the worker really qualifies as an independent contractor. However, if you've formed an S corporation for your business and work as its employee, you may take the deduction from your corporate distributions.

You Must Have Qualified Business Income

Individuals who earn income through pass-through businesses may qualify to deduct from their income tax up to 20% of their qualified business income (QBI) from each pass-through business they own. However, your actual deduction may be less depending on your taxable income and occupation. (I.R.C. § 199A.) QBI is the net income (profit) your pass-through business earns during the year. You determine this by subtracting all your regular business deductions from your total business income.

QBI does not include:

- short-term or long-term capital gain or loss—for example, capital gain (or loss) earned from selling business property
- dividend income
- interest income
- wages paid to S corporation shareholders
- guaranteed payments to partners in partnerships or LLC members, or
- business income earned outside the United States.

If you're a member of a multimember LLC, partnership, LLP, or S corporation, your QBI is determined at the shareholder-partner level. This means each shareholder, partner, or other owner takes into account his or her pro rata share of the pass-through business's income, deductions, gains, and losses.

Ordinarily, QBI is determined separately for each separate business you own (but non-service business owners have the option of combining multiple businesses; see below). If one or more of your businesses lose money, you deduct the loss from the QBI from your profitable businesses. If you have a qualified business loss—that is, your net QBI is zero or less—you get no pass-through deduction for the year. Any loss is carried forward to the next year and the pass-through deduction for that next year (or the next future year with positive QBI) is reduced (but not below zero) by 20% of the loss.

> **EXAMPLE:** During 2020, George earned $20,000 in QBI from his home-based Bitcoin mining business and had a $50,000 loss from his bakery business. He has a $30,000 qualified business loss, so he gets no pass-through deduction for 2020 and his loss must be carried forward to 2021. His pass-through deduction for 2021 must reduced by 20% of his $30,000 loss, or $6,000.

You Must Have Taxable Income

To determine your pass-through deduction, you must first figure your total taxable income for the year (not counting the pass-through deduction). This is your total taxable income from all sources (business, investment, and job income) minus deductions, including the standard deduction ($12,400 for singles and $24,800 for marrieds filing jointly in 2020). However, you do not include net capital gains for the year in your taxable income (such amounts already receive preferential tax treatment). If you're married and file jointly, include your spouse's income in your taxable income.

Your pass-through deduction can never exceed 20% of your taxable income. This limitation will apply, and reduce your pass-through deduction to less than 20% of QBI, if you don't have enough nonbusiness income to offset your personal deductions which reduce your taxable income below the amount of your qualified business income.

> **EXAMPLE:** Larry earned $100,000 in profit from his home-based consulting business in 2020. He had no other income and took the standard deduction. His taxable income is $87,600 ($100,000–$12,400 standard deduction = $87,600). Even though Larry had $100,000 in QBI, his pass-through deduction cannot exceed 20% of $87,600, or $17,520. If Larry had $12,400 in additional nonbusiness income, he would have had $100,000 in taxable income and qualified for the full 20% of QBI deduction, or $20,000.

Deduction for Taxable Income Up to $163,300 ($326,600 if Married)

If your 2020 taxable income is at or below $163,300 if single or $326,600 if married filing jointly, your pass-through deduction is equal to 20% of your qualified business income (QBI). However, as discussed above, the deduction may not exceed 20% of your taxable income.

> **EXAMPLE:** Tom is single and operates his public relations business as a sole proprietorship. His business earns $100,000 in qualified business income during 2020. He also earned $32,400 in investment income and took the $12,400 standard deduction. His total taxable income for the year is $120,000 (($100,000 + $32,400) – $12,400 = $120,000). His pass-through deduction is 20% x $100,000 = $20,000. He may deduct $20,000 from his taxable income.

If your taxable income is at or below the $163,300/$326,600 thresholds, that's all there is to the pass-through deduction. You're effectively taxed on only 80% of your business income.

Deduction for Income Above $163,300 ($326,600 if Married)

If your 2020 taxable income exceeds $163,300 if single or $326,600 if married, calculating your deduction is much more complicated and depends on your total income, the type of work you do, and whether you have employees or business property.

Are You a Specified Service Business?

First of all, you need to determine whether your business is a "specified service trade or business," or SSTB. SSTBs are not favored under the pass-through deduction. Indeed, they lose the deduction entirely at certain income levels. There are no such limitations on pass-through owners who are not specified service businesses.

There are several specific types of business activities that are SSTBs:
- health (doctors, dentists, nurses, and other health professionals)
- law
- accounting
- actuarial science
- performing arts
- consulting
- athletics
- financial services
- brokerage services
- trading or dealing in securities, partnership interests, or commodities
- investing and investment management, or
- trading and dealing in securities or commodities.

There is a final catchall category that includes any business where the *principal* asset is the reputation or skill of one or more of its owners or employees. IRS regulations very narrowly define the catch-all category to include only cases where a person:
- receives fees or other income for endorsing products or services
- licenses his or her image, likeness, name, signature, voice, or trademark, or
- receives fees or other income for appearing at an event or on radio, television, or another media format.

This eliminates most people from falling within the catch-all category.

Architecture and engineering services are expressly not included in the list of personal services. Also not included are real estate brokers, real property managers, and insurance brokers.

If the same business sells products or merchandise and also provides services that fall within one of the SSTB categories, the business will not be treated as an SSTB so long as less than 10% of the gross receipts of the business come from providing the service.

Deduction for Non-Service Businesses (Income Above $163,300/$326,600)

If your business is not included in the list of specified service businesses, and your taxable income is over the $163,300/$326,600 thresholds, how you figure your pass-through deduction depends on your taxable income.

Taxable Income Above $213,300 ($426,600 if Married)

If your 2020 taxable income exceeds $213,300 (single) or $426,600 (married filing jointly), your maximum possible pass-through deduction is 20% of your QBI, just like at the lower income levels. However, when your income is this high, a W-2 wage/business property limitation takes full effect. Your deduction is limited to the greater of:

- 50% of the W-2 employee wages paid by your business, or
- 25% of W-2 wages PLUS 2.5% of the acquisition cost of your depreciable business property.

Thus, if you have neither employees nor depreciable property, you get no deduction.

W-2 wages means the total wages and benefits reported by the employer to the Social Security Administration. Most home-based businesses have no employees.

The business property must be depreciable long-term property used in the production of income—the real property or equipment used in the business (not inventory). If you own your home and take the home office deduction for your business, including depreciation for your home office, you can count your home office as business property for this deduction. (See Chapter 6 for a detailed discussion of the home office deduction.)

You multiply 2.5% times your property's unadjusted basis—the original acquisition cost, minus the cost of land, if any. The unadjusted basis of a tax deductible home office is based on the percentage of the home used for the office. For example, if you use 10% of your home for your home office, and the home cost $300,000, not counting the land, your unadjusted basis for your home office is $30,000.

The 2.5% deduction can be taken during the entire depreciation period for the property—the depreciation period for a home office is 39 years. The depreciation period for personal property such as business equipment or furniture is much shorter—five or seven years. However, for purposes of the pass-through deduction, the depreciation period can be no shorter than ten years. Thus, property with a depreciation period of five or seven years still counts for the deduction for a full ten years after purchase. You can't count any property you sell during the year.

> **EXAMPLE:** Hal and Wanda are married and file jointly. Their taxable income this year is $500,000, including $400,000 in QBI they earned in profit from their interior design business. They have one part-time employee who they paid $25,000 in wages. They run their business from their home office, which accounts for 20% of the space of their entire home. They take the home office deduction for the space, which had an unadjusted basis of $100,000 (20% of their home which cost $500,000 not counting the cost of the land). Their maximum possible pass-through deduction is 20% of their $400,000 QBI, which equals $80,000. However, since their taxable income was over $426,600, their pass-through deduction is limited to the greater of (1) 50% of the W-2 wages they pay their employee, or (2) 25% of W-2 wages plus 2.5% of their home office's $100,000 basis. Option (1) is $12,500 (50% x $25,000 = $12,500); (2) is $8,750 (25% x $25,000) + (2.5% x $100,000) = $8,750. Thus, (1) is greater, so their pass-through deduction is $12,500.

Taxable Income $163,301 to $213,300 ($326,601 to $426,600 if Married)

If your 2020 taxable income is $163,301 to $213,300 (single) or $326,301 to $426,600 (married filing jointly), the W-2 wages/property limitation is phased in—that is, only part of your deduction is subject to the limit and the rest is based on 20% of your QBI. The phase-in range is $50,000 for singles and $100,000 for marrieds. For example, the limit would be 50% phased in for married taxpayers with taxable income of $376,600 ($50,000 over $326,600, which equals 50% of the $100,000 phase-in range). At the top of the income range ($213,300 for singles, $426,600 for marrieds), your entire deduction is subject to the W-2 wages/business property limit. Thus, if you have no W-2 wages or business property, you get no deduction.

To calculate the phase-in, first determine what the amount of your deduction would be if the W-2 wages/property limit didn't apply at all —this is 20% x your QBI. Next, calculate your deduction as if the W-2 wages/property limit applied in full. Your phase-in amount is based on the difference between these two calculations multiplied by your phase-in percentage.

> **EXAMPLE:** Assume that Hal and Wanda from the above example had $356,600 in QBI this year, and no other income. Their phase-in percentage is 30% because their $356,600 QBI is $30,000 over the $326,600 limit ($30,000 ÷ $100,000 phase-in range = 30%). Their deduction if the W-2 wages/property limit didn't apply would be 20% of their $356,600 QBI, which equals $71,320. Their fully limited deduction based on W-2 wages is $12,500 (50% of $25,000 W-2 wages = $12,500). They should lose 30% of the difference between the full deduction of $71,320 and the fully limited deduction of $12,500. The difference amounts to $17,334 (30% x ($71,320– $12,500) = $17,646). Thus, they should lose $17,646 from the full $71,320 deduction. Sid and Nancy can take a $53,674 pass-through deduction on their return.

Deduction for Specified Service Business Owners (Income Above $163,300/$326,600)

If your business is a specified service business, and your taxable income exceeds $163,300 (single) or $326,600 (married), your pass-through deduction is gradually phased out up to $213,300/$426,600 of QBI.

At the top of the income range, you get no deduction at all. That is, if your total income exceeds $213,300 (single) or $426,600 (married), you get no deduction. This was intended to prevent highly compensated employees who provide personal services from having their employers reclassify them as independent contractors so they could benefit from the pass-through deduction. There is no such phase-out of the entire deduction for non-service providers.

To calculate your deduction, you start by using the same formula as for non-service providers discussed above. Your maximum possible deduction is 20% of your QBI. However, your deduction may not exceed the greater of:

- 50% of your share W-2 employee wages paid by the business, or
- 25% W-2 wages PLUS 2.5% of the acquisition cost of depreciable property used in the business.

Thus, if you have no employees or depreciable business property, you get no deduction.

Next, you calculate the phase-out of the deduction. If you're married and have employees or property, your deduction is phased-out by 1% for every $1,000 your income exceeds the $326,600 threshold. When your income reaches $426,600, if you're married, you get no deduction. If you're single, your deduction is reduced by 2% for every $1,000 your income exceeds the $163,300 threshold and you get no deduction if your income reaches $210,701 or more.

> EXAMPLE: Mark is married and files jointly. He earned $356,600 in taxable income this year. His sole proprietorship consulting business earned $356,600 and paid $100,000 to employees. Consulting is one of the specified service businesses, so his pass-through deduction is subject to the phase-out. His $351,400 taxable income is $30,000, or 30%, over the $326,600 threshold. Before the phase-out, his deduction is limited to 50% of the W-2 wages he paid, which was $50,000 (50% x $100,000 W-2 wages = $50,000). Since his phase-out percentage is 30%, he gets 70% of the full deduction, or $35,000 (70% x $50,000 = $35,000).

Pass-Through Deduction Thresholds, Limits, and Phase-Ins (2020)

	Taxable Income: Single: Up to $163,300 Married: Up to $326,600	Taxable Income: Single: $163,301–$213,300 Married: $326,601–$426,600	Taxable Income: Single: $213,301 or more Married: $426,601 or more
Specified Service Business	Full 20% deduction No W-2/property limit	20% deduction subject to phase-out, W-2/property limit applied	No deduction
Non-Specified Service Business	Full 20% deduction No W-2/property limit	20% deduction subject to phase-in of W-2/property limit	20% deduction permitted but fully subject to W-2/property limit

Taking the Pass-Through Deduction

The pass-through deduction is a personal deduction you may take on your Form 1040 whether or not you itemize. To compute and claim the deduction, you must complete IRS Form 8995, *Qualified Business Income Deduction Simplified Computation.* But if your taxable income exceeds the applicable threshold amount, you should file Form 8995-A, *Qualified Business Income Deduction.* You then transfer the amount of the deduction to a line on your Form 1040.

The pass-through deduction is not an "above the line" deduction on the first page of Form 1040 that reduces your adjusted gross income (AGI). Thus, for example, it does not reduce your income for purposes of qualifying for Affordable Care Act (Obamacare) health insurance credits. Moreover, the deduction only reduces income taxes, not Social Security or Medicare taxes.

Strategies to Maximize the Pass-Through Deduction

There are many planning strategies high-income pass-through owners can take to preserve and maximize the pass-through deduction.

Keep Service Business Income Below $213,300/$426,600 Threshold

Be sure to keep track of your taxable income during the year. If your business is a specified service business, it's absolutely vital to keep your taxable income for the year at or below the cut-off amount: $213,300 for singles or $426,600 for marrieds filing jointly. If you earn one dollar more than this you get no deduction. Ideally, your taxable income should be at or below $163,300 (single) or $326,600 (married) so you can avoid the phase-in of the W-2 employee/property limitation and qualify for the full 20% of QBI deduction (the only exception would be if you have employees).

Your taxable income is your total income (not including capital gains) minus your deductions. If you don't itemize, this would include your standard deduction ($12,400 for singles, $24,800 for marrieds in 2020). Thus, if you take the standard deduction, you could have $175,700 in income (single) or $351,400 (married) and come within the income limits to qualify for the 20% of QBI deduction.

If your income is at or near these limits, there are lots of things you can do to reduce your taxable income for the year. For example, you can:

- Contribute to retirement accounts such as IRAs and 401(k)s—your contributions are deducted from your taxable income subject to annual limits (in 2020, business owners can contribute up to $57,000 to retirement plans).
- Give money to charity if you're so inclined (make sure you're able to itemize your personal deductions).
- Avoid billing clients or collecting amounts due your business near the end of the year.

• Increase your business deductions to reduce your taxable income—
for example, buy equipment or other property for your business
(all the long-term personal property you buy for your business is
100% deductible in one year using 100% bonus depreciation or
Section 179 expensing).

Form an S Corporation

If your business is not a service business and your taxable income is over
$163,300 (single) or $213,600 (married filing jointly), your pass-through
deduction will be fully or partly subject to the W-2 wage/property
limitation. If you don't pay W-2 wages and/or own depreciable property,
you could form an S corporation to operate your business and work as its
employee. Your employee income would constitute W-2 wages on which
you can base all or part of your pass-through deduction. Tax experts have
calculated that 28.57% of S corporation income should be paid as W-2
wages to maximize the pass-through deduction. Why not pay even more
as wages? Paying more actually results in a smaller deduction because
the total pass-through deduction may not exceed 20% of your qualified
business income: The wages an S corporation pays its owners don't count
as qualified business income. However, wages S corporations pay owner/
employees must be reasonable—depending on the circumstances, paying
28.57% of income as shareholder wages may be too much or too little.

> EXAMPLE: Mary, a married taxpayer, buys and sells goods online. She
> operates the business from home and has no employees. She earned $415,000
> in profit from the business and earned $44,400 in other income. Her taxable
> income is $425,000 ($459,400–$24,400 standard deduction = $425,000).
> At this income level, the W-2/property limitation is completely phased in.
> That is, her pass-through deduction is limited to 50% of W-2 wages or 25%
> of W-2 wages plus 2.5% of depreciable property. If her business is a sole
> proprietorship or LLC, she would get no pass-through deduction since she
> has no employees or depreciable property. She has formed an S corporation,
> of which she is the sole shareholder and employee. The corporation pays
> her $118,275 in W-2 wages, leaving $296,725 in qualified business income
> for the corporation. She is entitled to a pass-through deduction of 50% x
> her W-2 wages, which is $59,138 (which is also 20% of her corporation's QBI).

If you have a service business, the S corporation strategy only works if your taxable income is in the phase-out range: $163,301 to $213,300 for single taxpayers and $326,601 to $426,600 for marrieds filing jointly. If your taxable income is higher than this, you get no pass-through deduction. If it's lower than the phase-out threshold amount, the deduction is equal to 20% of your QBI, with no W-2 wage/property limit; so paying W-2 wages will not increase your deduction.

Sole proprietors, owners of LLCs taxed as partnerships, or partners in partnerships cannot pay themselves W-2 wages. Thus, S corporations (or LLCs taxed as S corporations) can be far more advantageous than these other business forms at higher income levels where the W-2 wage limitation applies. It's not clear that Congress actually intended to favor S corporations over the other pass-through entities in this way. It's possible the rules may be changed in the future to eliminate this advantage.

Combine Multiple Non-Service Businesses

If you own multiple non-service businesses, you have the option of combining (aggregating) them for purposes of the pass-through deduction. There is no benefit from doing this if your taxable income is no more than $163,300 for singles and $326,600 for married joint filers. But, if your income is higher than this, the pass-through deduction is based wholly or partly on how much you pay your employees and how much business property you own.

Thus, combining multiple businesses at these income levels can result in a larger pass-through deduction than computing the deduction separately for each business. For example, if one business has lots of profit and few employees and/or property, and another has little profit and many employees and/or property, combining them can result in a larger deduction.

You can combine (aggregate) multiple business only if the same person or group of people owns 50% or more of each business for a majority of the year, which must include the last day of the year. None of the businesses may be specified service businesses (see the list above) and they must share the same tax year. In addition, at least two of the following requirements must be satisfied:

- the businesses provide products, property, or services that are the same or customarily offered together, or
- the businesses share facilities or significant centralized business elements, such as personnel, accounting, legal, manufacturing, purchasing, human resources, or information technology resources, or
- the businesses are operated in coordination with, or reliance upon, one or more of the businesses in the combined group (for example, supply chain interdependencies).

The same people do not need to own an interest in each business that is being combined.

You must file an election with your tax return each year listing the businesses being aggregated. Despite the annual election requirement, the election is irrevocable. This means it can't be changed from year to year unless there is a material change in circumstances. However, new businesses can be added to the existing group if they meet the above requirements. For this reason, you must think carefully before using this strategy. It might be beneficial one year, but result in smaller pass-through deductions in future years if your circumstances change.

File a Separate Return

The vast majority of married people file joint returns in which their income and deductions are combined. However, married couples have the option of filing separate tax returns. When they do this, each spouse reports and pays tax on their income, credits, and deductions on their own return. In some cases, a married person could qualify for the pass-through deduction by filing a separate return rather than filing jointly with his or her spouse.

EXAMPLE: Jack and Jill are a married couple who live in New York. Jack earns $100,000 per year from his consulting business. His wife Jill earns $300,000 from her medical practice. They also earned $100,000 from investments. They both have service businesses and their combined income of $500,000 is well over the $426,600 cutoff for the pass-through deduction for service businesses. Thus, if they file a joint return, they get no pass-through deduction. However, if they each file separately, Jack will have only $100,000 of business income on his return, plus $50,000 in investment income. His $150,000 in taxable income puts him well under the $163,300 threshold for married taxpayers filing separately. Thus, he will be entitled to a 20% pass-through deduction on his $100,000 consulting income, a $20,000 deduction.

This strategy won't work if you live in one of the nine community property states: Arizona, California, Idaho, Louisiana, Nevada, New Mexico, Texas, Washington, and Wisconsin. Reason: In a community property state, the income spouses earn is split evenly between them when they file separately, as are expenses (unless they are paid by one spouse with his or her separate noncommunity funds—for example, money earned or inherited before marriage). Thus, if Jack and Jill from the above example lived in California, they would have to evenly split their $500,000 total income, leaving them each with $250,000, well over the $213,300 limit to qualify for the pass-through deduction for a service business for single filers.

Also, there are several tax disadvantages when a married couple files separately. So creating a pass-through deduction, where none was available when filing jointly, may not lower a couple's taxes. You need to compare your total tax liability when filing jointly and separately to see which filing status is best.

Getting Around Town:
Car and Local Travel Expenses

T hat expensive car parked in your garage doesn't just look great—
it could also give you a great tax deduction. This chapter shows
you how to deduct expenses for *local transportation*—that is,
business trips that don't require you to stay away from home overnight.
These rules apply to local business trips using any means of transportation,
but this chapter focuses primarily on car expenses, the most common type
of deduction for local business travel. Overnight trips (whether by car or
other means) are covered in Chapter 9.

RESOURCE

Different rules apply to corporate employees. This chapter covers
local transportation deductions by business owners—sole proprietors, partners
in partnerships, or LLC members—not by corporate employees. Starting in
2018, if you have incorporated your business and work as its employee, you may
not deduct your work-related local transportation expenses on your personal
tax return. Instead, you should have your corporation reimburse you for your
expenses. See Chapter 11.

CAUTION

Transportation expenses are a red flag for the IRS. Transportation
expenses are the number-one item that IRS auditors look at when they examine
small business tax returns. These expenses can be substantial—and it is easy to
overstate them—so the IRS will look very carefully to make sure that you're not
bending the rules. Your first line of defense against an audit is to keep good records to back up your deductions. This is something no tax preparation program
or accountant can do for you—you must develop good record-keeping habits
and follow them faithfully to stay out of trouble with the IRS. You can find information on record keeping in Chapter 15.

Deductible Local Transportation Expenses

Local transportation costs are deductible as business operating expenses if they are ordinary and necessary for your business, trade, or profession. The cost must be common, helpful, and appropriate for your business. (See Chapter 4 for a detailed discussion of the ordinary and necessary requirement.) It makes no difference what type of transportation you use to make the local trips—car, van, pickup, truck, motorcycle, taxi, bus, or train—or whether the vehicle you use is owned or leased. You can deduct these costs as long as they are ordinary and necessary and meet the other requirements discussed below.

Travel Must Be for Business

You can only deduct local trips that are for business—that is, travel to a business location. Personal trips—for example, to the supermarket or the gym—are not deductible as business travel expenses. A business location is any place where you perform business-related tasks, such as:

- the place where you have your principal place of business, including a home office
- other places where you work, including temporary job sites
- places where you meet with clients or customers
- the bank where you do business banking
- a local college where you take work-related classes
- the store where you buy business supplies, or
- the warehouse or other place where you keep business inventory.

Starting a New Business

The cost of local travel before you start your business, such as travel to investigate starting a new business, is not a currently deductible business operating expense. It is a start-up expense subject to special deduction rules. (See Chapter 3 for information on deducting start-up costs.)

As explained below, you can take the largest deduction for local business trip expenses if you have a home office.

Moreover, you don't have to do all the driving yourself to get a car expense deduction. Any use of your car by another person qualifies as a deductible business expense if any of the following are true:

- It is directly connected with your business.
- It is properly reported by you as income to the other person (and, if you have to, you withhold tax on the income)— for example, where an employee uses your car (see Chapter 11).
- You are paid a fair market rental for use of your car.

Thus, for example, you can count as business mileage a car trip your employee, spouse, or child takes to deliver an item for your business or for any other business purpose.

Trips From Your Home Office

If, like most home businesspeople, you have a home office that qualifies as your principal place of business, you can deduct the cost of any trips you make from home to another business location. You can get a lot of travel deductions this way. For example, you can deduct the cost of driving from home to a client's office or to attend a business-related seminar.

Your home office will qualify as your principal place of business if it is the place where you earn most of your income or perform most of your business administrative or management tasks. Virtually all home businesses should be able to qualify under either or both of these criteria.

> EXAMPLE: Kim, a personal trainer, spends most of her time working with her clients at their homes or gyms. But she maintains a home office where she does the administrative work for her business, such as billing, scheduling appointments, and creating written exercise programs for her clients. She may deduct the cost of driving from home to meet with clients and back home again.

If You Have No Regular Workplace

If you have no regular office—whether inside or outside your home—the location of your first business contact of the day is considered your office for tax purposes. Transportation expenses from your home to this first business contact are commuting expenses, which are not deductible. The same is true for your last business contact of the day—your trip home is nondeductible commute travel. You can deduct the cost of all your other trips during the day between clients or customers.

> EXAMPLE: Jim is an encyclopedia salesman who works in the Houston metropolitan area. He works out of his car, with no office at home or anywhere else. One day, he makes ten sales calls by car. His trip from home to his first sales contact of the day is a nondeductible commuting expense. His next nine trips are deductible, and his trip home from his last sales contact is a nondeductible personal commuting expense.

There is an easy way to get around this rule about the first and last trip of the day: Open a home office. That way, all of your trips are deductible.

> EXAMPLE: Jim creates an office at home where he performs administrative tasks for his sales business, such as bookkeeping. He may now deduct the cost of all of his business trips during the day, including driving from home to his first business contact and back home from his last contact of the day.

The Standard Mileage Rate

If you drive a car, panel truck, van, pickup, or an SUV for business (as most people do), you have two options for deducting your vehicle expenses: You can figure your deduction both ways the first year before deciding which method to use on your tax return.

Let's start with the easy one—the standard mileage rate. This method works best for people who don't want to bother with a lot of record keeping or calculations. But this ease comes at a price—it can result in a lower deduction than you might be entitled to if you used the actual expense method. However, this isn't always the case. The standard mileage rate may give you a larger deduction if you drive many business miles each year, especially if you drive an inexpensive car. (See "The Actual Expense Method," below.)

But, even if the standard mileage rate does give you a lower deduction, the difference is often so small that it doesn't justify the extra record keeping you will have to do using the actual expense method.

How the Standard Mileage Rate Works

To use the standard mileage rate, you deduct a specified number of cents for every business mile you drive. For 2020, the standard mileage rate is 57.5 cents per mile.

To figure out your deduction, simply multiply your business miles by the applicable standard mileage rate. The rate is the same whether you own or lease your car.

> EXAMPLE: Ed, a self-employed salesperson, drove his car 10,000 miles for business during 2020. To determine his car expense deduction, he simply multiplies his business mileage by 57.5 cents. His deduction is $5,750 (57.5 cents x 10,000 = $5,750).

The big advantage of the standard mileage rate is that it requires very little record keeping. You need only to keep track of how many business miles you drive and the dates, not the actual expenses for your car, such as gas, maintenance, or repairs.

If you choose the standard mileage rate, you cannot deduct actual car operating expenses—for example, maintenance and repairs, gasoline and its taxes, oil, insurance, and vehicle registration fees. All of these items are factored into the rate set by the IRS. And you can't deduct the cost of the car through regular or bonus depreciation or Section 179 expensing because the car's depreciation is also factored into the standard mileage rate (as are lease payments for a leased car).

The only actual expenses you can deduct (because these costs aren't included in the standard mileage rate) are:

- interest on a car loan
- parking fees and tolls for business trips (but you can't deduct parking ticket fines or the cost of parking your car at your place of work), and
- personal property tax you paid when you bought the vehicle, based on its value—this is often included as part of your auto registration fee.

Interest on an automobile loan is usually the largest of these expenses. Unfortunately, many people fail to deduct this because of confusion about the tax law. Taxpayers are not allowed to deduct interest on a loan for a car that is for personal use, so many people believe they also can't deduct interest on a business car. This is not the case. You may deduct interest on a loan for a car you use in your business. This is a business interest expense deduction, not part of the mileage deduction. But there is one exception—if you're an employee, you may not deduct interest on a car loan even if you use the car 100% for your job.

If you use your car for both business and personal trips, you can deduct only the business use percentage of the above-mentioned interest and taxes.

EXAMPLE: Ralph uses his car 50% for his home business and 50% for personal trips. He uses the standard mileage rate to deduct his car expenses. He pays $3,000 a year in interest on his car loan. He may deduct 50% of this amount, or $1,500, as a business operating expense, in addition to his business mileage deduction.

Requirements to Use the Standard Mileage Rate

You must use the standard mileage rate in the first year you use a car for business or you are forever foreclosed from using that method for that car. If you use the standard mileage rate the first year, you can switch to the actual expense method in a later year, and then switch back and forth between the two methods after that, provided the requirements listed below are met. For this reason, if you're not sure which method you want to use, it's a good idea to use the standard mileage rate the first year you use the car for business. This leaves all your options open for later years. However, this rule does not apply to leased cars. If you lease your car, you must use the standard mileage rate for the entire remainder of the lease period if you use it in the first year.

Keep in mind, however, that if you switch to the actual expense method after using the standard mileage rate, you'll have to reduce the tax basis of your car by a portion of the standard mileage rate deductions you already received. This will reduce your depreciation deduction.

There are some restrictions on switching back to the standard mileage rate after you have used the actual expense method. You can switch back to the standard mileage rate only if you used the straight-line method of depreciation during the years you used the actual expense method. This depreciation method gives you equal depreciation deductions every year, rather than the larger deductions you get in the early years using accelerated depreciation methods. You can't switch back to the standard mileage rate after using the actual expense method if you took accelerated depreciation, a Section 179 deduction, or bonus depreciation.

As a practical matter, once you switch from the standard rate to the actual expense method it's nearly impossible to switch back to the standard rate.

The Actual Expense Method

Instead of using the standard mileage rate, you can deduct the actual cost of using your car for business. This requires more record keeping, but it can result in a higher deduction. It all depends on the cost of your vehicle and how much you drive for business. As a general rule, the standard mileage rate results in a larger deduction if you drive many business miles, particularly if your car is cheap to operate. However, as a result of the Tax Cuts and Jobs Act, the actual expense method can result in much larger deductions than the standard mileage rate during the first several years you own a car.

How the Actual Expense Method Works

As the name implies, under the actual expense method, you deduct the actual costs you incur each year to operate your car, plus depreciation. If you use this method, you must keep careful track of all of your car expenses during the year, including:

- gas and oil
- repairs and maintenance
- depreciation of your original vehicle and improvements (see "Vehicle Depreciation Deductions," below)
- car repair tools
- license fees
- parking fees for business trips
- registration fees
- tires
- insurance
- garage rent
- tolls for business trips
- car washing
- lease payments
- interest on car loans
- towing charges, and
- auto club dues.

Business Travel by Motorcycle or Bicycle

You must use the actual expense method if you ride a motorcycle or bicycle—the standard mileage rate is only for passenger vehicles. However, the limits on depreciation for passenger automobiles (discussed in "Vehicle Depreciation Deductions," below) do not apply to bicycles or motorcycles. You may depreciate these items just like any other business property. Or, if you wish, you can deduct the cost of a motorcycle or bicycle in the year that you purchase it under Section 179. (See Chapter 5 for more on depreciation and Section 179.)

	Watch Those Tickets	
	You may not deduct the cost of driving violations or parking tickets, even if you were on business when you got the ticket. Government fines and penalties are never deductible, as a matter of public policy.	

When you do your taxes, add up the cost of all these items. For everything but parking fees and tolls, multiply the total cost of each item by your car's business use percentage. You determine your business use percentage by keeping track of all the miles you drive for business during the year and the total mileage driven. You divide the business mileage by your total mileage to figure your business use percentage. For parking fees and tolls that are business related, include (and deduct) the full cost. The total is your deductible transportation expense for the year.

> **EXAMPLE:** Laura, a salesperson, drove her car 10,000 miles for her business and a total of 20,000 in one year. Her business use percentage is 50% (20,000 ÷ 10,000 = 50%). She can deduct 50% of the actual costs of operating her car, plus the full cost of any business-related tolls and parking fees. Her expenses amount to $10,000 for the year, so she gets a $5,000 deduction, plus $1,000 in tolls and parking for business.

If you have a car that you use only for business, you may deduct 100% of your actual car costs. Be careful here. If you own just one car, it's hard to successfully claim that you use it only for business. The IRS is not likely to believe that you walk or take public transportation everywhere, except when you're on business. If you're a sole proprietor, the IRS will know how many cars you own because sole proprietors who claim transportation expenses must provide this information on their Schedule C. (See "Reporting Transportation Expenses on Your Tax Return," below.)

Record-Keeping Requirements

When you deduct actual car expenses, you must keep records of all the costs of owning and operating your car. This includes not only the number of business miles and total miles you drive, but also gas, repair, parking, insurance, tolls, and any other car expenses. (You'll find more information on record-keeping requirements in Chapter 15.)

Vehicle Depreciation Deductions

Using the actual expense method, you can deduct the cost of your vehicle. However, you can't deduct the entire cost in the year when you purchase your car. Instead, you must deduct the cost a portion at a time over several years, using a process called depreciation. For a detailed discussion of depreciation, see Chapter 5.

Leasing a Car

If you lease a car that you use in your business, you can use the actual expense method to deduct the portion of each lease payment that reflects the business percentage use of the car. You cannot deduct any part of a lease payment that is for commuting or personal use of the car.

> EXAMPLE: John pays $400 a month to lease a Lexus. He uses it 50% for his dental tool sales business and 50% for personal purposes. He may deduct half of his lease payments ($200 a month) as a local transportation expense for his sales business.

Leasing companies typically require you to make an advance or down payment to lease a car. You can deduct a percentage of this cost as well, but you must spread the deduction out equally over the entire lease period.

TIP
You may use either the actual expense method or the standard mileage rate when you lease a car for business. However, if you want to use the standard mileage rate, you must use it the first year you lease the car and continue to use it for the entire lease term. If you use the standard mileage method, you can't deduct any portion of your lease payments. Instead, this cost is covered by the standard mileage rate set by the IRS. (See "The Standard Mileage Rate," above.)

Other Local Transportation Expenses

You don't have to drive a car or another vehicle to get a tax deduction for local business trips. You can deduct the cost of travel by bus or other public transit, taxi, train, ferry, motorcycle, bicycle, or any other means. However, all the rules limiting deductions for travel by car (discussed in "Deductible Local Transportation Expenses," above) also apply to other transportation methods. This means, for example, that you can't deduct the cost of commuting from your home to your office or other permanent work location. The same record-keeping requirements apply as well.

Reporting Transportation Expenses on Your Tax Return

How you report transportation expenses on your tax return will depend on how your business is organized.

Sole Proprietors

If, like most home businesspeople, you're a sole proprietor or owner of a one-person LLC, you list your car expenses on Schedule C, *Profit or Loss From Business*. Schedule C asks more questions about this deduction than almost any other deduction (reflecting the IRS's general suspicion about auto deductions). Part IV of Schedule C is reproduced below. If you answer "yes" to Question 45 and "no" to Question 46, you cannot claim to use your single car 100% for business. If you answer "no" to Questions 47a or 47b, you do not qualify for the deduction.

You must also file IRS Form 4562, *Depreciation and Amortization*, to report your Section 179 and depreciation deductions for the vehicle.

Part IV	Information on Your Vehicle. Complete this part **only** if you are claiming car or truck expenses on line 9 and are not required to file Form 4562 for this business. See the instructions for line 13 to find out if you must file Form 4562.

43   When did you place your vehicle in service for business purposes? (month, day, year)   ▶ _____/_____/_____

44   Of the total number of miles you drove your vehicle during 2012, enter the number of miles you used your vehicle for:

a   Business _____   b Commuting (see instructions) _____   c Other _____

45   Was your vehicle available for personal use during off-duty hours? . . . .   ☐ Yes   ☐ No

46   Do you (or your spouse) have another vehicle available for personal use?. . . . .   ☐ Yes   ☐ No

47a   Do you have evidence to support your deduction? . . . .   ☐ Yes   ☐ No

b   If "Yes," is the evidence written?   . . . .   ☐ Yes   ☐ No

LLCs and Partnerships

If you organize your business as a partnership or multimember LLC, you don't file Schedule C. Instead, you deduct your unreimbursed car expenses (and any other unreimbursed business expenses) on IRS Schedule E (Part II) and attach it to your personal tax return. You must attach a separate schedule to Schedule E listing the car and other business expenses you're deducting.

How to Reduce Your Schedule C Auto Deduction

If you deduct the interest you pay on a car loan, you have the option of reporting the amount in two different places on your Schedule C: You can lump it in with all your other car expenses on Line 9 of the schedule, titled "Car and truck expenses," or you can list it separately on Line 16b as an "other interest" cost. Reporting your interest expense separately from your other car expenses reduces the total car expense shown on your Schedule C. This can help avoid an IRS audit.

Any transportation expense for which your partnership or LLC reimbursed you must be listed on the partnership or LLC tax return, IRS Form 1065, *U.S. Return of Partnership Income.* These deductions pass through to you along with other partnership deductions.

Corporations

If your business is incorporated, you will ordinarily be its employee. Starting 2018 through 2025, you cannot deduct any transportation expenses for which the corporation does not reimburse you as miscellaneous itemized expenses on Schedule A. (See "Employing Your Family or Yourself," in Chapter 11, for more on working for your corporation.)

When Clients or Customers Reimburse You

Some small business owners have their local travel expenses reimbursed by their clients or customers. You need not include such reimbursements in your income if you provide an adequate accounting of the expenses to your client and comply with the accountable plan rules. Basically, this requires that you submit all your documentation to the client in a timely manner, and return any excess payments. Accountable plans are covered in detail in Chapter 11. Record-keeping rules for business driving are covered in Chapter 15.

> EXAMPLE: Erica, a sole proprietor accountant, is hired by Acme Corp. to handle an audit. She keeps a complete mileage log showing that she drove 500 miles while working on the audit. Acme reimburses Erica $250 for the business mileage. Erica need not include this amount in her income for the year. Acme may deduct it as a business expense.

If you do not adequately account to your client for these expenses, you must include any reimbursements or allowances in your income. They should also be included in any 1099-MISC form the client provides to the IRS reporting how much you were paid. The client can still deduct the reimbursement as compensation paid to you. You may deduct the expenses on your own return, but you'll need documentation to back them up in the event of an audit.

Leaving Town: Business Travel

I f you travel overnight for business, you can deduct your airfare, hotel bills, and other expenses. If you plan your trip carefully, you can even mix business with pleasure and still take a deduction. However, IRS auditors closely scrutinize deductions for overnight business travel—and many taxpayers get caught claiming these deductions without proper records to back them up. To stay within the law (and avoid unwanted attention from the IRS), you need to know how this deduction works and how to properly document your travel expenses.

What Is Business Travel?

For tax purposes, business travel occurs when you travel away from your tax home overnight for business. You don't have to travel any set distance to take a travel expense deduction. However, you can't take this deduction if you just spend the night in a motel across town. You must travel outside your city limits. If you don't live in a city, you must go outside the general area where your business is located.

You must stay away overnight or at least long enough to require a stop for sleep or rest. You cannot satisfy the rest requirement by merely napping in your car.

> EXAMPLE: Phyllis, a home-based salesperson who lives in Los Angeles, flies to San Francisco to meet potential clients, spends the night in a hotel, and returns home the following day. Her trip is a deductible travel expense.

If you don't stay overnight, your trip will not qualify as business travel and your expenses will not be deductible as business travel expenses subject to one exception for lodging expenses—see "New IRS Rule on Deducting Lodging Expenses," below. This does not necessarily mean that you can't take a tax deduction. Local business trips are also deductible (see Chapter 8), but you are entitled to deduct only your transportation expenses—the cost of driving or using some other means of transportation. You may not deduct meals or other expenses like you can when you travel for business and stay overnight.

EXAMPLE: Philip drives from his home office in Los Angeles to a business meeting in San Diego and returns the same day. His 200-mile round trip is a deductible local business trip. He may deduct his expenses for the 200 business miles he drove, but he can't deduct the breakfast he bought on the way to San Diego.

RELATED TOPIC

How to deduct local travel. For a detailed discussion of tax deductions for local business travel, see Chapter 8.

New IRS Rule on Deducting Lodging Expenses

For decades, the rule has been that you can deduct business travel expenses, such as hotel or other lodging expenses, only when you travel away from your tax home overnight for your business. However, the IRS has created an exception to this rule. It now allows local lodging expenses—that is, hotel or other lodging expenses while an individual is not away from his or her tax home—to be deducted if all of the following apply:

- The lodging is necessary for the person to participate fully in, or be available for, a bona fide business meeting, conference, training activity, or other business function.
- The lodging lasts for no more than five calendar days and does not recur more than once per calendar quarter.
- In the case of an employee, the employer requires the person to remain at the activity or function overnight.
- The lodging is not lavish or extravagant and does not provide any significant element of personal pleasure, recreation, or benefit. (IRS Reg. § 1.162-32(a).)

EXAMPLE: Acme, Inc., conducts a three-day training session for its freelance salespeople at a hotel near its main office. Some salespeople attending the training are not traveling away from home. Acme requires all attendees to remain at the hotel overnight, at their own expense, for the bona fide purpose of facilitating the training. The salespeople may deduct the cost as a business expense.

Where Is Your Tax Home?

Your tax home is the entire city or general area where your principal place of business is located. If you run your business out of your residence, your tax home is the city or area where you live.

The IRS doesn't care how far you travel for business. You'll get a deduction as long as you travel outside your tax home's city limits and stay overnight. Thus, even if you're just traveling across town, you'll qualify for a deduction if you manage to stay outside your city limits or if you fall within the new IRS exception (see "New IRS Rule on Deducting Lodging Expenses," above).

> **EXAMPLE:** Pete, a tax adviser, works from his home in San Francisco. He travels to Oakland for an all-day meeting with a client. At the end of the meeting, he decides to spend the night in an Oakland hotel rather than brave the traffic back to San Francisco. Pete's stay qualifies as a business trip even though the distance between his San Francisco office and the Oakland business meeting is only eight miles. Pete can deduct his hotel and meal expenses.

If you don't live in a city, your tax home covers the general area where you reside—typically, the area within about 40 miles of your home.

No Main Place of Business

Some people have no main place of business—for example, a salesperson who is always on the road, traveling from sales contact to sales contact. In this situation, your home (main residence) can qualify as your tax home, as long as you:

- perform part of your business there and live at home while doing business in that area
- have living expenses at your home that you must duplicate because your business requires you to travel away from home, and
- satisfy one of the following three requirements:
  - You have not abandoned the area where your home is located—that is, you work in the area or have other contacts there.
  - You have family living in the home.
  - You often live in the home yourself.

EXAMPLE: Ruth is a liquor salesperson whose territory includes the entire southern United States. She has a home in Miami, Florida, where her mother lives. Ruth's sales territory includes Florida. She uses her home for her business when she is in the Miami area and lives in it when making sales calls in the area. She spends about 12 weeks a year at home and is on the road the rest of the time. Ruth's Miami home is her tax home because she satisfies all three factors listed above: (1) She does business in the Miami area and stays in her Miami home when doing so; (2) she has duplicate living expenses; and (3) she has family living at the home.

Even if you satisfy only two of the three factors, your home may still qualify as your tax home, depending on all the facts and circumstances.

EXAMPLE: Assume that Ruth's sales territory is the Northeast, and she does no work in the Miami area, where her home is located. She fails the first factor, but satisfies the second two. Her Miami home would still probably qualify as her tax home.

If you can't satisfy at least two of the three factors, you have no tax home. You are a transient for tax purposes. This means you cannot deduct any travel expenses, because you are never considered to be traveling away from home. Obviously, this is not a good situation to find yourself in, taxwise.

EXAMPLE: James Henderson was a stagehand for a traveling ice skating show. He spent most of his time on the road, but spent two to three months a year living rent free in his parents' home in Boise, Idaho. Both the IRS and the courts found that he was a transient for tax purposes because he failed to satisfy the first two of the three criteria listed above: (1) He did no work in Boise, and (2) because he paid no rent to live in his parents' house, he had no home living expenses that he had to duplicate while on the road. Thus, Henderson was not entitled to a tax deduction for his travel expenses. (*Henderson v. Comm'r.*, 143 F.3d 497 (9th Cir. 1998).)

If you travel a lot for business, you should do everything you can to avoid being classified as a transient. This means you must take steps to satisfy at least two of the three factors listed above. For example, Henderson might have avoided his transient status if he had paid his parents for his room (thereby resulting in duplicate expenses).

Temporary Work Locations

You may regularly work both at your tax home and at another location, such as a client's office or a temporary job site. It may not always be practical to return from this other worksite to your tax home at the end of each workday. Your overnight stays at these temporary work locations qualify as business travel as long as your work there is truly temporary—that is, it is reasonably expected to last no more than one year. In this situation, your tax home does not change, and you are considered to be traveling away from home for the entire period you spend at the temporary work location.

> EXAMPLE: Betty is a self-employed sexual harassment educator. She works out of her home office in Chicago, Illinois. She is hired to conduct sexual harassment training and counseling for a large company in Indianapolis, Indiana. The job is expected to last three months. Betty's assignment is temporary and Chicago remains her tax home. She may deduct the expenses she incurs traveling to and staying in Indianapolis.

Even if the job ends up lasting more than one year, the job location will be treated as temporary, and you can still take your travel deductions, if you reasonably expected the job to last less than one year when you took it. However, if at some later point the job is expected to exceed one year, then the job location will be treated as temporary only until the earlier of: (1) when your expectations changed, or (2) 12 months.

> EXAMPLE: Dominic, a self-employed computer expert who lived in Louisiana, took on a project as an independent contractor for a company located in Houston, about 320 miles away from his home. The project was expected to last nine to ten months, although Dominic was hired on a month-to-month basis. Due to technological delays, the project ended up taking 13 months.

Nevertheless, the tax court held that Houston was a temporary work location for Dominic because he reasonably expected the project to last less than one year when he took it. Thus, the court held he was entitled to deduct his travel expenses from Louisiana to Houston for the first 12 months. (*Senulis v. Comm'r.*, T.C. Summ. Op. 2009-97 (2009).)

On the other hand, if you reasonably expect your work at the other location to last more than one year, that location becomes your new tax home and you cannot deduct your travel expenses while there.

> **EXAMPLE:** Carl is a Seattle-based plumbing contractor. He is hired to install the plumbing in a new subdivision in Boise, Idaho, and the job is expected to take 18 months. Boise is now Carl's tax home, and he may not deduct his travel expenses while staying there.

If you return to your tax home from a temporary work location on your days off, you are not considered away from home while you are in your hometown. You cannot deduct the cost of meals and lodging there. However, you can deduct your expenses, including meals and lodging, for travel between your temporary work location and your tax home. You can claim these expenses up to the amount it would have cost you to stay at your temporary work location. In addition, if you continue to pay for your hotel room during your visit home, you can deduct that cost.

Your Trip Must Be for Business

Your trip must be primarily for business to be deductible. This means that you must have a business purpose in mind before leaving on the trip, and you must actually do some business while you're away.

You have a business purpose if the trip is intended to benefit your business in some way. Examples of business purposes include:

- finding new customers or markets for your products or services
- dealing with existing customers or clients
- learning new skills to help in your business
- contacting people who could help your business, such as potential investors, or
- checking out what the competition is doing.

> EXAMPLE: A taxpayer who manufactured and sold weightlifting equipment was entitled to deduct the cost of attending the summer Olympics in Rome because the purpose of the trip was to find new customers for his product line. (*Hoffman v. Comm'r.*, 798 F.2d 784 (3d Cir. 1962).)

It's not enough to claim that you had a business purpose for your trip. You must also be able to show that you actually spent some time on business activities while at your destination. Acceptable business activities include:

- visiting or working with existing or potential clients or customers
- attending trade shows or conventions, or
- attending professional seminars or business conventions that are clearly connected to your business.

On the other hand, business activities do not include:

- sightseeing
- recreational activities that you attend by yourself or with family or friends, or
- attending personal investment seminars or political events.

Use common sense when deciding whether to claim that a trip is for business. If you're audited, the IRS is likely to question any trip that doesn't have some logical connection to your existing business.

Travel for a New Business or Location

You must actually be in business to have deductible business trips. Trips you take to investigate a potential new business or to actually start or acquire a new business are not currently deductible business travel expenses. However, they may be deductible as business start-up expenses, which means you can deduct up to $5,000 of these expenses the first year you're in business if your total start-up expenses are less than $50,000. (See Chapter 3 for more on deducting start-up costs.)

That Trip to Europe Was Not for Business

Oliver Bentley and his foster son spent approximately $7,500 for an extensive European trip. When they got back, they tried to make money off their travel by attempting to arrange student tours to Europe. They contacted travel agents and distributed flyers, but the business never got off the ground. When Bentley did his taxes for the year, he took a $5,127 tax deduction for the trip, claiming it was primarily for this business. The IRS and the tax court both disagreed. Bentley could not claim a business travel deduction because he did not have an existing business when he took the trip, and the costs of investigating a new business venture are not currently deductible. (*Bentley v. Comm'r.*, TC Memo 1988-444.)

Travel as an Education Expense

You may deduct the cost of traveling to an educational activity directly related to your business. For example, a French translator can deduct the cost of traveling to France to attend formal French language classes. However, you can't take a trip and claim that the travel itself constitutes a form of education and is therefore deductible. For example, a French translator who travels to France may not take a business travel deduction if the purpose of the trip is to see the sights and become familiar with French language and culture. (See Chapter 14 for more on education expenses.)

Visiting Business Colleagues

Visiting business colleagues or competitors may be a legitimate business purpose for a trip. But you can't just socialize with them—you must use your visit to learn new skills, check out what your competitors are doing, seek investors, or attempt to get new customers or clients.

Deductible Travel Expenses

Subject to the limits covered in "How Much You Can Deduct," below, virtually all of your business travel expenses are deductible. These costs fall into two broad categories: your transportation expenses and the expenses you incur at your destination.

Transportation expenses are the costs of getting to and from your destination—for example:

- fares for airplanes, trains, or buses
- driving expenses, including car rentals
- shipping costs for your personal luggage or samples, displays, or other things you need for your business, and
- 50% of meals and beverages, and 100% of lodging expenses you incur while en route to your final destination.

If you drive your own car to your destination, you may deduct your costs by using the standard mileage rate or by deducting your actual expenses. You may also deduct your mileage while at your destination. (See Chapter 8 for more on mileage deductions.)

You may also deduct the expenses you incur to stay alive (food and lodging) and to do business while at your destination. Destination expenses include:

- hotel or other lodging expenses for business days
- 50% of meal and beverage expenses (see "How Much You Can Deduct," below)
- taxi, public transportation, and car rental expenses at your destination
- telephone, Internet, and fax expenses
- computer rental fees
- laundry and dry cleaning expenses, and
- tips you pay on any of the other costs.

You may not deduct entertainment expenses when you travel, even if you incur them for business purposes. Thus, you can't deduct the cost of a nightclub, concert, or ball game while on the road, even if you take a client or business associate along. The Tax Cuts and Jobs Act eliminated all such entertainment deductions starting in 2018.

Traveling First Class or Steerage

To be deductible, business travel expenses must be ordinary and necessary. This means that the trip and the expenses you incur must be helpful and appropriate for your business, not necessarily indispensable. You may not deduct lavish or extravagant expenses, but the IRS gives you a great deal of leeway here. You may, if you wish, travel first class, stay at four-star hotels, and eat at expensive restaurants. On the other hand, you're also entitled to be a cheapskate—for example, you could stay with a friend or relative at your destination to save on hotel charges and still deduct your meals and other expenses.

Taking People With You

You may deduct the expenses you pay for a person who travels with you only if he or she:

- is your employee
- has a genuine business reason for going on the trip with you, and
- would otherwise be allowed to deduct the travel expenses.

These rules apply to your family as well. This means you can deduct the expense of taking your spouse or child or another relative only if the person is your employee and has a genuine business reason for going on a trip with you. Typing notes or assisting in entertaining customers is not enough to warrant a deduction; the work must be essential to your business. For example, if you hire your son as a salesperson for your product or service and he calls on prospective customers during the trip, both your expenses and his are deductible.

If you bring your family along simply to enjoy the trip, you may still deduct your own business expenses as if you were traveling alone—and you don't have to reduce your deductions, even if others get a free ride with you. For example, if you drive to your destination, you can deduct the entire cost of the drive, even if your family rides along with you. Similarly, you can deduct the full cost of a single hotel room even if you obtain a larger, more expensive room for your whole family.

How Much You Can Deduct

If you spend all of your time at your destination on business, you may deduct 100% of your expenses (except meal expenses, which are only 50% deductible—see "Fifty Percent Limit on Meal Expenses," below). However, things get more complicated if you mix business and pleasure. Different rules apply to your transportation expenses and the expenses you incur while at your destination ("destination expenses"). The rules also depend on whether you travel to another country or remain in the United States.

Reimbursement for Business Travel Expenses

If a client or customer reimburses you for all or part of your business travel expenses, you get no deduction for the amount of the reimbursement—the client gets the deduction. However, you don't have to count the reimbursed amounts as business income.

> EXAMPLE: Clarence, a documents examiner, travels from Philadelphia to Nashville, Tennessee, to testify in a case for a client, Acme Corporation. He stays in Nashville for two weeks and incurs $5,000 in travel expenses. He bills Acme for this amount and receives the reimbursement. Clarence may not deduct the cost of the trip, but he also doesn't have to report the $5,000 reimbursement from Acme as business income. Acme may deduct the $5,000 as a business expense.

Travel Within the United States

Business travel within the United States is subject to an all or nothing rule: You may deduct 100% of your transportation expenses only if you spend *more than half of your time* on business activities while at your destination. In other words, your business days must outnumber your personal days. If you spend more time on personal activities than on business, you get no transportation deduction.

You may also deduct the destination expenses you incur on days when you do business. Expenses incurred on personal days at your destination are nondeductible personal expenses. (See "Calculating Time Spent on Business," below, for the rules used to determine what constitutes a business day.)

> **EXAMPLE:** Tom works out of his Atlanta home. He takes the train for a business trip to New Orleans. He spends six days in New Orleans, where he spends all of his time on business, and spends $400 for his hotel, meals, and other living expenses. On the way home, he stops in Mobile for three days to visit his parents and spends $100 for lodging and meals there. His round-trip train fare is $250. Tom's trip consisted of six business days and three personal days, so he spent more than half of the trip on business. He can deduct 100% of his train fare and the entire $400 he spent while on business in New Orleans. He may not, however, deduct the $100 he spent while visiting his parents.

If your trip is primarily a vacation—that is, you spend more than half of your time on personal activities—the entire cost of the trip is a nondeductible personal expense. However, you may deduct destination expenses that are directly related to your business. This includes things like the cost of renting a computer for business work. It doesn't include transportation, lodging, or food.

As long as your trip is primarily for business, you can add a vacation to the end of the trip, make a side trip purely for fun, or enjoy evenings at the theater or ballet, and still deduct your entire airfare. What you spend while having fun is not deductible, but you can deduct all of your business and transportation expenses.

> **EXAMPLE:** Bill flies to Miami for a four-day business meeting. He spends three extra days in Miami swimming and enjoying the sights. Because he spent over half his time on business—four days out of seven—the cost of his flight is entirely deductible, as are his hotel and meal costs during the business meeting. He may not deduct his hotel, meal, or other expenses during his vacation days.

Travel Outside the United States

Travel outside the United States is subject to more flexible rules than travel within the country. The rules for deducting your transportation expenses depend on how long you stay at your destination.

Trips for Up to Seven Days

If you travel outside the United States for *no more than seven days,* you can deduct 100% of your airfare or other transportation expenses, as long as you spend part of the time on business. You can spend a majority of your time on personal activities, as long as you spend at least some time on business. Seven days means seven consecutive days, not counting the day you leave but counting the day you return to the United States. You may also deduct the destination expenses you incur on the days you do business. (See "Calculating Time Spent on Business," below, for the rules used to determine what constitutes a business day.)

> **EXAMPLE:** Billie flies from Portland, Oregon, to Vancouver, Canada. She spends four days sightseeing in Vancouver and one day visiting suppliers for her import-export business. She may deduct 100% of her airfare, but she can deduct her lodging, meal, and other expenses from her stay in Vancouver for only the one day when she did business.

Trips for More Than Seven Days

The IRS does not want to subsidize foreign vacations, so more stringent rules apply if your foreign trip lasts more than one week. For these longer trips, the magic number is 75%: If you spend more than 75% of your time on business at your foreign destination, you can deduct what it would have cost to make the trip if you had not engaged in any personal activities. This means you may deduct 100% of your airfare or other transportation expenses, plus your living expenses while you were on business and any other business-related expenses.

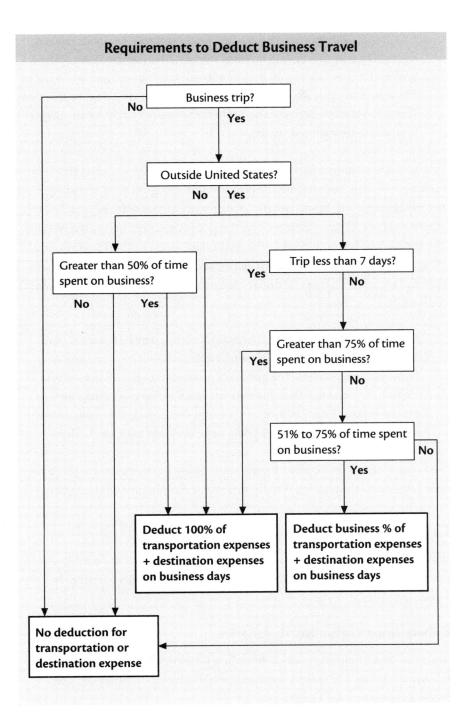

> **EXAMPLE:** Sean flies from Boston to Dublin, Ireland. He spends one day sightseeing and nine days in business meetings. He has spent 90% of his time on business, so he may deduct 100% of his airfare to Dublin and all of the living and other expenses he incurred during the nine days he spent on business. He may not deduct any of his expenses (including hotel charges) for the day he spent sightseeing.

If you spend more than 50%—but less than 75%—of your time on business, you can deduct only the business percentage of your transportation and other costs. You figure out this percentage by counting the number of business days and the number of personal days to come up with a fraction. The number of business days is the numerator (top number) and the total number of days away from home is the denominator (bottom number). For ease in determining the dollar amount of your deduction, you can convert this fraction into a percentage.

> **EXAMPLE:** Sam flies from Las Vegas to London, where he spends six days on business and four days sightseeing. He spent 6/10 of his total time away from home on business. The fraction 6/10 converts to 60% (6 ÷ 10 = 0.60). He therefore spent 60% of his time on business. He can deduct 60% of his travel costs—that is, 60% of his round-trip airfare, hotel, and other expenses. The trip cost him $3,000, so he gets an $1,800 deduction.

If you spend 50% or less of your time doing business on a foreign trip that lasts more than seven days, you cannot deduct any of your costs.

Conventions

The cost of traveling to and staying at a convention are deductible just like the cost of any other business trip, as long as you satisfy the following rules.

Conventions Within North America

You may deduct the expense of attending a convention in North America if your attendance benefits your business. You may not, however, deduct any expenses for your family.

How do you know if a convention benefits your business? Look at the convention agenda or program (and be sure to save a copy). The agenda does not have to specifically address what you do in your business, but it must be sufficiently related to show that your attendance was for business purposes. Examples of conventions that don't benefit your business include those for investment, political, or social purposes.

You probably learned in school that North America consists of the United States, Canada, and Mexico. However, for convention expense purposes, North America includes much of the Caribbean and many other great vacation destinations.

Foreign Conventions

More stringent rules apply if you attend a convention outside of North America. You can take a deduction for a foreign convention only if both of the following are true:

- The convention is directly related to your business (rather than merely benefiting it).
- It's as reasonable for the convention to be held outside of North America as in North America.

To determine whether it's reasonable to hold the convention outside of North America, the IRS looks at the purposes of the meeting and the sponsoring group, the activities at the convention, where the sponsors live, and where other meetings have been or will be held.

As a general rule, if you want a tax deduction, avoid attending a convention outside of North America unless there is a darn good reason for holding it there. For example, it would be hard to justify holding a convention for New York court reporters in Tahiti. On the other hand, it would probably be okay for a meeting of American travel writers to be held in Paris.

Travel by Ship

Forget about taking a tax deduction for a pure pleasure cruise. You may, however, be able to deduct part of the cost of a cruise if you attend business conventions, seminars, or similar meetings directly related to your business while on board. (Personal investment or financial planning seminars don't qualify.)

But there is a major restriction: You must travel on a U.S.-registered ship that stops only in ports in the United States or its possessions, such as Puerto Rico or the U.S. Virgin Islands. If a cruise sponsor promises you'll be able to deduct your trip, investigate carefully to make sure it meets these requirements.

To deduct your business-related cruise expenses, you must file a signed note with your tax return from the meeting or seminar sponsor listing the business meetings scheduled each day aboard ship and certifying how many hours you spent in attendance. Make sure to get this statement from the meeting sponsor. Your annual deduction for attending conventions, seminars, or similar meetings on ships cannot exceed $2,000.

Calculating Time Spent on Business

To calculate how much time you spend on business while on a trip, you must compare the number of days you spend on business to the number of days you spend on personal activities. A day is considered a business day if you:

- work for more than four hours
- must be at a particular place for your business—for example, to attend a business meeting—even if you spend most of the day on personal activities
- spend more than four hours on business travel (business travel time begins when you leave home and ends when you reach your hotel, or vice versa)
- drive at least 300 miles for business (you can average your mileage—for example, if you drive 600 miles to your destination in two days, you may claim two 300-mile days, even if you drove 500 miles on one day and 100 miles on the other)
- spend more than four hours on some combination of travel and work
- are prevented from working because of circumstances beyond your control, such as a transit strike or terrorist act, and

- stay at your destination between workdays if it would have cost more to go home and return than to remain where you are (this "sandwich" rule allows you to count weekends as business days if you work at your travel destination during the previous and following weeks; see "Maximizing Your Business Travel Deductions," below).

EXAMPLE: Mike, a home-based inventor who hates flying, travels by car from his home in Reno, Nevada, to Cleveland, Ohio, for a meeting with a potential investor concerning his latest invention: diapers for pet birds. He makes the 2,100-mile drive in six days, arriving in Cleveland on Saturday night. He has his meeting with the investor for one hour on Monday. The investor is intrigued with his idea, but wants him to flesh out his business plan. Mike works on this for five hours on Tuesday and three hours on Wednesday, spending the rest of his time resting and sightseeing. He has his second investor meeting on Thursday, which lasts two hours. He spends the rest of the day sightseeing and then drives straight home on Friday. Mike's trip consisted of 15 business days: 11 travel days, one sandwiched day (the Sunday before his first meeting), two meeting days, and one day when he worked more than four hours. He had one personal day—the day when he spent only three hours working.

Be sure to keep track of your time while you're away. You can do this by taking notes on your calendar or travel diary. (See Chapter 15 for a detailed discussion of record keeping while traveling.)

Fifty Percent Limit on Meal Expenses

The IRS figures that you have to eat, whether you're at home or away on a business trip. Because meals you eat at home ordinarily aren't deductible, the IRS won't let you deduct all of your food expenses while traveling. Instead, you can deduct only 50% of your meal expenses while on a business trip. There are two ways to calculate your meal expense deduction: You can keep track of your actual expenses or use a daily rate set by the federal government. Either way, you can only deduct 50% of that cost.

Deducting Actual Meal Expenses

If you use the actual expense method, you must keep track of what you spend on meals (including tips and tax) while traveling and at your business destination. When you do your taxes, you add these amounts together and deduct half of the total.

> **EXAMPLE:** Frank goes on a business trip from Santa Fe, New Mexico, to Reno, Nevada. He gets there by car. While on the road, he spends $200 for meals. In Reno, he spends another $200. His total meal expense for the trip is $400. He may deduct half of this amount, or $200.

If you combine a business trip with a vacation, you may deduct only those meals you eat while on business—for example, meals you eat while attending business meetings or doing other business-related work. Meals that constitute business entertainment (for example, if you take a client out to a business lunch) are subject to the rules on entertainment expenses covered in Chapter 7.

You do not necessarily have to keep every receipt for your business meals, but you need to keep careful track of what you spend, and you should be able to prove that the meal was for business. See Chapter 15 for a detailed discussion of record keeping for meal expenses.

Using the Standard Meal Allowance

When you use the actual expense method, you must keep track of what you spend for each meal. This can be a lot of work, so the IRS provides an alternative method of deducting meals: Instead of deducting your actual expenses, you can deduct a set amount for each day of your business trip. This amount is called the standard meal allowance. It covers your expenses for business meals, beverages, tax, and tips. The amount of the allowance depends on where and when you travel.

The advantage of using the standard meal allowance is that you don't have to keep track of how much you spend on meals and tips. However, you have to keep records to prove the time, place, and business purpose of your travel. (See Chapter 15 for more on record keeping.)

The disadvantage is that the standard meal allowance is based on what federal workers are allowed to charge for meals while traveling, and is therefore relatively modest. In 2020, the full rate federal workers could charge for domestic travel ranged from $55 per day for travel in the least expensive areas to up to $76 for high-cost areas, which includes most major cities. And because you can deduct only half of your meal expenses, your deduction is limited to one-half of the standard meal allowance.

The standard meal allowance rates are generally higher for travel outside the continental United States—that is, Alaska, Hawaii, and foreign countries. For example, in 2020, the allowance for Paris, France was $169. In contrast, travelers to Baghdad were permitted only $11 per day.

The standard meal allowance includes $5 per day for incidental expenses—tips you pay to porters, bellhops, maids, and transportation workers. If you wish, you can use the actual expense method for your meal costs and the $5 incidental expense rate for your tips. However, you'd have to be a pretty stingy tipper for this amount to be adequate.

You Don't Have to Spend Your Whole Allowance

When you use the standard meal allowance, you get to deduct the whole amount, regardless of what you spend. If you spend more than the daily allowance, you are limited to the allowance amount. But if you spend less, you still get to deduct the full allowance amount. For example, if you travel to New York City and live on bread and water, you may still deduct $38 (half of the $76 per diem rate) for each business day. This strategy will not only save you money; you'll lose weight as well.

The standard meal allowance is revised each year. You can find the current rates for travel within the United States on the U.S. General Services Administration website at www.gsa.gov (look for the link to "Per Diem Rates"). The rates for foreign travel are set by the U.S. State Department. When you look at these rate listings, you'll see several categories of numbers. You want the "M & IE Rate"—short for meals and incidental expenses. Rates are also provided for lodging, but these don't apply to nongovernmental travelers.

You can claim the standard meal allowance only for business days. If you travel to more than one location in one day, use the rate in effect for the area where you spend the night. Remember, you are allowed to deduct only 50% of the standard meal allowance from your taxes as a business expense.

> **EXAMPLE:** Art travels from Los Angeles to Chicago for a five-day business conference. Chicago is a high-cost locality, so the daily meal and incidental expense (M & IE) rate is $76. Art figures his deduction by multiplying the daily rate by five and dividing this in half: 5 days × $76 = $380; $380 × 50% = $190.

If you use the standard meal allowance, you must use it for *all of the business trips you take during the year*. You can't use it for some trips and use the actual expense method for others. For example, you can't use the standard allowance when you go to an inexpensive destination and the actual expense method when you go to a pricey one.

Because the standard meal allowance is relatively small, it's better to use it only if you travel exclusively to low-cost areas, or if you are simply unable or unwilling to keep track of what you actually spend for meals.

Maximizing Your Business Travel Deductions

Here are some simple strategies you can use to maximize your business travel deductions.

Plan Ahead

Plan your itinerary carefully before you leave to make sure your trip qualifies as a business trip. For example, if you're traveling within the United States, you must spend more than half of your time on business for your transportation to be deductible. If you know you're going to spend three days on business, arrange to spend no more than two days on personal activities so that your trip meets the requirements. If you're traveling overseas for more than 14 days, you'll have to spend at least 75% of your time on business to deduct your transportation—you may be able to do this by using strategies to maximize your business days (see "Maximize Your Business Days," below).

Make a Paper Trail

If you are audited by the IRS, you will probably be questioned about business travel deductions. Of course, you'll need to have records showing what you spent for your trips (see Chapter 15 for a detailed discussion). However, you'll also need documents proving that your trip was for your existing business. You can prove this by:

- making a note in your calendar or daily planner of every business meeting you attend or other business-related work you do—be sure to note the time you spend on each business activity
- obtaining and saving business cards from anyone you meet while on business
- noting in your calendar or daily planner the names of all the people you meet for business on your trip
- keeping the programs or agendas from any conventions or training seminars you attend, as well as any notes you made
- keeping copies of thank-you notes you send to the business contacts you met on your trips, and
- keeping copies of business-related correspondence or emails you sent or received before the trip.

Maximize Your Business Days

If you mix business with pleasure on your trip, you have to make sure that you have enough business days to deduct your transportation costs. You'll need to spend more than 50% of your days on business on domestic trips and more than 75% for foreign trips of more than 14 days.

You don't have to work all day for that day to count as a business day: Any day in which you work at least four hours is a business day, even if you goof off the rest of time. The day will count as a business day for purposes of determining whether your transportation expenses are deductible, and you can deduct your lodging, meal, and other expenses during the day, even though you worked only four hours.

You can easily maximize your business days by taking advantage of this rule. For example, you can:

- work no more than four hours in any one day whenever possible
- spread your business over several days—for example, if you need to be present at three meetings, try to spread them over two or three days instead of one, and
- avoid using the fastest form of transportation to your business destination—travel days count as business days, so you'll add business days to your trip if you drive instead of fly. Remember, there's no law that says you have to take the quickest means of transportation to your destination.

Take Advantage of the Sandwich Day Rule

Days when you do no business-related work still count as business days if they are sandwiched between workdays, as long as it was cheaper to spend that day away than to go back home. If you work on Friday and Monday, this rule allows you to count Saturday and Sunday as business days, even if you don't do any work.

EXAMPLE: Kim flies from Houston to Honolulu, Hawaii, for a business convention. She arrives on Wednesday and returns the following Wednesday. She does not attend any convention activities during the weekend and goes to the beach instead. Nevertheless, because it was cheaper for her to stay in Hawaii than to fly back to Houston for the weekend and return to Hawaii, she may count Saturday and Sunday as business days. This means she can deduct her lodging and meal expenses for those days (but not the cost of renting a surfboard).

Travel Expenses Reimbursed by Clients or Customers

Business owners who travel while performing services for a client or customer often have their expenses reimbursed by the client. You need not include such reimbursements in your income if you provide an adequate accounting of the expenses to your client and comply with the accountable plan rules. Basically, this requires that you submit all your documentation to the client in a timely manner, and return any excess payments. Accountable plans are covered in detail in Chapter 11. Record-keeping rules for long-distance travel are covered in Chapter 15.

> **EXAMPLE:** Farley, a home-based architect, incurs $5,000 in travel expenses while working on a new shopping center for a client. He keeps complete and accurate records of his expenses which he provides to his client who reimburses him the $5,000. Farley need not include the $5,000 in his income for the year. Farley's client may deduct the reimbursement as a business expense.

If you do not adequately account to your client for these expenses, you must include any reimbursements or allowances in your income, and they should also be included in any 1099-MISC form the client is required to provide the IRS reporting how much you were paid (see Chapter 11). The client can still deduct the reimbursement as compensation paid to you. You may deduct the expenses on your own return, but you'll need documentation to back them up in the event of an audit.

Inventory

This chapter covers inventory, including how to determine which of your purchases constitute inventory, how to value your inventory, and how to calculate your deduction for inventory costs.

SKIP AHEAD

Service providers can skip ahead. If your home business involves making or buying goods to sell to customers—even if your primary business is to provide services—you need to read this chapter and learn about inventories. If you only provide services to your clients or customers, then you don't need to worry about inventories. You can skip ahead to Chapter 11.

What Is Inventory?

Inventory (also called merchandise) is the goods and products that a business owns to sell to customers in the ordinary course of business. It includes almost anything a business offers for sale, except for real estate. It makes no difference whether you manufacture the goods yourself or buy finished goods to resell to customers. Inventory includes not only finished merchandise, but also unfinished work in progress, as well as the raw materials and supplies that will become part of the finished merchandise.

Only things to which you hold title—that is, things you own—constitute inventory. Inventory includes items you haven't yet received or paid for, as long as you own them. For example, an item you buy with a credit card counts as inventory, even if you haven't paid the bill yet. However, if you buy merchandise that is sent C.O.D., you acquire ownership only after the goods are delivered and paid for. Similarly, goods that you hold on consignment are not part of your inventory because you don't own them.

> EXAMPLE: Ava owns a home-based crafts business—she makes her own crafts and buys finished products from others, which she then sells at crafts fairs and on her website. Ava's inventory consists of the finished

crafts she has for sale, the unfinished crafts she is working on, and the raw material she will eventually use to create finished crafts. Raw materials that she has on order (but has not paid for) are not inventory. Neither is Ava's craft-making equipment, such as her leather hole punch and jewelry tools, nor the computer she uses to keep track of sales and maintain her website. These items are part of her business assets, not merchandise that she is offering for sale to customers. Jewelry pieces that Ava is selling in her store on consignment also don't count as inventory because they still belong to the craftspeople who made them, not to Ava.

Supplies Are Not Inventory

Materials and supplies that do not physically become part of the merchandise a business sells are not included in inventory. This includes:

- parts and other components acquired to maintain, repair, or improve business property
- fuel, lubricants, water, or similar items that are reasonably expected to be consumed in 12 months or less
- property that has an economic useful life of 12 months or less, and
- property with an acquisition or production cost of $200 or less. (IRS Reg. 1.162-3T(c)(1).)

Unless they are incidental supplies (as described in "Incidental Supplies," below), the cost of these supplies must be deducted *in the year in which they are used or consumed*, which is not necessarily the year when you purchase them. This means that you must keep track of how much material you use each year.

EXAMPLE: Ava decides to tan her own leather, which she will use to create leather pouches to sell to customers. She orders large amounts of various expensive chemicals needed for the tanning process. In one year, she spent $5,000 for the tanning chemicals, but used only half of them. She may deduct $2,500 of the cost of the chemicals that year. She may not deduct the cost of the remaining chemicals until she uses them.

Incidental Supplies

There is an important exception to the rule that the cost of materials and supplies may be deducted only as they are used or consumed. You may deduct the entire cost of supplies that are *incidental* to your business in the year when you purchase them. Supplies are incidental if you:

- do *not* keep a record of when you use the supplies
- do not take a physical inventory of the supplies at the beginning and end of the tax year, and
- deduct the cost of supplies in the year you purchase them and doing so does not distort your taxable income (IRS Reg. 1.162-3T(a)(2)).

> EXAMPLE: This year, Ava purchases $100 worth of lightbulbs to light her home workspace. She does not keep a record of how many lightbulbs she uses each year or take a physical inventory of how many she has on hand at year's end. The lightbulbs are incidental supplies. Ava may deduct the entire $100 for the year, regardless of how many lightbulbs she actually used that year.

Long-Term Assets

Long-term assets are things that last for more than one year—for example, equipment, tools, office furniture, vehicles, and buildings. Long-term assets that you purchase to use in your business are not a part of your inventory. They are deductible capital expenses that you may depreciate over several years or, in many cases, deduct in a single year using bonus depreciation or Section 179. (See Chapter 5 for more on deducting long-term assets.)

> EXAMPLE: Ava buys a new computer to help her keep track of her sales. The computer is not part of Ava's inventory because she bought it to use in her business, not to resell to customers. Because it will last for more than one year, it's a long-term asset. She may deduct the cost in one year using bonus depreciation or Section 179, or deduct it over several years using regular depreciation.

Deducting Inventory Costs

Before 2018, you were not allowed to deduct inventory costs in the same way you deduct other costs of doing business, such as your office rent or employee salaries. Instead you had to maintain inventory on your books and deduct it only in the year it was sold, which could be long after it was purchased. However, the Tax Cuts and Jobs Act changed this longstanding rule for smaller businesses. If the average annual gross receipts earned by your business over the past three years total less than $26 million, you now have two alternative ways to treat inventory:

- as nonincidental materials and supplies, or
- the same way it is treated in your financial statements or books and records. (I.R.C. § 471(c).)

Nonincidental Materials and Supplies Deduction

Businesses with less than $26 million in gross receipts may use the cash method of accounting and treat inventory as nonincidental materials and supplies. You deduct the cost of inventory treated as materials and supplies in the year in which it is first used or consumed in your business operations.

The impact of such treatment is greatest for businesses that manufacture products for sale. They may deduct the cost of purchased raw materials when the materials move out of storage into the work-in-process. For businesses that buy finished merchandise for resale, the impact is not so great. Their inventory is used or consumed when it is sold to customers. Thus, they get no deduction until the merchandise is sold, the same as under regular inventory rules.

However, there are other advantages to this method. The uniform capitalization rules, which require that a portion of overhead and other indirect costs be apportioned to inventory, do not apply. As a result, all the direct labor and overhead costs incurred in producing the goods should be deductible as incurred.

Moreover, once you adopt the cash method of accounting, you may elect to use the de minimis safe harbor to deduct inventory that cost no more than $2,500 per item as shown on your invoice (see Chapter 5).

If your business previously used the accrual method of accounting, you must obtain IRS permission to change to the cash method and start deducting inventory as nonincidental materials and supplies. You do so filing IRS Form 3115, *Application for Change in Accounting Method.* The change is automatically accepted by the IRS, which has adopted simplified filing procedures. (See Rev. Proc. 2018-40.) Nevertheless, it is wise to have a tax pro help with this complex form. The form has to be filed by the due date of the business's tax return for the year (plus extensions).

Books and Records Deduction for Inventory

The second alternative method businesses with less than $26 million in gross receipts may use is to deduct inventory:
- in accordance with their applicable financial statement, or
- if they don't have an applicable financial statement, in conformance with their books and records prepared in accordance with their accounting procedures. (I.R.C. § 471(c)(1)(B).)

An "applicable financial statement" is something larger businesses have; it includes audited financial statements and annual filings with the SEC and other government agencies by large businesses. Since smaller businesses don't have such statements, they may deduct inventory the same way it is treated in their books and records.

Here's what could make this provision revolutionary: All businesses with less than $26 million in gross receipts are now allowed to use the cash method of accounting. Those that do so use this method in their financial statements and books and records.

With the cash method of accounting system, income is reported when cash is received and expenses reported when cash is paid. Thus, inventory is expensed on a business's books when it is purchased. A sale (income) is shown on the books when purchased inventory is sold and cash received. There is no need to calculate cost of goods sold at the end of the year, and the uniform capitalization rules (requiring indirect costs be apportioned to inventory) do not apply. In other words, smaller businesses that use the cash method can deduct all of their inventory in the year it is purchased, instead of waiting until it is sold.

> **EXAMPLE:** Barbee owns a crafts business—she makes her own crafts and buys finished products from others, which she then sells. This year, she spent $28,000 on inventory. Barbee doesn't have an applicable financial statement, but she prepares her books and records in accordance with the cash method of accounting. Barbee may deduct her entire $28,000 inventory expense in the current year, since this is how she accounts for the expense in her books and records. She includes in income only the inventory items she sold during the year.

If a current deduction for inventory is in fact allowed, it would be a big change in the tax law. It is not entirely clear if this was actually intended by Congress when it wrote the Tax Cuts and Jobs Act. The IRS needs to provide guidance on how this provision will be implemented—something it has yet to do. It's wise to wait until the IRS makes it position clear before you start deducting all your inventory the year you pay for it.

If you need to switch from the accrual to the cash method of accounting, you'll need to file IRS Form 3115, *Application for Change in Accounting Method*. As discussed above, the change is automatically accepted by the IRS.

Merchandise to Include in Inventory	
Include the following merchandise in inventory:	**Do not include the following items in inventory:**
Purchased merchandise if title has passed to you, even if the merchandise is in transit or you do not have physical possession of it for some other reason	Goods you have sold, if title has passed to the buyer
	Goods consigned to you
Merchandise you've agreed to sell but have not separated from other similar merchandise you own to supply to the buyer	Goods ordered for future delivery, if you do not yet have title
	Assets such as land, buildings, and equipment used in your business
Goods you have placed with another person or business to sell on consignment	Supplies that do not physically become part of the item intended for sale
Goods held for sale in display rooms, merchandise mart rooms, or booths located away from your place of business	

Maintaining an Inventory

If you don't deduct inventoriable items as nonincidental materials and supplies or use the cash method in accordance with your books and records, you must maintain an inventory. You then deduct the cost of inventory only as it is sold. You must carry unsold inventory items as an asset on your books. You can deduct the cost of these items only when they are sold or become worthless (as a business loss).

You must report the cost of goods sold on your tax return using the following formula:

	Inventory at beginning of year
Plus:	Purchases or additions during the year
Minus:	Goods withdrawn from sale for personal use
Equals:	Cost of goods available for sale
Minus:	Inventory at end of year
Equals:	Cost of goods sold

EXAMPLE: Ava had $1,000 in inventory at the beginning of the year and purchased another $28,000 of inventory during the year. She removed $500 of inventory for her own personal use (to give away as Christmas presents). The cost of the inventory she had left at the end of the year is $10,500. She would calculate her cost of goods sold as follows:

Inventory at beginning of year		$ 1,000
Purchases or additions during the year	+	28,000
Goods withdrawn from sale for personal use	–	500
Cost of goods available for sale	=	28,500
Inventory at end of year	–	10,500
Cost of goods sold	=	$18,000

Note that all of these costs are based on what Ava paid for her inventory, not what she sold it for (which was substantially greater).

Determining the Value of Inventory

To use the equation in "Maintaining an Inventory," above, you must be able to calculate the value of the inventory you have left at the end of the year. There is no single way to do this—standard methods for tracking inventory vary according to the type and size of business involved. As long as your inventory methods are consistent from year to year, the IRS doesn't care which method you use.

Taking Physical Inventory

You need to know how much inventory you have at the beginning and end of each tax year to figure your cost of goods sold. If, like most businesses, you use the calendar year as your tax year, this means that you need to figure out your inventory each December 31. Unless you hold a New Year's Eve sale, your inventory on January 1 will usually be the same as the prior year's ending inventory—your inventory on December 31. Any differences must be explained in a schedule attached to your tax return.

Until recently, the IRS required all businesses that sold or manufactured goods to make a physical inventory of the merchandise they owned—that is, to actually count it. This process, often called "taking inventory," is usually done at the end of the year, although it doesn't have to be. Nor is it necessary to count every single item in stock. Businesses can make a physical inventory of a portion of their total merchandise, then extrapolate their total inventory from the sample.

The IRS no longer requires small businesses to take physical inventories. But even small businesses must keep track of how much inventory they buy and sell to determine their cost of goods sold for the year. With modern inventory software, it is possible for a business to keep a continuous record of the goods on hand during the year. Keep copies of your invoices and receipts to prove to the IRS that you correctly accounted for your inventory, in case you are audited.

Identifying Inventory Items Sold During the Year

The second step in figuring out your cost of goods sold is to identify which inventory items were sold during the year. There are several ways to do this. You can specifically track each item that is sold during the year. This is generally done only by businesses that sell a relatively small number of high-cost items each year, such as automobile dealers or jewelers.

If you don't want to identify specific items by their invoices, you must make an assumption about which items were sold during the year and which items remain in stock. Small businesses ordinarily use the first-in, first-out (FIFO) method. The FIFO method assumes that the first items you purchased or produced are the first items that you sold, consumed, or otherwise disposed of.

> EXAMPLE: Ava purchased three leather pouches to sell to customers during 2018. She bought the first pouch on February 1 for $5, the second on March 1 for $6, and the third on April 1 for $7. At the end of the year, Ava finds that she only has one of these pouches left in stock. Using the FIFO method, she assumes that the first two pouches that she bought were the first ones sold. This means that in 2018, she sold two pouches that cost her $11 and has one pouch left in her inventory that cost $7.

Another method of identifying inventory makes the opposite assumption. Under the last-in, first-out (LIFO) method, you assume that the last items purchased or produced were the first to sell. This method is not favored by the IRS. You may use it only if you use the accrual method of accounting (see Chapter 15) and take physical inventory. To use the LIFO method, you must file IRS Form 970, *Application to Use LIFO Inventory Method*, and follow some very complex tax rules.

Valuing Your Inventory

You must also determine the value of the inventory you sold during the year. The value of your inventory is a major factor in figuring out your taxable income, so the method that you use is very important. The two most common methods are the cost method and the lower of cost or market method. A new business that doesn't use LIFO to determine which goods were sold (see above) may choose either method to value its inventory. You must use the same method to value your entire inventory, and you cannot change the method from year to year without first obtaining IRS approval.

Cost Method

As the name indicates, when you use the cost method, your inventory cost is the amount that you paid for the merchandise. Note that this is not the same as what you sold it for, which will (hopefully!) be higher.

Using the cost method is relatively easy when you purchase goods to resell. To calculate the value of each item, start with the invoice price. Add the cost of transportation, shipping, and other money you had to spend to acquire the items. Subtract any discounts you received.

Things get much more complicated if you manufacture goods to sell. In this situation, you must include all direct and indirect costs associated with the goods. This includes:

- the cost of products or raw materials, including the cost of having them shipped to you
- the cost of storing the products you sell, and
- direct labor costs (including contributions to pension or annuity plans) for workers who produce the products. This does not include your own salary, unless you are a corporate employee.

In addition, larger businesses (those with more than $10 million in gross receipts) must include an amount for depreciation on machinery used to produce the products and factory overhead expenses. If your home business makes this much money, obtain an accountant's help.

Lower of Cost or Market Method

What if the retail value of your inventory goes down during the year? This could happen, for example, if your inventory becomes obsolete or falls out of fashion. In this event, you may use the lower of cost or market method to value your inventory. Under this method, you compare the market (retail) value of each item on hand on the inventory date with its cost, and use the lower value as its inventory value. By using the lower of these two numbers, your inventory will be worth less and your deductible expenses will be greater, thereby reducing your taxable income.

EXAMPLE: Ava purchased a jeweled belt for $1,000. Due to a change in fashion, Ava finds she can sell the belt for only $500. Using the lower of cost or market method, she may value the belt at $500.

However, you can't simply make up an inventory item's market value. You must establish the market value of your inventory through objective evidence, such as the actual sales price for similar items.

RESOURCE
For more information on inventory, refer to:

- *The Accounting Game,* by Darrell Mullis and Judith Orloff (Sourcebooks, Inc.)
- *Small Time Operator,* by Bernard B. Kamoroff (Taylor Trade Publishing)
- IRS Publication 334, *Tax Guide for Small Business* (Chapter 7), and
- IRS Publication 538, *Accounting Periods and Methods.*

Hiring Help: Employees and Independent Contractors

A nne has a highly successful home business selling used clothing on eBay. In fact, business is so good that she needs help keeping up with her orders. She hires John, a high school kid, to work ten hours per week helping her with fulfillment. Now, she has to figure out how to treat John—and the money she pays him—for tax purposes.

This chapter is about the host of tax rules that apply to home business owners like Anne who hire people, whether as employees or independent contractors. These rules apply when you hire strangers or family members, or when your incorporated business hires you.

Employees Versus Independent Contractors

As far as the IRS is concerned, there are only two types of people you can hire to help in your home business: employees and independent contractors. You must understand the difference between these two categories because the tax rules are very different for each. If you hire an employee, you become subject to a wide array of state and federal tax requirements. You must withhold taxes from your employee's earnings, and pay other taxes yourself. You must also comply with complex and burdensome bookkeeping and reporting requirements. If you hire an independent contractor, none of these requirements apply. Tax deductions related to the two types differ as well. Independent contractors (ICs) go by a variety of names: self-employed, freelancers, free agents, consultants, entrepreneurs, or business owners. What they all have in common is that they are people who are in business for themselves. In contrast, an employee works for someone else's business.

Initially, it's up to you to determine whether any person you hire is an employee or an IC. However, your decision about how to classify a worker is subject to review by various government agencies, including:

- the IRS
- your state's tax department
- your state's unemployment compensation insurance agency, and
- your state's workers' compensation insurance agency.

These agencies are mostly interested in whether you have classified workers as independent contractors when you should have classified them as employees. The reason is that you must pay money to each of these agencies for employees, but not for independent contractors. The more workers that are classified as employees, the more money flows into the agencies' coffers. In the case of taxing agencies, employers must withhold tax from employees' paychecks and hand it over to the government; ICs pay their own taxes, which means the government must wait longer to get its money and faces the possibility that ICs won't declare their income or will otherwise cheat on their taxes. If an agency determines that you misclassified an employee as an IC, you may have to pay back taxes, fines, and penalties.

Scrutinizing agencies use various tests to determine whether a worker is an IC or an employee. The determining factor is usually whether you have the right to control the worker. If you have the right to *direct and control* the way a worker performs—both the final results of the job and the details of when, where, and how the work is done—then the worker is your employee. On the other hand, if you have only the right to accept or reject the final results the worker achieves, then that person is an IC.

An employer may not always exercise its right of control. For example, if an employee is experienced and well trained, the employer may not feel the need to closely supervise him or her. But the employer still has the right to step in at any time, which distinguishes an employment relationship from an IC arrangement.

> EXAMPLE: Anne hires John to help her fill orders and ship her clothing items to customers. John works ten hours per week in Anne's home office and warehouse (which is located in her garage). Anne carefully trains John, a 17-year-old, in how to take orders and ship the ordered items. When John first starts work, Anne closely supervises how he does his job. Virtually every aspect of John's behavior on the job is under Anne's control, including what time he arrives at and leaves work, when he takes a lunch break, and the sequence of tasks he must perform. If John proves to be an able and conscientious worker, Anne may choose not to look over his shoulder very often. But Anne has the right to do so at any time. John is Anne's employee.

IRS Test for Worker Status		
	Workers will more likely be considered ICs if:	**Workers will more likely be considered employees if:**
Behavioral Control	• You do not give them instructions. • You do not provide them with training.	• You give them instructions they must follow about how to do the work. • You give them detailed training.
Financial Control	• They have a significant investment in equipment and facilities. • They pay business or travel expenses themselves. • They make their services available to the public. • They are paid by the job. • They have opportunity for profit or loss.	• You provide them with equipment and facilities free of charge. • You reimburse their business or travel expenses. • They make no effort to market their services to the public. • You pay them by the hour or another unit of time. • They have no opportunity for profit or loss—for example, because they're paid by the hour and have all expenses reimbursed.
Relationship Between You and the Worker	• They don't receive employee benefits such as health insurance. • They sign a client agreement with your firm. • They can't quit or be fired at will. • They perform services that are not part of your regular business activities.	• They receive employee benefits. • They have no written client agreement. • They can quit at any time without incurring any liability to you. • They can be fired at any time. • They perform services that are part of your core business.

In contrast, a worker is an independent contractor if the hiring business does not have the right to control the person on the job. Because the worker is an independent businessperson not solely dependent on you (the hiring party) for a living, your control is limited to accepting or rejecting the final results the IC achieves.

> EXAMPLE: Anne hires Maya, a bookkeeper, to keep her business's books. Anne is only one of Maya's many clients. Anne doesn't tell Maya how to do her bookkeeping tasks; Maya is a professional who already knows how to do her work. Maya sets her own hours, provides her own equipment, and works from her own home office. Maya is an independent contractor.
>
> Because Maya is clearly running her own business, it's virtually certain that Anne does not have the right to control the way Maya performs her bookkeeping services. Anne's control is limited to accepting or rejecting the final result. If Anne doesn't like the work Maya has done, she can refuse to pay her.

There's no clear cut way for auditors to figure out whether you have the right to control a worker you hire. After all, they can't look into your mind to see whether you are controlling a worker (or whether you believe that you have the right to do so). They rely instead on indirect or circumstantial evidence indicating control or lack of it—for example, whether you provide a worker with tools and equipment, where the work is performed, how the worker is paid, and whether you can fire the worker. The chart above shows the primary factors used by the IRS and most other government agencies to determine if you have the right to control a worker.

> CAUTION
> **Part-time workers and temps can be employees.** Don't assume that a person you hire to work part time or for a short period automatically qualifies as an IC. People who work for you only temporarily or part time are your employees if you have the right to control the way they work.

> **RESOURCE**
>
> **Need more information about independent contractors?** For a detailed discussion of the practical and legal issues business owners face when hiring ICs, see *Working With Independent Contractors*, by Stephen Fishman (Nolo).

Tax Deductions for Employee Pay and Benefits

Only 9% of home businesses hire employees, according to a study sponsored by the Small Business Administration. However, the tax law provides valuable deductions for those who do have employees. You may deduct most or all of what you pay an employee as a business expense. Thus, for example, if you pay an employee $25,000 per year in salary and benefits, you'll ordinarily get a $25,000 tax deduction. In some cases, you can also get an additional pass-through deduction equal to 50% of what you pay your employees (see Chapter 7). You should factor this into your calculations whenever you're thinking about hiring employees or deciding how much to pay them.

You may pay your employees in the form of salaries, sales commissions, bonuses, vacation allowances, sick pay (as long as it's not covered by insurance), or fringe benefits. For tax deduction purposes, it doesn't really matter how you measure or make the payments.

Most of the time, amounts you pay employees to work in your business will be business operating expenses. These expenses are currently deductible as long as they are:

- ordinary and necessary
- reasonable in amount
- paid for services actually performed, and
- actually paid or incurred in the year the deduction is claimed (as shown by your payroll records).

(See Chapter 4 for more on business operating expenses.)

An employee's services are ordinary and necessary if they are common, accepted, helpful, and appropriate for your business; they don't have to be indispensable. An employee's pay is reasonable if the amount is within the range that other businesses pay for similar services. These requirements usually won't pose a problem when you hire an employee to perform any legitimate business function.

> **EXAMPLE:** Victor, a lawyer who works from home, hires Kim to work as a paralegal and pays her $2,500 per month—what such workers are typically paid in the area. Victor can deduct Kim's $2,500 monthly salary as a business operating expense. If Kim works a full year, Victor will get a $30,000 deduction.

Payments to employees for personal services are not deductible as business expenses.

> **EXAMPLE:** Victor hires Samantha to work as a live-in nanny for his three children. Samantha is Victor's employee, but her services are personal, not related to his business. Thus, Victor may not deduct her pay as a business expense.

Special rules (described in "Employing Your Family or Yourself," later in this chapter) apply if you hire family members to work in your business or hire yourself as an employee.

Payroll Taxes

Whenever you hire an employee, you become an unpaid tax collector for the government. You are required to withhold and pay both federal and state taxes for the worker. These taxes are called payroll taxes or employment taxes. Federal payroll taxes consist of:

- Social Security and Medicare taxes—also known as FICA
- unemployment taxes—also known as FUTA, and
- federal income taxes—also known as FITW.

You must periodically pay FICA, FUTA, and FITW to the IRS, either electronically or by making federal tax deposits at specified banks, which then transmit the money to the IRS. You are entitled to deduct as a business expense payroll taxes that you pay yourself. You get no deductions for taxes you withhold from employees' pay.

Every year, employers must file IRS Form W-2, *Wage and Tax Statement*, for each of their workers. The form shows the IRS how much a worker was paid and how much tax was withheld.

RESOURCE

IRS Publication 15, Circular E, *Employer's Tax Guide*, provides detailed information on payroll tax requirements. You can get a free copy by calling the IRS at 800-TAX-FORM, by calling or visiting your local IRS office, or by downloading it from the IRS website, www.irs.gov.

Employer's FICA Contributions

FICA is an acronym for Federal Income Contributions Act, the law requiring employers and employees to pay Social Security and Medicare taxes.

FICA taxes consist of a 12.4% Social Security tax on income up to an annual ceiling. In 2020, the annual Social Security ceiling was $137,700. Medicare taxes are not subject to any income ceiling and are levied at a 2.9% rate up to an annual ceiling—$200,000 for single taxpayers and $250,000 for married couples filing jointly. Income above these ceilings is taxed at a 3.8% rate. For 2020, this combines to a total 15.3% tax on employment income up to the Social Security tax ceiling.

Ordinarily, an employer and employee split the cost of FICA taxes—the employer pays half and withholds the other half from the employee's pay. This means that each pays 7.65% up to the Social Security tax ceiling. You are entitled to deduct (as a business operating expense) the portion of the tax that you pay yourself.

The ceiling for the Social Security tax changes annually. You can find out what the Social Security tax ceiling is for the current year from IRS Publication 15, Circular E, *Employer's Tax Guide*; the amount is printed right on the first page.

Deferral of 2020 Employer FICA Contributions

Due to the coronavirus (COVID-19) pandemic, employers have the option of deferring their 2020 FICA payments. All such payments due beginning on March 27, 2020 (the date the CARES Act was signed into law) and ending on December 31, 2020, can be deferred. Half of the deferred payroll taxes are due on December 31, 2021, with the remainder due on December 31, 2022. The deferral applies only to the employer portion of FICA taxes. Employers must continue to withhold their employees' contributions and deposit the money with the IRS.

FUTA

FUTA is an acronym for the Federal Unemployment Tax Act, the law that establishes federal unemployment taxes. Most employers must pay both state and federal unemployment taxes. Even if you're exempt from the state tax, you may still have to pay the federal tax. Employers alone are responsible for FUTA—you may not collect or deduct it from employees' wages.

You must pay FUTA taxes if either of the following is true:

- You pay $1,500 or more to employees during any calendar quarter— that is, any three-month period beginning with January, April, July, or October.
- You had one or more employees for at least some part of a day in any 20 or more different weeks during the year. The weeks don't have to be consecutive, nor does the employee have to be the same each week.

The FUTA tax rate is 6%. In practice, you rarely pay this much. You are given a credit of 5.4% if you pay the applicable state unemployment tax in full and on time. This means that the actual FUTA tax rate is usually 0.6%. In 2020, the FUTA tax was assessed on only the first $7,000 of an employee's annual wages. Therefore, the full amount of the tax is $42 per year per employee.

FITW

FITW is an acronym for Federal Income Tax Withholding. You must calculate and withhold federal income tax from your employees' paychecks. Employees are solely responsible for paying federal income tax. Your only responsibility is to withhold the funds and remit them to the government. You get no deductions for FITW; it wasn't your money to begin with.

State Payroll Taxes

Employers in every state are required to pay and withhold state payroll taxes. These taxes include:

- state unemployment compensation taxes in all states
- state income tax withholding in most states, and
- state disability taxes in a few states.

Employers in every state are required to contribute to a state unemployment insurance fund. Employees make no contributions, except in Alaska, New Jersey, Pennsylvania, and Rhode Island, where employers must withhold small employee contributions from employees' paychecks. The employer contributions are a deductible business expense.

If your payroll is very small—less than $1,500 per calendar quarter—you probably won't have to pay unemployment compensation taxes. In most states, you must pay state unemployment taxes for employees if you're paying federal FUTA taxes. However, some states have stricter requirements. Contact your state labor department for the exact rules and payroll amounts.

All states except Alaska, Florida, Nevada, South Dakota, Texas, Washington, and Wyoming have income taxation. If your state has income taxes, you must withhold the applicable amount from your employees' paychecks and pay it to the state taxing authority. Each state has its own income tax withholding forms and procedures. Contact your state tax department for information. Of course, employers get no deductions for withholding their employees' state income taxes.

California, Hawaii, New Jersey, New York, Rhode Island, and Washington state (starting in 2019) have state disability insurance programs that provide employees with coverage for injuries or illnesses that are not related to work. Employers in these states must withhold their employees' disability insurance contributions from their pay. Employers must also make their own contributions in Hawaii, New Jersey, New York, and Washington state (starting in 2019) and these employer contributions are deductible.

In addition, subject to some important exceptions, employers in all states must provide their employees with workers' compensation insurance to cover work-related injuries. Workers' compensation is not a payroll tax. Employers must purchase a workers' compensation policy from a private insurer or the state workers' compensation fund. Your workers' compensation insurance premiums are deductible as a business insurance expense (see Chapter 14).

> **CAUTION**
>
> **Employers in California must withhold for parental leave.** California was the first state to require paid family leave. Employers in California must withhold money from their employees' paychecks (as part of the state's disability insurance program) to fund this leave program. For more information on the program, go to www.edd.ca.gov.

> **TIP**
>
> **Bookkeeping expenses are deductible.** Figuring out how much to withhold, doing the necessary record keeping, and filling out the required forms can be complicated. If you have a computer, software programs such as *QuickBooks* or *QuickPay* can help with all the calculations and print out your employees' checks and IRS forms. You can also hire a bookkeeper or payroll tax service to do the work. Amounts you pay a bookkeeper or payroll tax service are deductible business operating expenses. Moreover, the cost will be quite small if you only have a few employees. You can find these services in the phone book or on the Internet under payroll tax services. You can also find a list of payroll service providers on the IRS website at www.irs.gov/efile. Be aware, however,

that even if you hire a payroll service, you remain personally liable if your payroll taxes are not paid on time. The IRS recommends that employers: (1) keep their company address on file with the IRS, rather than the address of the payroll service provider, so that the company will be contacted by the IRS if there are any problems; (2) require the payroll service provider to post a fiduciary bond in case it defaults on its obligation to pay any penalties and interest due to IRS deficiency notices; and (3) ask the service provider to enroll in and use the Electronic Federal Tax Payment System (EFTPS) so the employer can confirm payments made on its behalf (see www.eftps.gov for more information).

Employee Fringe Benefits

You don't have to provide any fringe benefits to your employees—not even health insurance (except in Hawaii and Massachusetts), sick pay, or vacation. But, large employers (those with at least 50 or more employees) are required to provide health insurance to their full-time employees or pay a penalty to the IRS. This shouldn't impact any home businesses. However, the tax law encourages you to provide employee benefits by allowing you to deduct the cost as a business expense. (You should deduct these expenses as employee benefits, not employee compensation.) Moreover, your employees do not have to treat the value of their fringe benefits as taxable income. So you get a deduction and your employees get tax-free goodies. In contrast, if you're a business owner (a sole proprietor, a partner in a partnership, an LLC member, or a greater than 2% shareholder of an S corporation), you must include in your income, and pay tax on, the value of any fringe benefits your company provides you—the only exception is for de minimis (minor) fringes. Tax-free employee fringe benefits include:
- health insurance
- accident insurance
- Health Savings Accounts (see Chapter 12)
- dependent care assistance
- educational assistance

- group term life insurance coverage—limits apply based on the policy value
- qualified employee benefit plans, including profit-sharing plans, stock bonus plans, and money purchase plans
- employee stock options
- lodging on your business premises
- achievement awards
- commuting benefits (not deductible by the employer starting in 2018)
- employee discounts on the goods or services you sell
- supplemental unemployment benefits
- de minimis (low-cost) fringe benefits, such as low-value birthday or holiday gifts, event tickets, traditional awards (such as a retirement gift), other special occasion gifts, and coffee and soft drinks, and
- "cafeteria" plans that allow employees to choose among two or more of the tax-qualified benefits listed above, or receive reimbursement for specified expenses. Since 2011, small employers (those with 100 or fewer employees) have been able to offer their employees a simple cafeteria plan—a plan not subject to the non-discrimination requirements of traditional cafeteria plans.

Health insurance is by far the most important tax-free employee fringe benefit; it is discussed in detail in Chapter 12. See IRS Publication 15-B, *Employer's Tax Guide to Fringe Benefits*, for more information on the other types of benefits.

Employees may also be supplied with working condition fringe benefits. These are property and services you provide to an employee so that the employee can perform his or her job. A working condition fringe benefit is tax free to an employee to the extent the employee would be able to deduct the cost of the property or services as a business or depreciation expense if he or she had paid for it. If the employee uses the benefit 100% for work, it is tax free. But the value of any personal use of a working condition fringe benefit must be included in the employee's compensation and he or she must pay tax on it. The employee must meet any documentation requirements that apply to the deduction.

Special Coronavirus Pandemic Employer Tax Credits

To help blunt the devastating economic impact of the coronavirus (COVID-19) pandemic, Congress implemented temporary tax credits for employers who maintained their payrolls and provided paid sick leave and family leave during 2020. These credits can be claimed by home business owners who have employees, including family members as described below. These credits are refundable, meaning the IRS will pay you any amount in excess of your employer's tax liability.

Sick Leave and Family Leave Credits: The Family First Coronavirus Response Act requires employers with less than 500 full-time employees to provide:

- up to 80 hours of paid sick leave at full pay if an employee is unable to work due to quarantine, COVID-19 symptoms, or the need to seek medical advice
- up to 80 hours of paid sick leave at two-thirds full pay if an employee is unable to work in order to care for a person under quarantine or a child under 18 years old whose school is closed or child care provider unavailable due to COVID-19, and
- up to ten additional weeks of paid family and medical leave at two-thirds full pay to employees unable to work or telework due to the need to care for a child under 18 years old whose school or child care provider is closed or unavailable due to COVID-19.

Employers may claim a tax credit to cover the cost of such sick and family leave, plus the cost to maintain employee health insurance coverage during the leave period. The employee full-pay sick leave credit is capped at $510 per day. The two-thirds full pay credit to care for others and child care leave credit are capped at $200 per day. You can reduce your employer payroll tax payments to immediately collect the credit. You may also file a request for an accelerated payment of the credit from the IRS. Such employer sick leave and emergency leave payments to employees don't count as wages for Social Security and Medicare tax purposes, thus they don't add to your employer payroll tax burden. This credit is not available to employers who also receive the paid family and medical leave credit that took effect in 2018. (I.R.C. § 45S.)

> ### Special Coronavirus Pandemic Employer Tax Credits (continued)
>
> **Employee Retention Credit:** Under the CARES Act, any employer, regardless of size, may claim a refundable credit if, during March 13, 2020 through December 31, 2020, it:
>
> - fully or partially suspended operations during any calendar quarter in 2020 due to a government COVID-19 related order, or
> - experienced 50% or greater decline in gross receipts (compared with 2019) during a calendar quarter—the decline need not have been due to the pandemic.
>
> The credit is 50% of up to $10,000 in employee wages (including health plan expenses) paid from March 31, 2020 through December 31, 2020. Thus, the credit is capped at $5,000 per employee. However, if you received loans under the SBA Paycheck Protection Program (PPP loans), you don't qualify for this credit. Also, the credit may not be claimed for the same employee wages used to qualify for the 100% sick leave and family leave credit. Thus, you should first claim the sick leave and family leave credit and then claim the employee retention credit for other eligible wages.

Employing Your Family or Yourself

Whoever said "never hire your relatives" must not have read the tax code. The tax law promotes family togetherness by making it highly advantageous for home business owners to hire family members. And when you have a home business, hiring your spouse, children, or other relatives can be very convenient for everyone (and eliminate the commute!).

Employing Your Children

Believe it or not, your children can be a great tax savings device. Indeed, as a result of the Tax Cuts and Jobs Act, you can save more tax by hiring your children than ever before. Here's how: If you hire your children as employees to do legitimate work in your business, you may deduct their salaries from your business income as a business expense. Your child will have to pay tax on his or her salary only to the extent it exceeds the standard deduction amount for the year: As a result of the Tax Cuts and Jobs Act, this is a whopping $12,400 in 2020. Moreover, if your child is under the age of 18, you won't have to withhold or pay any FICA (Social Security or Medicare) tax on the salary (subject to a couple of exceptions).

What About Child Labor Laws?

You're probably aware that certain types of child labor are illegal under federal and state law. However, these laws generally don't apply to children under the age of 16 who are employed by their parents, unless the child is employed in mining, manufacturing, or a hazardous occupation. Hazardous occupations include driving a motor vehicle; being an outside helper on a motor vehicle; operating various power-driven machines, including machines for woodworking, metal forming, sawing, and baking; or roofing, wrecking, excavation, demolition, and ship-breaking operations.

A child who is at least 16 may be employed in any nonhazardous occupation. Children at least 17 years of age may spend up to 20% of their time driving cars and trucks weighing less than 6,000 pounds as part of their job if they have licenses and no tickets, drive only in daylight hours, and go no more than 30 miles from home. They may not perform dangerous driving maneuvers (such as towing) or do regular route deliveries. For detailed information, see the Department of Labor website, www.dol.gov.

These rules allow you to shift part of your business income from your own tax bracket to your child's bracket, which should be much lower than yours (unless you earn little or no income). This can result in substantial tax savings. If you pay your child no more than the standard deduction amount—$12,400 in 2020—there will be no tax due at all. Moreover, in 2020, a child need only pay a 10% tax on taxable earned income up to $9,875—taxable income means total income minus the standard deduction. Thus, a child could earn up to $22,275 (the $12,400 standard deduction amount + $9,875) and pay only a 10% income tax on $9,875 of it—that's $987.50 in tax on $22,275 in income.

EXAMPLE: Carol hires Mark, her 16-year-old son, to perform computer inputting services for her medical record transcription business, which she owns as a sole proprietor. He works ten hours per week and she pays him $20 per hour (the going rate for such work). Over the course of a year, she pays him a total of $9,000. She need not pay FICA tax for Mark because he's not yet 18. When she does her taxes for the year, she may deduct his $9,000 salary from her business income as a business expense. Mark need not pay tax on his income since it is less than the $12,400 standard deduction. Had Carol not hired Mark and done the work herself, she would have lost her $9,000 deduction and had to pay income tax and self-employment taxes on this amount—a 37.3% tax in her tax bracket (22% federal income tax + 15.3% self-employment tax = 37.3%). Thus, she would have had to pay an additional $3,357 in federal taxes. Depending on the state where Carol lives, she likely would have had to pay a state income tax as well.

No Payroll Taxes

One of the advantages of hiring your child is that you need not pay FICA taxes for your child under the age of 18 who works in your trade or business, or your partnership, if it's owned solely by you and your spouse.

EXAMPLE: Lisa, a 16-year-old, makes deliveries for her mother's mail order business, which is operated as a sole proprietorship. Although Lisa is her mother's employee, her mother need not pay FICA taxes on her salary until she turns 18.

Moreover, you need not pay federal unemployment (FUTA) taxes for services performed by your child who is under 21 years old.

However, these rules do not apply—and you must pay both FICA and FUTA—if you hire your child to work for:

- your corporation, or
- your partnership, unless all the partners are parents of the child.

EXAMPLE: Ron works in a home-based computer repair business that is co-owned by his mother and her partner, Ralph, who is no relation to the family. The business must pay FICA and FUTA taxes for Ron because he is working for a partnership and not all of the partners are his parents.

You need not pay FICA or FUTA if you've formed a one-member limited liability company and hire your child to work for it. For tax purposes, a one-member LLC is a "disregarded entity"—that is, it's treated as if it didn't exist.

No Withholding

In addition, if your child has no unearned income (for example, interest or dividend income), you must withhold income taxes from your child's pay only if it exceeds the standard deduction for the year. The standard deduction was $12,400 in 2020 and is adjusted every year for inflation. Children who are paid less than this amount need not pay any income taxes on their earnings. However, you must withhold income taxes if your child has more than $350 in unearned income for the year and his or her total income exceeds $1,100 (2020).

> EXAMPLE: Connie, a 15-year-old girl, is paid $4,000 a year to help out in her parents' home business. She has no income from interest or any other unearned income. Her parents need not withhold income taxes from Connie's salary.
>
> If Connie is paid $4,000 in salary and has $500 in interest income, her parents must withhold income taxes from her salary because she has more than $350 in unearned income and her total income for the year was more than $1,100.

Employing Your Spouse

You don't get the benefits of income shifting when you employ your spouse in your business because your income is combined when you file a joint tax return. You'll also have to pay FICA taxes on your spouse's wages, so you get no savings there either. However, you need not pay FUTA tax if you employ your spouse in your unincorporated business. This tax is usually less than $50 per year, so this is not much of a savings.

The real advantage of hiring your spouse is in the realm of employee benefits. You can provide your spouse with any or all of the employee benefits discussed in "Tax Deductions for Employee Pay and Benefits," above. You can take a tax deduction for the cost of the benefit, and your spouse doesn't have to declare the benefit as income, provided the IRS requirements are satisfied. This is a particularly valuable tool for health insurance—you can give your spouse health insurance coverage as an employee benefit. (See Chapter 12 for a detailed discussion.)

Another benefit of hiring your spouse is that you can take business trips together and deduct the cost as a business expense, as long as your spouse's presence was necessary (for your business, not for you, personally).

Rules to Follow When Employing Your Family

The IRS is well aware of the tax benefits of hiring a spouse or child, so it's on the lookout for taxpayers who claim the benefit without meeting the requirements. If the IRS concludes that your spouse or children aren't really employees, you'll lose your tax deductions for their salary and benefits. And they'll have to pay tax on their benefits. To avoid this, you should observe the following simple rules.

Rule 1: Your Child or Spouse Must Be a Real Employee

First of all, your child or spouse must be a bona fide employee. Their work must be ordinary and necessary for your business, and their pay must be compensation for services actually performed. Their services don't have to be indispensable, but they must be common, accepted, helpful, and appropriate for your business. Any real work for your business can qualify—for example, you could employ your child or spouse to clean your office, answer the phone, stuff envelopes, input data, or make deliveries. You get no business deductions when you pay your child for personal services, such as babysitting or mowing your lawn at home. On the other hand, money you pay for yard work performed on business property could be deductible as a business expense.

The IRS won't believe that an extremely young child is a legitimate employee. How young is too young? The IRS has accepted that a seven-year-old child may be an employee, but probably won't believe that children younger than seven are performing any useful work for your business.

You should keep track of the work and hours your children or spouse perform by having them fill out time sheets or time cards. You can find these in stationery stores or you can create a time sheet yourself. There are also many time sheet apps you can use. It should list the date, the services performed, and the time spent performing the services. Although not legally required, it's also a good idea to have your spouse or child sign a written employment agreement specifying his or her job duties and hours. These duties should be related only to your business.

Rule 2: Compensation Must Be Reasonable

When you hire your children, it is advantageous (tax wise) to pay them as much as possible. That way, you can shift more of your income to your children, who are probably in a much lower income tax bracket. Conversely, you want to pay your spouse as little as possible, because you get no benefits from income shifting; you and your spouse are in the same income tax bracket (assuming you file a joint return, as the vast majority of married people do). Moreover, your spouse will have to pay the employee's share of Social Security taxes on his or her salary—an amount that is not tax deductible. This tax is 7.65% up to the annual ceiling. (As your spouse's employer, you'll have to pay employment taxes on your spouse's salary as well, but these taxes are deductible business expenses.) The absolute minimum you can pay your spouse is the minimum wage in your area. On the other hand, at higher income levels the pass-through tax deduction is based on the amount you pay your employees; so, to maximize this deduction, you may wish to pay your spouse more. (See Chapter 7.)

However, you can't just pay whatever amount will result in the lowest tax bill: Your spouse's and/or your child's total compensation must be reasonable. Total compensation means the sum of the salary plus all the fringe benefits you provide your spouse, including health insurance and medical expense reimbursements, if any. You shouldn't have a problem as long as you don't pay more than you'd pay a stranger for the same work. In other words, don't try paying your child $100 per hour for office cleaning just to get a big tax deduction. Find out what workers who perform similar services in your area are being paid. For example, if you plan to hire your teenager to do computer inputting, check with an employment agency or temp agency in your area to see what these workers are being paid.

To prove how much you paid (and that you actually paid it), you should pay your child or spouse by check or electronic deposit, not cash. Do this once or twice a month, just as you would for any other employee. The funds should be deposited in a bank account in your child's or spouse's name. Your child's bank account may be a trust account.

Rule 3: Comply With Legal Requirements for Employers

You must comply with most of the same legal requirements when you hire a child or spouse as you do when you hire a stranger. Schedule the following:

- **At the time you hire.** When you first hire your child or spouse, you must fill out IRS Form W-4. You (the employer) use it to determine how much tax you must withhold from the employee's salary. A child who is exempt from withholding should write "exempt" in the space provided and complete and sign the rest of the form. You must also complete U.S. Citizenship and Immigration Services Form I-9, *Employment Eligibility Verification*, verifying that the employee is a U.S. citizen or is otherwise eligible to work in the United States. Keep both forms. You must also record your employee's Social Security number. If your child doesn't have a number, you must apply for one. In addition, you must have an Employer Identification Number (EIN). If you don't have one, you may obtain it by filing IRS Form SS-4.

- **Every payday.** You'll need to withhold income tax from your child's pay only if it exceeds a specified amount (see "Employing Your Children," above). You don't have to withhold FICA taxes for children younger than 18. You must withhold income tax and FICA for your spouse, but not FUTA tax. If the amounts withheld plus the employer's share of payroll taxes exceed $2,500 during a calendar quarter, you must deposit the amounts monthly by making federal tax deposits electronically with the IRS. You can make these deposits yourself using the IRS's free Electronic Federal Tax Payment System (EFTPS) (see www.eftps.gov). If you do not want to use EFTPS, you can arrange for your tax professional, financial institution, payroll service, or other trusted third party to make electronic deposits on your behalf.

- **Every calendar quarter.** If you withhold tax from your child's or spouse's pay, you must deposit it with the IRS or a specified bank. If you deposit more than $1,000 a year, you must file Form 941, *Employer's Quarterly Federal Tax Return*, with the IRS, showing how much the employee was paid during the quarter and how much tax you withheld and deposited. If you need to deposit less than $2,500 during a calendar quarter, you can make your payment along with the Form 941, instead of paying monthly. Employers with total employment tax liability of $1,000 or less may file employment tax returns once a year instead of quarterly. Use new IRS Form 944, *Employer's Annual Federal Tax Return*. You must receive written notice from the IRS to file Form 944 instead of Form 941. If you haven't been notified but believe you qualify to file Form 944, visit www.irs.gov and enter "file employment taxes annually" in the search box.

- **Each year.** By January 31 of each year, you must complete and give your employee a copy of IRS Form W-2, *Wage and Tax Statement*, showing how much you paid the employee and how much tax was withheld. You must also file copies of the W-2 forms with the IRS and Social Security Administration by February 28. You must include IRS Form W-3, *Transmittal of Wage and Tax Statements*, with the copy you file with the Social Security Administration. If your child is exempt from withholding, a new W-4 form must be completed each year. You must also file Form 940, *Employer's Annual Federal Unemployment (FUTA) Tax Return*. The due date is January 31; however, if you deposited all of the FUTA tax when due, you have ten additional days to file. You must file a Form 940 for your child even though you are not required to withhold any unemployment taxes from his or her pay. If your child is your only employee, enter his or her wages as "exempt" from unemployment tax.

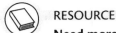

RESOURCE

Need more information on employing family members?
IRS Publication 15, Circular E, *Employer's Tax Guide*, and Publication 929, *Tax Rules for Children and Dependents*, provide detailed information on these requirements. You can get free copies by calling the IRS at 800-TAX-FORM, by calling or visiting your local IRS office, or by downloading them from the IRS website, www.irs.gov.

Employing Yourself

If, like the vast majority of home business owners, you are a sole proprietor, partner in a partnership, or member of a limited liability company (LLC), you are *not* an employee of your business. You are a business owner. However, if you have incorporated your business, whether as a regular C corporation or an S corporation, you are an employee of your corporation if you actively work in the business. In effect, you will be employing yourself. This has important tax consequences.

Your Company Must Pay Payroll Taxes

Your incorporated business must treat you just like any other employee for tax purposes. This means it must withhold income and FICA taxes from your pay and pay half of your FICA tax itself. It must also pay FUTA taxes for you. It gets a tax deduction for its contributions, just like any other employer (see "Tax Deductions for Employee Pay and Benefits," above). Your corporation—not you personally—must pay these payroll taxes.

You can't avoid these payroll taxes by working for free. The corporation must pay you at least a reasonable salary—what similar companies pay for the same services.

Tax Deductions for Your Salary and Benefits

When you're an employee, your incorporated business can deduct your salary as a business expense. However, you will have to pay income tax on your salary, so you won't realize a net tax savings.

But being an employee can have a significant upside. You'll be eligible for all of the tax-advantaged employee benefits discussed in "Tax Deductions for Employee Pay and Benefits," above. This means that your corporation can provide you with benefits, like health insurance, and deduct the expense (see Chapter 12). If your corporation is a regular C corporation, you won't have to pay income tax on the value of your employee benefits. However, most employees of S corporations must pay tax on their employee benefits, so you probably won't get an overall tax savings. Employees of an S corporation who own less than 2% of the corporate stock don't have to pay tax on benefits, but it's unlikely you'll have this little stock in your own S corporation.

You Can't Deduct Your Draw

If you're a sole proprietor, a partner, or an LLC member, you do not pay yourself a salary. If you want money from your business, you simply withdraw it from your business bank account. This is called a "draw." Because you are not an employee of your business, your draws are not employee compensation and are not deductible as business expenses.

Your Employee Expenses

Your corporation should reimburse you or pay directly for any expenses you incur while working for your corporation—for example, when you travel on company business.

If you comply with the requirements for an accountable plan, your corporation gets to deduct the expense and you don't have to count the reimbursement as income to you. If you fail to follow the rules, you must treat any reimbursements as employee income subject to tax. You may not deduct any expenses you incur as an employee on your own personal tax return. This deduction was eliminated by the Tax Cuts and Jobs Act starting in 2018 through 2025.

Tax Deductions When You Hire Independent Contractors

Anyone you hire to help in your home business who does not qualify as an employee is an independent contractor for tax purposes. As far as tax deductions are concerned, hiring independent contractors is very simple. Most of the time, the money you pay to an IC to perform services for your business will be deductible as a business operating expense. These expenses are deductible as long as they are ordinary, necessary, and reasonable in amount. (See "Tax Deductions for Employee Pay and Benefits," above, for more on this rule.)

> EXAMPLE: Emily, a graphic designer, hires Don, an attorney, to sue a client who failed to pay her. He collects $5,000 and she pays him $1,500 of this amount. The $1,500 is an ordinary and necessary business operating expense—Emily may deduct it from her business income for the year.

Of course, you get no business deduction if you hire an IC to perform personal services.

> EXAMPLE: Emily pays lawyer Don $2,000 to write her personal will. Because this is a personal expense, Emily cannot deduct the $2,000 from her business income.

If you hire an IC to perform services during the start-up phase of your business, to manufacture inventory, or as part of a long-term asset purchase, you can't deduct payments to the IC as operating expenses. Instead, you must follow the rules to deduct these amounts as start-up expenses, inventory, or long-term assets, respectively.

No Deductions for ICs' Taxes

When you hire an independent contractor, you don't have to withhold or pay any state or federal payroll taxes on the IC's behalf. Therefore, you get no deductions for the IC's taxes; the IC is responsible for paying them.

However, if you pay an unincorporated IC $600 or more during the year for business-related services by cash, check, or direct deposit, you must:

- obtain the IC's taxpayer identification number, and
- file IRS Form 1099-NEC, *Nonemployee Compensation*, telling the IRS how much you paid the IC (before 2020, Form 1099-MISC was filed instead of Form 1099-NEC).

You need not file a 1099 form if you pay an independent contractor electronically through a third-party payment organization—for example, through PayPal—or by credit card. The IRS may impose a $250 fine if you intentionally fail to file a Form 1099 when required. You could also be subject to more severe penalties if the IRS later audits you and determines that you misclassified the worker.

If you're not sure whether you must file a Form 1099-NEC for a worker, go ahead and file one. You lose nothing by doing so—and you'll save yourself the consequences of failing to file if you were legally required to do so.

RESOURCE

Need more information on reporting requirements for ICs? For a detailed discussion of how to file a 1099 form—and the consequences of not filing one—see *Working With Independent Contractors*, by Stephen Fishman (Nolo).

Paying Independent Contractors' Expenses

Independent contractors often incur expenses while performing services for their clients—for example, for travel, photocopying, phone calls, or materials. Although many ICs want their clients to separately reimburse them for such expenses, it's better for you not to do so. ICs who pay their own expenses are less likely to be viewed as your employees by the IRS or other government agencies. Instead of reimbursing expenses, pay ICs enough so they can cover their own expenses.

However, it's customary in some businesses and professions for the client to reimburse the IC for expenses. For example, a lawyer who handles a business lawsuit will usually seek reimbursement for expenses such as photocopying, court reporters, and travel. If this is the case, you may pay these reimbursements without too much concern about misclassification problems.

When you reimburse an IC for a business-related expense, you get the deduction for the expense, not the IC. Unless the IC fails to follow the adequate accounting rules discussed below, you should not include the amount of the reimbursement on the 1099 form you file with the IRS reporting how much you paid the IC, because the reimbursement is not considered income for the IC. Make sure to require ICs to document expenses with receipts and save them in case the IRS questions the payments.

The rules differ depending on whether the IC provides you with an "adequate accounting."

Adequate Accounting for Travel and Meal Expenses

To make an adequate accounting of travel and meal expenses, an IC must comply with all the record-keeping rules applicable to business owners and employees. You must document the date, amount, place, and business purpose of the expense, and show the business relationship of the people at a business meal. (See Chapter 7.) The IRS is particularly suspicious of travel and meal expenses, so there are special documentation requirements for these. (See Chapter 15 for more on record keeping.) You are not required to save the IC's expense records. You may deduct the IC's travel and meal expenses as your own business expenses for these items. (But remember that meal expenses are only 50% deductible.) You do not include the amount of the reimbursement you pay the IC on the Form 1099 you file with the IRS reporting how much you paid the IC.

> EXAMPLE: Tim, a writer, hires Mary, a self-employed book publicity consultant, to help him promote his latest book. In the course of her work, Mary incurs $5,000 in travel expenses while meeting potential contacts. She makes an adequate accounting of these expenses and Tim reimburses her the $5,000. Tim may deduct the $5,000 as a travel expense for his business; Mary gets no deduction. When Tim fills out the 1099 form telling the IRS how much he paid Mary, he does not include the $5,000.

No Adequate Accounting for Travel and Meal Expenses

If an IC doesn't properly document travel or meal expenses, you are probably not under any legal obligation to pay him or her. However, if you decide to pay some of these expenses, you may deduct the full amount as IC payments, provided these expenses are ordinary, necessary, and reasonable in amount. The IC should provide you with some type of records to establish this. You are not deducting these expenses as travel or meal expenses, so the 50% limit on these deductions does not apply. However, you must include the amount of the reimbursement as income paid to the IC on the IC's 1099 form.

What If You Get Sick?
Deducting Medical Expenses

f you own a home business or are thinking about starting one, one of the most important problems you face is how you'll pay for your health insurance and other medical expenses. There are at least four possibilities:

- If you have a job that provides health insurance coverage, you can keep it (and your coverage).
- If your spouse has a job that provides health coverage, you can obtain coverage through him or her (one-third of all home business owners obtain their health coverage this way).
- If you're under 26 years of age, your parents can cover you under their health insurance policy.
- You can purchase your own health insurance.

This chapter explains how the Affordable Care Act (Obamacare) affects home business owners, and the array of tax deductions and strategies available to them to help lower their health care costs.

The Affordable Care Act (ACA)

The Patient Protection and Affordable Care Act (ACA) enacted by Congress in 2010 (also referred to as Obamacare) took effect in 2014. The ACA affects all businesses, no matter how large or small, including home-based businesses. Congress has tweaked the ACA and eliminated one of its major provisions—the individual mandate—starting in 2019. Otherwise, the ACA remains largely in place.

Here are key things to know about the ACA:

- Starting in 2019, individuals who fail to obtain health insurance for themselves and their dependents were no longer required to pay a penalty to the IRS (but a few states impose penalties).
- It requires most individuals to obtain health insurance for themselves and their dependents during 2018 or pay a penalty.
- It requires larger businesses to provide their employees with health coverage or pay substantial penalties.
- It imposes minimum standards for health coverage.
- You may obtain health coverage through a health insurance exchange.
- You may qualify for a premium tax credit to help you pay for your coverage.

RESOURCE

For more information on all aspects of the ACA, see www.healthcare.gov.

Federal Individual Health Insurance Mandate Terminated

Since 2014, one of the ACA's principal features was the individual health insurance mandate. Subject to certain exceptions, all Americans were required to obtain at least minimal comprehensive health insurance coverage or they pay a penalty to the IRS. Congress effectively eliminated the individual mandate starting in 2019 by reducing the penalty for noncompliance to zero. Thus, during 2019 and later, individuals who fail to obtain health coverage are not penalized by the federal government. As far as the federal government is concerned, an individual's decision whether to obtain health insurance will be purely voluntary, just as it was before the ACA was enacted.

However, some states have enacted their own state-wide health care individual mandates. These include California, the District of Columbia, Massachusetts, New Jersey, Rhode Island, and Vermont. If you live in any of these states, you may have to pay a penalty to the state if you don't have health insurance. Other states are considering implementing their own mandates—these likely won't take effect until 2020 or later.

The Employer Mandate

The ACA's employer mandate has not been changed. Businesses with at least 50 full-time employees (or a combination of full-time and part-time employees that's "equivalent" to at least 50 full-time employees), had to (1) provide at least 95% of their employees and their families with "minimum essential healthcare coverage," or (2) pay a tax penalty equal to $3,750 per year per employee (minus the first 30 employees). Few home-based businesses have 50 or more employees. For detailed guidance on how to determine whether your business has more than 50 full-time employees for ACA purposes, visit the IRS ACA Information Center for Applicable Large Employers (ALEs) at www.irs.gov/affordable-care-act/employers/aca-information-center-for-applicable-large-employers-ales.

Smaller employers—those with fewer than 50 full-time equivalent employees—are not subject to the ACA employer mandate. However, if they do elect to provide their employees with health coverage, they may qualify for tax credits. (See "Tax Credits for Employee Health Insurance," below.) Moreover, smaller employers may purchase coverage through state small business health insurance exchanges (also called "SHOP exchanges").

ACA Health Insurance Rules

To help everyone obtain coverage, starting in 2014, the ACA imposed the following rules on all health insurers and the coverage they provide. However, the Trump administration may loosen up these rules so that insurers can offer cheaper (and less comprehensive) coverage.

No preexisting condition exclusions. First, health insurers are not allowed to use your health status to deny you coverage. This means you can purchase health insurance regardless of any current or past health conditions.

Insurance premium rates. Insurers may vary their premiums based on the following factors only: your age (older people may be charged up to 300% more than the young), tobacco use, geography, and the number of family members covered. They may not charge you more based on your health status.

Minimal comprehensive coverage. All health insurers must offer comprehensive health insurance that provides at least the following ten essential health benefits:

- ambulatory ("walk-in") patient services
- emergency services
- hospitalization
- maternity/newborn care

- mental health and substance use disorder services
  (including behavioral health treatment)
- prescription drugs
- rehab and habilitative services/devices
- lab services
- preventive/wellness services and chronic disease management, and
- pediatric services (including oral and vision care).

No rescission. Your insurer can't cancel your insurance if you get sick.

No dollar caps. Health insurers cannot impose lifetime or annual dollar limits on their coverage. This means that no matter how much your health care costs, your insurer must pay for it all once you've paid your total annual out-of-pocket limit.

State Health Insurance Exchanges

Online health insurance exchanges (also called marketplaces) have been established to help individuals and small businesses obtain health coverage. These exchanges are not health insurance companies. Rather, they are a competitive marketplace set up by the government through which private insurers offer insurance to the public.

Several states have established their own online health care exchanges that they run themselves or with help from the federal government. The other states use the federal government's insurance exchange at www. healthcare.gov. Links to the appropriate online exchange are available at: www.healthcare.gov/get-coverage. The states and federal government have also established call centers for those who prefer to obtain information from a person over the phone.

You aren't required to obtain your health insurance through your state's exchange. You can obtain it on your own or through an insurance broker. You may have more choices if you shop outside your state's exchange, but you'll probably have to pay more. Moreover, you must obtain your insurance through a state exchange to qualify for health insurance premium credits.

The health insurance plans offered though state exchanges are standardized to enable consumers to better compare their costs. Four levels of coverage are available, each of which covers a specified percentage of an individual enrollee's covered benefits:

- Bronze, which covers 60% of covered benefits
- Silver, which covers 70% of covered benefits
- Gold, which covers 80% of covered benefits, and
- Platinum, which covers 90% of covered benefits.

In addition, people under 30 and some people with limited incomes may buy "catastrophic" health plans. Such a low-cost plan with a large deductible is intended to protect you from very high medical costs in case you have a serious medical problem.

Open Enrollment Periods

Under the ACA rules, unless you have a "qualifying life event" as described below, individual nongroup coverage for yourself and your dependents can be obtained only if you apply during the annual open enrollment period. This is so whether you obtain coverage from your state health insurance exchange or directly from a private health insurer. The open enrollment period for 2020 is over. In most states, the open enrollment period for 2021 coverage is November 1, 2020 to December 15, 2020; however, some states have longer open enrollment periods.

Qualifying Life Events

After the open enrollment period ends, individual nongroup health insurance coverage will be available for purchase only for an individual who has a "qualifying life event" during the year. Such events include:

- losing your existing health insurance coverage—for example, because you quit your job, were laid off, or your work hours were reduced below the level required for you to qualify for employer-provided coverage
- getting married, divorced, or legally separated
- giving birth to or adopting a child

- losing your coverage because you moved to another state or a part of the same state outside of your health plan service area
- losing eligibility for Medicaid—for example, because your income grew
- no longer being eligible to receive coverage as someone else's dependent—for example, you turn 26 and are no longer eligible for coverage through your parents' plan
- being timely enrolled in coverage through your state exchange, but your income increases or decreases enough to change your eligibility for subsidies, or
- becoming a U.S. citizen.

Once a qualifying life event occurs, you have 60 days to obtain individual coverage, either through your state health insurance exchange or private insurers. This period is called your "special enrollment opportunity."

Note carefully that the following are *not* qualifying life events:

- getting sick
- getting pregnant
- losing your coverage because you didn't pay your premiums, or
- voluntarily quitting your existing health coverage.

Thus, for example, you can't go without coverage past the open enrollment deadline and then decide you want to enroll because you get sick (or get pregnant; but after you have a child, you can obtain coverage).

Medicaid Enrollment

You can enroll in Medicaid or the Children's Health Insurance Program (CHIP) in your state at any time. There is no open enrollment period for these programs. Medicaid is publicly funded health care for low income and disabled Americans. The Medicaid eligibility rules vary from state to state. In 36 states and the District of Columbia, adults can get Medicaid if their income is up to 138% of the federal poverty level. This is $17,609 a year for individuals, or $36,156 for a family of four. Eligibility is determined by current monthly income, so individuals can qualify even if their annual income is over these levels. For more information, see www.healthcare.gov/medicaid-chip.

Health Insurance Premium Assistance Credits

To help moderate- and low-income people afford purchasing individual health coverage, a premium assistance credit is provided for those who purchase health insurance from a state exchange. The purpose of the credits is to ensure that moderate- and lower-income people don't have to spend more than a specified percentage of their household income on health insurance. These percentages range from 3.0% to 9.78%, depending on household income.

You'll be eligible for the premium credit if the following are true:

- Your household income is between 100% and 400% of the federal poverty level (FPL).
- You are not eligible for other affordable coverage.
- You file a joint tax return if you're married.

Almost half of American households have household incomes below 400% of FPL and can potentially qualify for these credits. The following chart shows the 2019 federal poverty levels that are used to determine eligibility for premium credits in 2020.

Household Size	400% of Federal Poverty Level (2019)
1	$49,960
2	67,640
3	85,320
4	103,000
For each additional person, add	**$17,680**

Based on the 2019 FPL, the credit would be available for individuals with household incomes below $49,960 and families of four with incomes below $103,000.

If you already have health coverage through an employer or your spouse's employer, you won't qualify for the health insurance credits, unless either of two important exceptions applies to you:

- Your employer's health plan covers less than 60% of the cost of covered benefits.
- Your share of the employer's premium that you must pay from your own pocket is more than 9.5% of your household income.

The IRS has created an interactive online questionnaire you can use to see if you qualify for the premium tax credit. It is available at www.irs. gov/uac/am-i-eligible-to-claim-the-premium-tax-credit.

Determining Your Household Income

To qualify for an ACA tax credit, you'll have to list your estimated household income for the following year in your application. You can base this amount on your most recently filed tax return. To figure your household income, you take your adjusted gross income amount listed on your return and add the following items to determine your modified adjusted gross income (MAGI):

- any tax-exempt interest you earned that year
- any nontaxable Social Security payments you received, and
- any foreign income you earned that was excluded from your income.

When you file your tax return the following year, you have to reconcile the MAGI you actually earned with the amount of credits you received. If you earned substantially more than you listed on your application, you may have to pay all or part of your credit payments back to the federal government. On the other hand, if you earned substantially less, you may be entitled to additional credit payments.

Although they are called credits, these payments are really a government-funded subsidy. You don't need to owe any income taxes to receive the credit. Moreover, unless you direct otherwise, the full credit amount for the year is paid by the federal government directly to your health insurance company when you enroll in your health insurance plan. This means that you will not need to wait until your taxes have been filed and processed to receive the credit; nor will you need to pay the full premium when you purchase health insurance and then wait to be reimbursed.

The amount of the credit is determined on a sliding scale based on your age, household size, and income. Those with the highest age and lowest incomes will receive the largest tax credits. The credit can be substantial.

You can get an estimate of the credit you qualify for at the Kaiser Health Reform Subsidy Calculator (http://kff.org/interactive/subsidy-calculator). To obtain the ACA credit, you'll need to obtain your health insurance through your state exchange.

The Personal Deduction for Medical Expenses

All taxpayers—whether or not they own a business—are entitled to a personal income tax deduction for medical and dental expenses for themselves and their dependents. Eligible expenses include both health insurance premiums and out-of-pocket expenses not covered by insurance (see "What HSA Funds Can Be Used For," later in this chapter, for a list of eligible expenses). However, there are two significant limitations on the deduction, which make it difficult to use for most taxpayers.

To take the personal deduction, you must comply with both of the following requirements:

- You must itemize your deductions on IRS Schedule A. You can itemize deductions only if all of your itemized deductions exceed the standard deduction for the year. The Tax Cuts and Jobs Act greatly increased the standard deduction to $24,800 for joint returns and $12,400 for single returns in 2020. Itemized deductions include medical expenses, home mortgage interest, state and local taxes (up to a $10,000 annual limit), charitable contributions, and a few others.

- All taxpayers who itemize can only deduct the amount of their medical and dental expenses that is more than 7.5% of their adjusted gross income (AGI). Your AGI is your net business income and other taxable income, minus deductions for retirement contributions and one-half of your self-employment taxes, plus a few other items (as shown at the bottom of your Form 1040).

> EXAMPLE: Al is a self-employed interior decorator whose adjusted gross income for 2020 is $100,000. He pays $1,000 per month for health insurance for himself and his wife. He spends another $4,000 in out-of-pocket medical and dental expenses for the year for a total of $16,000 in medical expenses. Al may deduct his medical expenses only if all of his itemized deductions exceed the $24,800 standard deduction for the year. If they do exceed the standard deduction, his personal medical expense deduction is limited to the amount he paid that exceeds $10,000 (7.5% × $100,000 = $7,500). Because he paid a total of $16,000 in medical expenses for the year, he may deduct only $8,500.

As you can see, unless your medical expenses are substantial, the 7.5% limitation eats up much of your deduction. The more money you make, the less you'll be able to deduct. For this reason, most home business owners need to look elsewhere for meaningful medical expense deductions.

Deducting Health Insurance Premiums

Health insurance premiums are the largest medical expense most people pay. There are several ways that home business owners can deduct these premiums.

Personal Income Tax Deduction for the Self-Employed

Self-employed people, whether or not they work at home, are allowed to deduct health insurance premiums (including dental and long-term care coverage) for themselves, their spouses, their dependents, and their children under age 27. Self-employed people who have Medicare coverage may deduct their Medicare premiums as part of the self-employed health insurance deduction—this includes all Medicare parts (not just Part B). In addition, this insurance can also cover your children up to age 26, whether or not they are your dependents. For these purposes, a child includes a son, daughter, or stepchild, an adopted child, or an eligible foster child.

Sole proprietors, partners in partnerships, LLC members, and S corporation shareholders who own more than 2% of the company stock can use this deduction. Only owners of regular C corporations may not take this deduction. And you get the deduction whether you purchase your health insurance policy as an individual or have your business obtain it for you.

> **EXAMPLE:** Kim is a sole proprietor who pays $10,000 each year for health insurance for herself, her husband, and her three children. Her business earns approximately $50,000 in profit each year. Every year, she may deduct her $10,000 annual health insurance expense from her gross income for federal and state income tax purposes. Since her combined federal and state income tax rate is 30%, this saves her $3,000 in income taxes each year. Kim may not deduct her premiums from her income when she figures her self-employment taxes.

Self-Employment Tax Primer

Ordinarily, self-employment taxes consist of a 12.4% Social Security tax on income up to an annual ceiling. In 2020, the annual Social Security ceiling is $139,700. Medicare taxes are not subject to any income ceiling and are levied at a 2.9% rate up to an annual ceiling ($200,000 for single taxpayers or $250,000 for married couples filing jointly), and a 3.8% tax on amounts over the ceiling. This combines to a total 15.3% tax on employment or self-employment income up to the Social Security tax ceiling. If you earn more than that ceiling, deducting your health insurance costs from your self-employment income will not give you a very significant tax savings, because you would have had to pay only a 2.9% or 3.8% tax on that income.

S corporation owners, partners in partnerships, and owners of multi-member LLCs taxed as partnerships can take this deduction only if their businesses pay for the health insurance directly or reimburse them for their payments. The amount of the payments must be reported as wages on an S corporation owner's W-2 form, and as guaranteed payments on the K-1 form provided to partners and multimember LLC owners by the partnership or LLC.

Business Income Limitation

There is a significant limitation on the health insurance deduction for the self-employed: You may deduct only as much as you earn from your business. If your business earns no money or incurs a loss, you get no deduction. Thus, if Kim from the above example earned only $3,000 in profit from her business, her self-employed deduction would be limited to that amount; she wouldn't be able to deduct the remaining $7,000 in premiums she paid for the year.

If your business is organized as an S corporation, your deduction is limited to the amount of wages you are paid by your corporation.

If you have more than one business, you cannot combine the income from all your businesses for purposes of the income limit. You may only use the income from a single business you designate to be the health insurance plan sponsor.

Designating Your Plan Sponsor

If you purchase your health insurance plan in the name of one of your businesses, that business will be the sponsor. However, the IRS says you may purchase your health coverage in your own name and still get the self-employed health insurance deduction. (IRS Chief Counsel Memo 200524001.) This may be advantageous because it allows you to pick which of your businesses will be the sponsor at the start of each year. Obviously, you should pick the business you think will earn the most money that year.

Moreover, if you have more than one business, you can have one business purchase medical insurance and the other purchase dental insurance and deduct 100% of the premiums for each policy subject to the income limits discussed above. This will be helpful if no single business earns enough income for you to deduct both policies through one business.

> **EXAMPLE:** Robert is a sole proprietor medical doctor who has a sideline business running a medical lab. He purchases a medical insurance policy for himself and his family with his medical practice as the sponsor. He also purchases a dental insurance plan with his lab business as the sponsor. He may deduct 100% of the premiums for each policy, subject to the income limits.

No Other Health Insurance Coverage

You may not take the self-employed health insurance deduction if you are eligible to participate in a subsidized health insurance plan maintained by your employer or your spouse's employer. This is so even if the plan requires co-payments, or you have to pay additional premiums to obtain all the coverage you need.

> **EXAMPLE:** Rich works as an employee editor at a publishing company and also has a part-time home business. He obtains insurance coverage for himself and his wife through his employer. However, he must pay $500 per month for his wife's coverage. This amount is not deductible under the self-employed health insurance deduction.

This rule applies separately to plans that provide long-term care insurance and those that do not. Thus, for example, if your spouse has employer-provided health insurance that does not include long-term care, you may purchase your own long-term care policy and deduct the premiums.

Tax Reporting

Because the self-employed health insurance deduction is a personal deduction, you take this deduction directly on your Form 1040 (it does not go on your Schedule C if you're a sole proprietor). If you itemize your deductions and do not claim 100% of your self-employed health insurance costs on your Form 1040, you may include the rest with your other medical expenses on Schedule A, subject to the 10% threshold. You would have to do this, for example, if your health insurance premiums exceeded your business income.

Deducting Health Insurance as a Business Expense

You can deduct health insurance costs as a currently deductible business expense if your business pays them on behalf of an employee. The benefit to treating these costs as a business expense is that you can deduct them from your business income for tax purposes. The premiums are an employee fringe benefit and are not taxable income for the employee. Thus, if you are an employee of your business, you can have your business pay your health insurance premiums and then deduct the cost as a business expense, reducing both your income and your self-employment taxes.

> EXAMPLE: Mona, a sole proprietor data miner, hires Milt to work as an employee in her business. She pays $250 per month to provide Milt with health insurance. The payments are a business expense that she can deduct from her business income. Milt need not count the value of the insurance as income or pay any tax on it. Mona deducts her $3,000 annual payments for Milt's insurance from her business income for both income tax and self-employment tax purposes. The $3,000 deduction saves her $720 in income taxes (she's in the 24% income tax bracket; 24% × $3,000 = $720). She also saves $459 in self-employment taxes (15.3% × $3,000 = $459).

Unfortunately, if (like the vast majority of home business owners) you are a sole proprietor, a partner in a partnership, an LLC member, or an S corporation shareholder with more than 2% of the company stock, you *cannot* be an employee of your own business for these purposes.

Thus, you cannot have your business provide you with health insurance and deduct the cost as a business expense.

You can still take the self-employed health insurance tax deduction discussed above, which will effectively wipe out the extra income tax you had to pay. But the self-employed health insurance deduction is a personal deduction, not a business deduction, and thus does not reduce your business income for self-employment tax purposes.

Form a C Corporation and Hire Yourself

If you want to convert your own health insurance premiums to a business expense, you must form a C corporation to run your business and have the corporation hire you as its employee. You can do this even if you're running a one-person home business. Alternatively, you may form an LLC and elect to be taxed as a C corporation.

As an employee of a C corporation, your corporation must pay you a salary, as well as the employer's share of Social Security and Medicare taxes. Your corporation deducts your health insurance premiums from its taxes—you don't deduct them from your personal taxes. Because you own the corporation, you get the benefit of the deduction.

There are disadvantages to incorporating, however: Incorporating costs money, you'll have to comply with more burdensome bookkeeping requirements, and you will have a more complex tax return. You'll also have to pay state and federal unemployment taxes for yourself—a tax you don't have to pay if you're not an employee of your business. And, depending on your state's requirements, you may have to provide yourself with workers' compensation coverage.

Because your health insurance is 100% deductible from your income taxes, it may not be worthwhile to incorporate just to save on Social Security and Medicare taxes. This is particularly true if your employee income would substantially exceed the Social Security tax ceiling—$132,900 in 2019. If you're in this situation, think about obtaining a Health Savings Account instead (see "Health Savings Accounts," below).

Disability Insurance

Disability insurance pays a monthly benefit to employees who are unable to work due to sickness or injury. You may provide disability insurance as an employee benefit to your workers, including your spouse, and deduct the premiums as a business expense. If your business is a C corporation, it may deduct disability payments made for you, its employee. However, any employees who collect disability benefits must include them in their taxable income.

Employing Your Spouse

If, like 90% of home business owners, you're a sole proprietor (or have formed an entity other than an S corporation to run your business), there's another way you can deduct health insurance costs as a business expense: Hire your spouse to work in your business as an employee and provide him or her with health insurance. The insurance should be purchased in the name of the spouse/employee, not in the employer's name. The policy can cover your spouse, you, your children, and other dependents as well. Moreover, the insurance can cover your children up to age 26, whether or not they are your dependents. Then you can deduct the cost of the health insurance as a business expense.

> **EXAMPLE:** Joe, a successful home-based financial consultant, hires his wife, Martha, to work as his employee assistant. He pays her $25,000 per year and provides her with a health insurance policy covering both of them and their two children. The annual policy premiums are $5,000. Joe may deduct the $5,000 as a business expense for his consulting practice, listing it as an expense on his Schedule C. He may deduct the $5,000 not only from his $80,000 income for income tax purposes, but also from his self-employment income.

If you do this and you're self-employed, do not take the health insurance deduction for self-employed people discussed in "Personal Income Tax Deduction for the Self-Employed," above. You're better off taxwise deducting all your health insurance premiums as a business expense because a business deduction reduces the amount of your income subject to self-employment taxes. The self-employed health insurance deduction is a personal deduction, not a business deduction, and thus does not reduce your business income for self-employment tax purposes.

There are a couple of catches to this deduction. This method ordinarily doesn't work if you have an S corporation because your spouse is deemed to be a shareholder of the corporation along with you and can't also be a corporate employee. In addition, your spouse must be a bona fide employee. In other words, he or she must do real work in your business, you must pay applicable payroll taxes, and you must otherwise treat your spouse like any other employee. (See Chapter 11 for a detailed discussion of your obligations to workers.)

You'll probably want to pay your spouse as low a salary as possible, because both of you will have to pay Social Security and Medicare taxes on that salary (but not on employee benefits like health insurance and medical expense reimbursements). You should, however, regularly pay your spouse at least some cash wages or the IRS could claim that your spouse is not a real employee. You can make the cash wages a relatively small part of your spouse's total compensation—wages plus fringe benefits like your medical reimbursement plan.

No matter how you pay your spouse, his or her total compensation must be reasonable—that is, you can't pay more than your spouse's services are worth. For example, you can't pay your spouse at a rate of $100 per hour for simple clerical work. Total compensation means the sum of the salary, plus all the fringe benefits you pay your spouse, including health insurance and medical expense reimbursements, if any.

Your Spouse May Not Be Your Partner

A marriage may be a partnership, but you can't be partners with your spouse in your business and also claim that he or she is your employee for purposes of health insurance deductions. If your spouse co-owns the business with you, he or she is treated as self-employed—not an employee—for purposes of health insurance. You and your spouse are co-owners if you file partnership returns for your business (IRS Form 1065) listing him or her as a partner, or if your spouse has made a substantial financial investment in your business with his or her own money.

Alternatively, spouses who jointly own a business may elect to be taxed as a "qualified joint venture." When this is done, both spouses are treated as sole proprietors for tax purposes. See Chapter 16 for more details.

Of course, if you're single, you won't be able to hire a spouse to take advantage of this method for turning health insurance costs into a business expense. However, if you're a single parent, you could hire your child and deduct the cost of your child's health insurance as a business expense. But your child's policy cannot cover you or other family members.

Sick and Family Leave Tax Credits for the Self-Employed

In response to the coronavirus (COVID-19) pandemic, Congress enacted the Families First Coronavirus Response Act, which includes special sick leave and family leave tax credits for the self-employed. These highly innovative tax credits are a temporary measure only available for 2020.

Sick Leave Credit

You qualify for the sick leave credit if you were unable to work or telework because:

- you were subject to a federal, state, or local COVID-19 quarantine or isolation order
- you were advised by a health care provider to self-quarantine due to COVID-19, or
- you experienced COVID-19 symptoms and sought a medical diagnosis.

The sick leave credit is equal to 100% of the average net self-employment income you earn per day during 2020 for a maximum of ten days (80 hours). The credit is capped at $510 per day. Thus, the maximum credit is $5,100.

Family Leave Credit

You qualify for the family leave credit if you were unable to work or telework because:

- you had to care for an individual who was subject to a COVID-19 quarantine or isolation order, or was advised by a health care provider to self-quarantine due to COVID-19, or
- you had to care for a son or daughter under 18 years of age whose school or place of care was closed (or child care provider was unavailable) due to COVID-19.

The family leave credit is equal to 67% of the average 2020 self-employment income you earn per day. But the credit is capped at $200 per day. The credit for caring for an individual other than a son or daughter is for a maximum of ten days (80 hours). The credit for taking care of a son or daughter is for a maximum of 12 weeks (60 days).

Calculating the Credit

To calculate either credit, you must determine your average 2020 daily net self-employment income. To do so, divide your total 2020 net self-employment income by 260. For example, if your 2020 net self-employment income is $70,000, your daily self-employment income is $269. Your sick pay credit is a maximum of ten days x $269 = $2,690. Your family leave credit is $200 per day for up to ten days or 60 days.

Claiming the Credit

The credits apply to both income and self-employment taxes (Social Security and Medicare tax). You may reduce your 2020 estimated tax payments by the amount of your credit. These credits are refundable—you get the full amount even if you end up with a negative tax liability. For example, if you owe $1,000 in total taxes and qualify for a $2,500 credit, you won't have to pay any estimated taxes and the IRS will send you a check for $1,500 after it processes your 2020 tax return.

Self-employed individuals who obtain loans through the SBA Paycheck Protection Program (PPP loans) may have a substantial portion of the loan forgiven—an amount equal to up to eight weeks of net profit earned during 2019. However, the forgiveness amount must be reduced by the amount of any sick leave or family leave credit that is claimed for 2020.

Tax Credits for Employee Health Insurance

The previous section explained how you can deduct health insurance costs for employees—including your spouse—as a business expense. Tax deductions are all well and good, but there is something even better: tax credits. Unlike a deduction, a tax credit is a dollar-for-dollar reduction in the amount you owe the IRS. In other words, a $1,000 credit saves you $1,000 on your taxes.

The ACA created a tax credit for small employers who pay for health insurance for their employees. Employers who qualify can claim a tax credit of up to 50% of their contributions to their employees' health insurance premiums, subject to certain limits. Obviously, if you qualify for the credit, you could save substantial taxes. The credit could be taken for two consecutive years. Thus, for example, if an employer first qualified for the credit in 2020, the credit would only be available to the employer in 2020 and 2021.

However, you can qualify for the health insurance credit only if your business has nonowner employees who are not your relatives.

For this purpose, a relative includes a child (or descendant of a child); spouse; sibling or stepsibling; parent (or ancestor of a parent); stepparent; niece or nephew; aunt or uncle; son-in-law, daughter-in-law; father-in-law, mother-in-law, brother-in-law, or sister-in-law.

This eliminates the great majority of home businesses. But, if you have employees in your home business who are not related to you, you may qualify for the credit. However, you can qualify for the credit only if you purchase your employees' health insurance through a Small Business Health Options Program (SHOP) Marketplace—these are health insurance exchanges specifically designed for employers with 50 or fewer full-time employees. For details, visit www.healthcare.gov/small-businesses/employers.

Health Reimbursement Arrangements

Health insurance usually doesn't cover all of your medical expenses. For example, it doesn't cover deductibles or co-payments—that is, amounts you must pay yourself before your insurance coverage kicks in. Many costs aren't covered by insurance at all, including fertility treatment and optometric care. As a result, the average family of four pays about $3,500 a year in out-of-pocket health-related expenses. One way to deduct these expenses is to establish a health reimbursement arrangement (HRA). Another way is to use a health savings account (discussed below).

An HRA is a plan under which an employer reimburses its employees for health or dental expenses. This can include health insurance, co-pays, and other medical expenses not covered by insurance.

Why would an employer do this? One good reason is that the reimbursements are deductible business expenses for the employer. Also, the employee doesn't have to include the reimbursements as taxable income (as long as the employee has not taken a deduction for these amounts as a personal medical expense).

There are three different types of HRAs:

- spouse-only HRAs for businesses with one employee-spouse
- Individual Coverage Health Reimbursement Arrangements (ICHRAS) for businesses with any number of employees, and
- Qualified Small Employer Health Reimbursement Arrangements (QSEHRAs) for businesses with up to 50 employees.

Spousal Health Reimbursement Accounts

The Affordable Care Act imposes various restrictions on the ability of employers to use HRAs. However, the ACA does not apply to HRAs established by businesses with only one employee. Thus, if you're married, you can hire your spouse as the sole employee of your business and provide him or her with an HRA that is not subject to these restrictions. However, this only works if your spouse is your only employee. And your business must be organized as a sole proprietorship, a partnership, an LLC, or a C corporation. This leaves out S corporations, but S corporations can take advantage of ICHRAs and QSEHRAs discussed below.

The plan may cover not only your spouse, but also you, your children, and other dependents. Moreover, your plan can cover your children up to age 26, whether or not they are your dependents. This allows your business to reimburse you and your family for out-of-pocket medical expenses and deduct the amounts as a business expense. And you don't have to include the reimbursements in your own taxable income. The IRS has ruled that this is perfectly legal. (Rev. Rul. 2002-45.)

> **EXAMPLE 1:** Jennifer has her own public relations business. She hires her husband, Paul, to work as her part-time employee assistant. She establishes an HRA covering Paul, herself, and their young child. Paul spends $12,000 for health insurance, copays, and uninsured health expenses. Jennifer reimburses Paul for the $12,000 as provided by their plan. Jennifer may deduct the $12,000 from her business income for the year, meaning she pays neither income nor self-employment tax on that amount. Paul need not include the $12,000 in his income—it's tax free to him. The deduction saves Jennifer and Paul $4,000 in taxes for the year.

> **CAUTION**
> **Your spouse must be a legitimate employee.** Your spouse must
> be a legitimate employee for your HRA to pass muster with the IRS. You can't
> simply hire your spouse on paper—he or she must do real work in your business.
> If you can't prove your spouse is a legitimate employee, the IRS will disallow your
> deductions in the event of an audit.

> **EXAMPLE 2:** Mr. Haeder, a sole proprietor attorney who practiced law
> from his home, claimed that he hired his wife as his employee to answer the
> telephone, greet visitors, type legal papers, and clean his office. Mrs. Haeder
> had no employment contract or set work schedule, did not keep track of her
> hours, and did not directly or regularly receive a salary. Instead, Mr. Haeder
> paid her the maximum amount she could deduct as an IRA contribution.
> Annually, he transferred money in his brokerage account to an IRA in his
> wife's name. For all but one of the years eventually audited by the IRS, no
> W-2 was issued to Mrs. Haeder. Mr. Haeder sponsored an HRA that covered
> out-of-pocket expenses for his wife, her children, and her spouse—that is,
> himself. Mrs. Haeder submitted bills for out-of-pocket medical expenses to her
> husband, which he reimbursed and attempted to deduct as business expenses.
>
> The IRS determined Mr. Haeder was not entitled to deduct the reimburse-
> ments under the HRA because Mrs. Haeder was not a bona fide employee.
> The tax court agreed, finding that there was no credible evidence that
> Mrs. Haeder performed any services other than those reasonably expected
> of a family member. (*Haeder v. Comm'r.,* TC Memo 2001-7 (2001).)

Make sure to comply with all the legal requirements for hiring
an employee, including providing workers' compensation insurance
(required in many states), paying any state unemployment insurance
premiums, and paying and withholding income tax. Your spouse-
employee should also submit a weekly time sheet showing the date,
work done, and time spent on that work. If this is too much trouble or
too expensive, forget about establishing an HRA.

The total amount your spouse is reimbursed under your HRA
can be the spouse's sole source of remuneration as your business's
employee. But the total amount must be reasonable for the work the

spouse does. If you don't pay your spouse-employee wages, you won't need to make payroll tax payments or filings. However, many tax pros prefer that the spouse-employee be paid at least a nominal salary and a W-2 filed with the IRS as added proof of employment.

You also need to make sure that you and your spouse do not end up being partners (co-owners) in the business. Your spouse cannot be your partner and your employee in the same business. You must own the business and your spouse must work under your direction and control. Factors that indicate that your spouse is your partner include joint ownership of business assets, joint sharing of profits, and joint control over business operations.

The HRA deduction is available only to your employees, not to you (the business owner). The only way you can qualify as an employee is if your business is a C corporation (see "Deducting Health Insurance as a Business Expense," above). If you don't have a spouse to employ, you could employ your child and provide him or her with a reimbursement plan. But the plan may not cover you or any other family members.

What Expenses May Be Reimbursed?

One of the great things about HRAs is that they can be used to reimburse employees for a wide variety of health-related expenses. Deductible medical expenses include any expense for the diagnosis, cure, mitigation, treatment, or prevention of disease; or any expense paid to affect the structure or function of the human body. (IRS Reg. 1.213.1(e).)

This includes, of course, premiums for health and accident insurance and health insurance deductibles and co-payments. But it also includes expenses for acupuncture, chiropractors, eyeglasses and contact lenses, dental treatment, laser eye surgery, psychiatric care, and treatment for learning disabilities. It includes prescription medications, but not over-the-counter nonprescription medications unless you have a prescription for them. You can draft your plan to include only those expenses you wish to reimburse. Presumably, though, you'd want to include as many expenses as possible if the plan covers only your spouse, yourself, and your family.

How to Establish a Spousal HRA

If an HRA sounds attractive to you, you should establish one as early in the year as possible because it applies only to medical expenses incurred *after* the date the plan is adopted. (Rev. Rul. 2002-58.) Forget about using a plan to reimburse your spouse or yourself for expenses you have already incurred. If you do, the reimbursement must be added to your spouse's income for tax purposes and you must pay employment tax on it.

A written HRA must be drawn up and adopted by your business. If your business is incorporated, the plan should be adopted by a corporate resolution approved by the corporation's board of directors. You can find a form for this purpose in *The Corporate Records Handbook,* by Anthony Mancuso (Nolo).

Sample Spousal HRA

A sample HRA is provided below.

Individual Coverage HRAs (ICHRAs)

If your business has more than one employee, you may not establish a spousal HRA. However, rules under the Affordable Care Act were amended effective January 1, 2020 to allow businesses with multiple employees to establish Individual Coverage Health Reimbursement Arrangements (ICHRAs). ICHRAs appear to be the Goldilocks of HRAs: Unlike spousal HRAs, you can use them for any number of employees, and they are not subject to most of the restrictions imposed on QSEHRAs (see below).

ICHRAs may be used by any business of whatever size. And, there are no caps on benefits. Here's how they work:

Health Reimbursement Arrangement

[_Your business name_] ("Employer") and [_employee's name_] ("Employee") enter into this health reimbursement arrangement (HRA) under which Employer agrees to reimburse Employee for medical expenses incurred by Employee and Employee's spouse and dependents, subject to the conditions and limitations set forth below.

1. Uninsured Expenses

Employer will reimburse eligible Employee and Employee's spouse and dependents only for medical expenses that are not covered by health or accident insurance.

2. Medical Expenses Defined

Medical expenses are those expenses defined by Internal Revenue Code Sec. 213(d).

3. Eligible Employee

This plan is a one-employee plan that does not include group health insurance. All full- and part-time employees of Employer may participate in this plan, but should the plan cover more than one eligible employee, it will be amended to purchase qualified Affordable Care Act "group health coverage" as a plan component.

4. Dependent Defined

Dependent is defined by IRC Section 152. It includes any member of an eligible Employee's family for whom the Employee and his or her spouse provide more than half of the financial support.

5. Submission of Claims

To obtain reimbursement under HRA, Employee shall submit to Employer, at least annually, all bills for medical care, including those for accident or health insurance. Such bills and other claims for reimbursement shall be verified by Employer prior to reimbursement. Employer, in its sole discretion, may terminate Employee's right to reimbursement if the Employee fails to comply.

6. Payments

At its option, Employer may pay the medical expenses directly to the medical provider or by purchasing insurance that pays Employee's expenses. Such a direct payment or provision of such insurance shall relieve Employer of all further liability for the expense.

7. Effective Date; Plan Year

This HRA shall take effect on [_date_] and operates on a calendar year basis thereafter. The HRA year is the same as the tax year of Employer. HRA records shall be kept on a calendar year basis.

8. Benefits Not Taxable

Employer intends that the benefits under this HRA shall qualify under IRC Sec. 105 so as to be excludable from the gross income of the Employee covered by the HRA.

9. Termination

Employer may terminate this HRA at any time. Medical expenses incurred prior to the date of termination shall be reimbursed by Employer. Employer is under no obligation to provide advance notice of termination.

_____   _____
Employer's Signature   Date

_____   _____
Employee's Signature   Date

Employees Obtain Individual Coverage

Employees must obtain their own individual health coverage to use ICHRAs. They can do this through their state health insurance exchange or elsewhere, including Medicare coverage. The employee can be the primary policyholder or be covered under a family member's individual policy. Employees must prove they have coverage each year.

However, employees who have ICHRAs will not be eligible for ACA premium tax credits. In contrast, employees who have QSEHRAs may receive tax credits, but the amount of the credit is reduced by the amount of HRA benefits received.

Employer Provides Monthly Allowance

The employer sets a monthly allowance of tax-free money the employees can use to pay for their health insurance coverage and other uninsured healthcare expenses. There are no caps on the amount of the allowance —it can be as big or small as desired.

Employer Reimburses Employees

Employees submit proof of their expenses and the employer reimburses them up to the allowance amount. The reimbursements are tax free to the employees and tax deductible by the employer.

Employer May Offer Different Allowances to Different Classes of Employees

Employers are not required to provide the same allowances to all employees. They can offer different amounts for different classes of employees, including:

- full-time
- part-time
- seasonal
- salaried
- hourly

- temporary employees working for a staffing firm
- employees covered under a collective bargaining agreement
- employees in a waiting period
- foreign employees who work abroad
- employees in different locations, based on rating areas, and
- a combination of two or more of the above.

HRA allowances must be the same for all employees within the same class. However, employers can make distinctions based on an employee's age or family size. For example, an employer can increase the allowance amount for older workers or those with more children or other dependents.

Establishing an ICHRA

The employer must give notice of the ICHRA to all employees at least 90 days before the beginning of the plan year. The notice must make clear that participating in the ICHRA makes the employee ineligible for ACA tax credits. The Department of Labor has created a model notice that employers may use. The notice and FAQs created by the IRS are at: www.irs.gov/newsroom/health-reimbursement-arrangements-hras.

Qualified Small Employer HRAs (QSEHRAs)

Another type of HRA for businesses with multiple employees is the Qualified Small Employer HRA, or QSEHRA. QSEHRAs became available in 2017. Unfortunately, there are far more restrictions on these plans than on spousal HRAs or ICHRAs. With a QSEHRA, an eligible small business can reimburse an employee's individually purchased health insurance and other deductible medical costs up to $5,250 per year for an individual and up to $10,600 for a family (these are the limits for 2020). The cost of the QSEHRA benefit must be entirely covered by the employer.

Which Employers May Offer QSEHRAs?

QSEHRAs may be offered only by employers with fewer than 50 full-time (or full-time equivalent) employees during the prior year and who do not offer a group health plan to any of their employees.

Which Employees May be Covered by QSEHRAs?

As with ICHRAs, only employees who obtain their own health insurance that meets the minimum requirements of the ACA (called minimum essential coverage) may benefit from a QSEHRA. Reimbursements paid to an employee without such coverage must be included in the employee's taxable income. Minimum essential coverage includes all individually purchased private insurance, government insurance such as Medicare, and the employee's or spouse's job-based insurance. The employees must provide their employer with proof that they have such coverage. Employees must also substantiate all medical expenses that are reimbursed. Reimbursements made under a QSEHRA must be reported to the IRS on the employee's W-2.

All eligible employees must be covered by the QSEHRA. This includes all employees except those who:

- have not completed 90 days of service
- are under age 25
- are part-time or seasonal employees
- are covered by a collective bargaining agreement if health benefits were the subject of good-faith bargaining, or
- are nonresident aliens with no earned income from sources within the United States.

Thus, QSEHRA benefits cannot be offered to only a select group, such as to only a company's owner and top level employees.

A QSEHRA plan may be used only for employees. It may not be used by sole proprietors, partners in partnerships, or members of limited liability companies (LLCs). However, until the IRS issues further guidance, a business organized as an S corporation may maintain a QSEHRA for its shareholder-employees who own more than 2% of the corporate stock.

How to Establish a QSEHRA

The employer begins a QSEHRA by giving all of its eligible employees written notice of the plan, which can also serve as the document establishing the plan. The notice must be given 90 days before the beginning of a plan year. The notice must:

- list the amount of the employee's permitted benefit for the year
- require the employee to provide information about the QSEHRA to any health insurance exchange to which the employee applies for advance payment of premium assistance tax credits to help pay for health insurance, and
- contain a warning that, if the employee is not covered under minimum essential coverage for any month, the employee may have to pay tax on any plan reimbursements.

An employer that fails to provide the required notice may be subject to a $50 per employee, per failure penalty, up to a $2,500 calendar year maximum for all such failures.

Health Savings Accounts

Another tax-advantaged method of buying health insurance has been available since 2004: health savings accounts (HSAs). HSAs can save you taxes, but they're not for everybody.

 **RESOURCE**
Need more information on health savings accounts? Check out IRS Publication 969, *Health Savings Accounts and Other Tax-Favored Health Plans,* available on the IRS website at www.irs.gov.

What Are Health Savings Accounts?

The HSA concept is very simple: Instead of relying on health insurance to pay small or routine medical expenses, you pay them yourself. To help you do this, you establish a health savings account with a health insurance company, a bank, or another financial institution. Your contributions to the account are tax deductible, and you don't have to pay tax on the interest or other money you earn on the money in your account. You can withdraw the money in your HSA to pay almost any kind of health-related expense, and you don't have to pay any tax on these withdrawals.

In case you or a family member develops a serious health problem, you must also obtain a health insurance policy with a high deductible— for 2020, at least $1,400 for individuals and $2,800 for families. You can use the money in your HSA to pay this large deductible and any co-payments you're required to make.

Using an HSA can save you money in two ways:

- You'll get a tax deduction for the money you deposit in your account.
- The premiums for your high-deductible health insurance policy may be less than those for traditional comprehensive coverage policies or HMO coverage (you may save as much as 40%).

Establishing Your HSA

To participate in the HSA program, you need two things:

- a high-deductible health plan that qualifies under the HSA rules, and
- an HSA account.

HSA-Qualified Plans

You can't have an HSA if you're covered by health insurance other than a high-deductible HSA plan—for example, if your spouse has family coverage for you from his or her job. So you may have to change your existing coverage to qualify for an HSA. However, you may get your own HSA if you are not covered by your spouse's health insurance. In addition, people eligible to receive Medicare may not participate in the HSA program.

You need to obtain a bare-bones health plan that meets the HSA criteria (is "HSA qualified"). You may obtain coverage from a health maintenance organization, preferred provider organization, or traditional plan. The key feature of an HSA-qualified health plan is that it has a relatively high annual deductible (the amount you must pay out of your own pocket before your insurance kicks in). In 2019, the minimum annual deductible for single people was $1,400 and $2,800 for families.

You can have a higher deductible if you wish, but there is an annual ceiling on the total amount you can have for your deductible plus other out-of-pocket expenses you're required to pay before your health plan provides coverage. (Such out-of-pocket expenses include co-payments, but do not include health insurance premiums.) For example, in 2020, the annual ceiling for an individual HSA plan was $6,900. This means that your annual deductible and other out-of-pocket expenses you're required to pay before your insurance kicks in cannot exceed that amount. Thus, if your annual deductible was $3,500, your other annual out-of-pocket expenses would have to be limited to $3,400. In 2020, the maximum limits were $6,900 for single people and $13,800 for families. All these numbers are adjusted for inflation each year.

In addition, your health insurance plan must be "HSA qualified." To become qualified, the insurer must agree to participate in the HSA program and give the roster of enrolled participants to the IRS. If your insurer fails to report to the IRS that you are enrolled in an HSA-qualified insurance plan, the IRS will not permit you to deduct your HSA contributions.

HSA-qualified health insurance policies should be clearly labeled as such on the cover page or declaration page of the policy. It might be possible to convert a high-deductible health insurance policy you already have to an HSA-qualified health insurance policy; ask your health insurer for details.

You can obtain an HSA-qualified health plan from health insurers that participate in the program. You can also contact your present health insurer to find out if it offers an HSA-qualified plan.

The premiums you pay for an HSA-qualified health plan are deductible to the same extent as any other health insurance premiums. This means that if you're self-employed, you may deduct your entire premium from your federal income tax as a special personal deduction. (See "Personal Income Tax Deduction for the Self-Employed," above.)

You can also deduct your contribution if your business is an LLC or a partnership, or if you've formed an S corporation. If your partnership or multimember LLC makes the contribution for you as a distribution of partnership or LLC funds, it is reported as a cash distribution to you on your Schedule K-1 (Form 1065). You may take a personal deduction for the HSA contribution on your tax return (IRS Form 1040) and the contribution is not subject to income or self-employment taxes.

However, the tax result is very different if the contribution is made as a guaranteed payment to the partner or LLC member. A guaranteed payment is like a salary paid to a partner or an LLC member for services performed for the partnership or LLC. The amount of a guaranteed payment is determined without reference to the partnership's or LLC's income. The partnership or LLC deducts the guaranteed payment on its return and lists it as a guaranteed payment to you on your Schedule K-1 (Form 1065). You must pay income and self-employment tax on the amount. You may take a personal income tax deduction on your Form 1040 for the HSA contribution.

Contributions by an S corporation to a shareholder-employee's HSA are treated as wages subject to income tax, but they normally are not subject to employment taxes. The shareholder can deduct the contribution on his or her personal tax return (IRS Form 1040) as an HSA contribution.

If you've formed a C corporation and work as its employee, your corporation can make a contribution to your HSA and deduct the amount as employee compensation. The contribution is not taxable to you. (See "HSAs for Employees," below.)

HSA Account

Once you have an HSA-qualified health insurance policy, you may open your HSA account. You must establish your HSA with a trustee. The HSA trustee keeps track of your deposits and withdrawals, produces annual statements, and reports your HSA deposits to the IRS.

Any person, insurance company, bank, or financial institution already approved by the IRS to be a trustee or custodian of an IRA is automatically approved to serve as an HSA trustee. Others may apply for approval under IRS procedures for HSAs.

Health insurers can administer both the health plan and the HSA. However, you don't have to have your HSA administered by your insurer. You can establish an HSA with a bank, an insurance company, a mutual fund, or another financial institution offering HSA products.

Whoever administers your account will usually give you a checkbook or debit card to use to withdraw funds from the account. You can also make withdrawals by mail or in person.

Look at the plans offered by several companies to see which offers the best deal. Compare the fees charged to set up the account, as well as any other charges (some companies may charge an annual service fee, for example). Ask about special promotions and discounts, and find out how the account is invested.

Making Contributions to Your HSA

Once you set up your HSA-qualified health plan and HSA account, you can start making contributions to your account. There is no minimum amount you are required to contribute each year; you may contribute nothing if you wish. But there are maximum limits on how much you may contribute each year:

- If you have individual coverage, the maximum you may contribute to your HSA is $3,500.
- If you have family coverage, the maximum you may contribute to your HSA each year is $7,100.

These maximums were for 2020. They are adjusted for inflation each year.

A taxpayer who has an HSA may make a one-time tax-free rollover of funds from his or her Individual Retirement Accounts (IRAs) to his or her HSA. The rollover amount is limited to the maximum HSA contribution for the year (minus any HSA contributions you've already made for the year).

Catch-Up Contributions

Individuals who are 55 to 65 years old have the option of making additional tax-free catch-up contributions to their HSA accounts of up to $1,000. This rule is intended to compensate for the fact that older folks won't have as many years to fund their accounts as younger taxpayers. If you're in this age group, it's wise to make these contributions if you can afford them, so your HSA account will have enough money to pay for future health expenses.

	Self Only	Family
Maximum Contribution	$3,550	$7,100
Catch-Up Contribution (55 and over)	$1,000	$1,000
Minimum Deductible	$1,400	$2,800
Maximum Out-of-Pocket Payments	$6,900	$13,800

Deducting HSA Contributions

The amounts you contribute each year to your HSA account, up to the annual limit, are deductible from your federal income taxes. This is a personal deduction you take on the first page of your IRS Form 1040. You deduct it from your gross income, just like a business deduction. This means you get the full deduction, whether or not you itemize your personal deductions.

> EXAMPLE: Martin, a self-employed artist, establishes an HSA for himself and his family with a $2,800 deductible. Every year, he contributes the maximum amount to his HSA account—$7,100 in 2020. Because he is in the 24% federal income tax bracket, this saves him $1,704 in federal income tax for 2020.

Where to Invest Your HSA Contributions

The contributions you make to your HSA account may be invested just like IRA contributions. You can invest in almost anything—money market accounts, bank certificates of deposit, stocks, bonds, mutual funds, Treasury bills, and notes. However, you can't invest in collectibles such as art, antiques, postage stamps, or other personal property. Most HSA funds are invested in money market accounts and certificates of deposit.

Withdrawing HSA Funds

If you or a family member needs health care, you can withdraw money from your HSA to pay your deductible or any other medical expenses. However, you cannot deduct qualified medical expenses as an itemized deduction on Schedule A (Form 1040) that is equal to the tax-free distribution from your HSA. You pay no federal tax on HSA withdrawals used to pay qualified medical expenses.

Qualified medical expenses are broadly defined to include many types of expenses ordinarily not covered by health insurance—for example, dental or optometric care. This is one of the great advantages of the HSA program over traditional health insurance.

No Approval Required

HSA participants don't have to obtain advance approval from their HSA trustee (whether their insurer or someone else) that an expense is a qualified medical expense before they withdraw funds from their accounts. You make that determination yourself. The trustee will report any distribution to you and the IRS on Form 1099-SA, *Distributions From an HSA, Archer MSA, or Medicare Advantage MSA*. You should keep records of your medical expenses to show that your withdrawals were for qualified medical expenses and are therefore excludable from your gross income.

However, you may not use HSA funds to purchase nonprescription medications.

Tax-Free Withdrawals

If you withdraw funds from your HSA to use for something other than qualified medical expenses, you must pay regular income tax on the withdrawal, plus a 20% penalty. For example, if you were in the 24% federal income tax bracket, you'd have to pay a 44% tax on your nonqualified withdrawals.

Once you reach the age of 65 or become disabled, you can withdraw your HSA funds for any reason without penalty. If you use the money for nonmedical expenses, you will have to pay regular income tax on the withdrawals. When you die, the money in your HSA account is transferred to the beneficiary you've named for the account. The transfer is tax free if the beneficiary is your surviving spouse. Other transfers are taxable.

If you elect to leave the HSA program, you can keep your HSA account and withdraw money from it tax free for health care expenses. However, you won't be able to make any additional contributions to the account.

What HSA Funds Can Be Used For

Ordinarily, you may not use HSA funds to purchase health insurance. However, there are three exceptions to this general rule. You can use HSA funds to pay for:

- a health plan during any period of continuation coverage required under any federal law—for example, when you are terminated from your job and purchase continuing health insurance coverage from your employer's health insurer, which the insurer is legally required to make available to you under COBRA
- long-term health care insurance, or
- health insurance premiums you pay while you are receiving unemployment compensation.

For a list of all the expenses that may be paid with HSA funds, see IRS Publication 969, *Health Savings Accounts and Other Tax-Favored Health Plans*. You can download it from the IRS website at www.irs.gov.

Are HSAs a Good Deal?

Should you get an HSA? It depends. HSAs are a very good deal if you're young or in good health, and you don't go to the doctor often or take many expensive medications. You can purchase a health plan with a high deductible, pay substantially lower premiums, and have the security of knowing that you can dip into your HSA if you get sick and have to pay the deductible or other uncovered medical expenses.

If you don't tap into the money, it will keep accumulating free of taxes. You also get the benefit of deducting your HSA contributions from your income taxes. And you can use your HSA funds to pay for many health-related expenses that aren't covered by traditional health insurance.

If you enjoy good health while you have your HSA, you may end up with a substantial amount in your account that you can withdraw without penalty for any purpose once you turn 65. Unlike all other existing tax-advantaged savings or retirement accounts, HSAs provide a tax break when funds are deposited *and* when they are withdrawn. No other account provides both a "front-end" and "back-end" tax break.

With IRAs, for example, you must pay tax either when you deposit or when you withdraw your money. This feature can make your HSA an extremely lucrative tax shelter—a kind of super IRA.

On the other hand, HSAs are not for everybody. You could be better off with traditional comprehensive health insurance if you or a member of your family has substantial medical expenses. When you are in this situation, you'll likely end up spending all or most of your HSA contributions each year and earn little or no interest on your account (but you'll still get a deduction for your contributions). Of course, whether traditional health insurance is better than an HSA depends on its cost, including the deductibles and co-payments you must make.

HSAs for Employees

Employers may provide HSAs to their employees. Any business, no matter how small, may participate in the HSA program. The employer purchases an HSA-qualified health plan for its employees, who establish their own individual HSA accounts. The employer may pay all or part of its employees' insurance premiums and make contributions to their HSA accounts. Employees may also make their own contributions to their individual accounts. The combined annual contributions of the employer and employee may not exceed the limits listed in "Making Contributions to Your HSA," above.

HSAs are portable when an employee changes employers. Contributions and earnings belong to the account holder, not the employer. An employer is required to report amounts contributed to an HSA on the employee's Form W-2.

Health insurance payments and HSA contributions made by a business on behalf of its employees are currently deductible business expenses. The employees do not have to report employer contributions to their HSA accounts as income. You deduct them on the "Employee benefit programs" line of your business income tax return. If you're filing Schedule C, this is on Part II, Line 14.

If you've formed a C corporation and work as its employee, your corporation may establish an HSA on your behalf and deduct its contributions on its own tax return. The contributions are not taxable to you, but you get no personal deduction for them. You do get a deduction, however, if you make contributions to your HSA account from your personal funds. You can't do this if you have an S corporation, an LLC, or a partnership because owners of these entities are not considered employees for employment benefit purposes.

Hiring Your Spouse

If you're a sole proprietor or have formed any business entity other than an S corporation, you may hire your spouse as your employee and have your business pay for an HSA-qualified family health plan for your spouse, you, and your children and other dependents. (Moreover, your HSA-qualified health plan can cover your children up to age 26, whether or not they are your dependents.) Your spouse then establishes an HSA, which your business may fully fund each year. The money your business spends for your spouse's health insurance premiums and to fund the HSA is a fully deductible business expense. This allows you to reduce both your income and self-employment taxes. (See "Personal Income Tax Deduction for the Self-Employed," above.)

Nondiscrimination Rules

If you have employees other than yourself, your spouse, or other family members, you'll need to comply with nondiscrimination rules—that is, you'll have to make comparable HSA contributions for all employees with HSA-qualified health coverage during the year. Contributions are considered comparable if they are either of the same amount or the same percentage of the deductible under the plan. The rule is applied separately to employees who work fewer than 30 hours per week. Employers who do not comply with these nondiscrimination rules are subject to a 35% excise tax.

Tax Reporting for HSAs

You must report to the IRS how much you deposit to and withdraw from your HSA each year. You make the report using IRS Form 8889, *Health Savings Accounts*. You'll also have to keep a record of the name and address of each person or company you pay with funds from your HSA.

Deductions That Can Help You Retire

When you own your own business, it's up to you to establish and fund your own pension plan to supplement the Social Security benefits you'll receive when you retire. The tax law helps you do this by providing tax deductions and other income tax benefits for your retirement account contributions and earnings.

This chapter provides a general overview of the retirement plan choices you have as a small business owner. Deciding what type of account to establish is just as important as deciding how to invest your money once you open your account—if not more so. Once you set up your retirement account, you can always change your investments within the account with little or no difficulty. But changing the type of retirement account you have may prove difficult and costly. So it's best to spend some time up front learning about your choices and deciding which type of plan will best meet your needs.

CAUTION

You should get professional help with your plan if you have employees (other than a spouse). Having employees makes it much more complicated to set up a retirement plan (see "Having Employees Complicates Matters Tremendously," below). Because of the many complex issues that come up when you have employees, any business owner with employees should turn to a professional consultant for help in choosing, establishing, and administering a retirement plan.

RESOURCE

For additional information on the tax aspects of retirement, check out these books and IRS guides:
- *IRAs, 401(k)s & Other Retirement Plans: Strategies for Taking Your Money Out,* by Twila Slesnick and John C. Suttle (Nolo)
- IRS Publication 560, *Retirement Plans for Small Business,* and
- IRS Publication 590, *Individual Retirement Arrangements.*

Why You Need a Retirement Plan (or Plans)

In all likelihood, you will receive Social Security benefits when you retire. However, Social Security will probably cover only half of your needs when you retire—possibly less depending upon your retirement lifestyle. You'll need to make up this shortfall with your own retirement investments.

When it comes to saving for retirement, small business owners are better off than employees of most companies. This is because the federal government has created several types of retirement accounts specifically designed for small business owners. These accounts provide enormous tax benefits that are intended to maximize the amount of money you can save during your working years for your retirement years. The amount you are allowed to contribute each year to your retirement account depends upon the type of account you establish and how much money you earn. If your business doesn't earn money, you won't be able to make any contributions—you must have income to fund retirement accounts.

The two biggest benefits that most of these plans provide—tax deductions for plan contributions and tax deferral on investment earnings—are discussed in more detail below.

Tax Deduction

Retirement accounts that comply with IRS requirements are called "tax qualified." You can deduct the amount you contribute to a tax-qualified retirement account from your income taxes (except for Roth IRAs and Roth 401(k)s—see "Traditional IRAs," below). If you are a sole proprietor, a partner in a partnership, or an LLC member, you can deduct from your personal income all contributions you make to a retirement account. If you have incorporated your business, the corporation can deduct as a business expense contributions that it makes on your behalf. Either way, you or your business get a substantial income tax savings.

> **EXAMPLE:** Art, a sole proprietor, contributes $10,000 this year to a qualified retirement account. He can deduct the entire amount from his personal income taxes. Because Art is in the 24% tax bracket, he saves $2,400 in income taxes for the year (24% × $10,000) and has also put away $10,000 toward his retirement.

Tax Deferral

In addition to the tax deduction you receive for putting money into a retirement account, there is another tremendous tax benefit to retirement accounts: tax deferral on earnings. When you earn money on an investment, you usually must pay taxes on those earnings in the year when you earn the money. For example, you must pay taxes on the interest you earn on a savings account or certificate of deposit in the year when the interest accrues. And when you sell an investment at a profit, you must pay income tax in that year on the gain you realize from the sale. For example, you must pay tax on the profit you earn from selling stock in the year when you sell the stock.

A different rule applies, however, for earnings you receive from a tax-qualified retirement account. You do not pay taxes on investment earnings from retirement accounts until you withdraw the funds. Most people withdraw these funds at retirement, so they are often in a lower income tax bracket when they pay tax on these earnings. This can result in substantial tax savings for people who would have had to pay higher taxes on these earnings if they had paid as the earnings accumulated.

> CAUTION
> **Retirement accounts have restrictions on withdrawals.** The tax deferral benefits you receive by putting your money in a retirement account come at a price: You're not supposed to withdraw the money until you are 59½ years old; and, after you turn 72, you must withdraw a certain minimum amount each year and pay tax on it (but, due to the coronavirus (COVID-19) pandemic, no such withdrawals are required for 2020). Stiff penalties are imposed if you fail to follow these rules. So, if you aren't prepared to give up your right to use this money freely, you should think about a taxable account instead, where there are no restrictions on your use of your money. You should also consider a Roth IRA or Roth 401(k)—you can withdraw your contributions to these accounts (but not earnings) at any time without penalty (see below).

Special Retirement Account Withdrawal Rules for 2020

Ordinarily, if you withdraw money from an IRA, 401(k), or other tax qualified retirement plan before age 59½ you must pay a 10% early withdrawal penalty plus regular income tax on the amount. However, due to the coronavirus (COVID-19) pandemic, Congress eliminated the penalty for pandemic-related withdrawals. You may withdraw up to $100,000 from your plan during 2020 without paying the 10% penalty if:

- you, your spouse, or dependent were diagnosed with COVID-19
- you experienced adverse financial consequences because you were quarantined, furloughed, laid off, or forced to reduce work hours due to COVID-19
- you were unable to work because of a lack of child care due to COVID-19 and experienced adverse financial consequences as a result, or
- you own or operate a business that closed or reduced operating hours due to COVID-19.

There are no income limits on who can make such withdrawals. And you can use the money for any purpose. You can make your withdrawal in one lump sum or take several smaller withdrawals up to $100,000 during 2020. If you have more than one retirement plan, you can make withdrawals from each up to the $100,000 aggregate limit.

You can't make such penalty-free withdrawals after 2020.

Ordinarily, when you withdraw money from a retirement plan (other than a Roth IRA or Roth 401(k)) you must pay all the tax due that year. However, you have three years to pay the income tax on your up-to-$100,000 2020 withdrawals. You can spread your tax payments equally over the three years, starting in 2020.

Moreover, you don't have to pay any tax at all on your withdrawal if you pay the entire amount back within three years of the withdrawal date. You can pay the money back in a lump sum or with multiple recontributions.

RESOURCE

For detailed guidance on distributions from retirement accounts,
refer to *IRAs, 401(k)s & Other Retirement Plans: Strategies for Taking Your Money
Out,* by Twila Slesnick and John C. Suttle (Nolo).

Individual Retirement Accounts (IRAs)

The simplest type of tax-deferred retirement account is the individual
retirement account (IRA). An IRA is a retirement account established
by an individual, not a business. You can have an IRA whether you're a
business owner or an employee in someone else's business. Moreover, you
can establish an IRA for yourself as an individual and also set up one or
more of the other types of retirement plans discussed below, which are
just for businesses.

An IRA is a trust or custodial account set up for the benefit of an
individual or his or her beneficiaries. The trustee or custodian administers
the account. The trustee can be a bank, mutual fund, or brokerage firm, or
another financial institution (such as an insurance company).

IRAs are extremely easy to set up and administer. You need a written
IRA agreement, but you don't have to file any tax forms with the IRS. The
financial institution you use to set up your account will usually ask you to
complete IRS Form 5305, *Traditional Individual Retirement Trust Account,*
which serves as an IRA agreement and meets all of the IRS requirements.
Keep the form in your records—you don't file it with the IRS.

Most financial institutions offer an array of IRA accounts that provide
for different types of investments. You can invest your IRA money in
just about anything—stocks, bonds, mutual funds, treasury bills and
notes, and bank certificates of deposit. However, you can't invest in
collectibles like art, antiques, stamps, or other personal property.

You can establish as many IRA accounts as you want, but there is a
maximum combined amount of money you can contribute to all of your
IRA accounts each year. The limit will be adjusted each year for inflation
in $500 increments.

There are different limits for workers who are at least 50 years old.
Anyone who is at least 50 years old at the end of the year can make an

increased annual contribution of $1,000 per year. This rule is intended to allow older people to catch up with younger folks who will have more years to make contributions at the higher levels.

Annual IRA Contribution Limits		
Tax Year	Under Age 50	Aged 50 or Over
2020	$6,000	$7,000

Having Employees Complicates Matters Tremendously

If you own your own business and have no employees (other than your spouse), you can probably choose, establish, and administer your own retirement plan with little or no assistance. The instant you add employees to the mix, however, virtually every aspect of your plan becomes more complex. This is primarily due to legal requirements called nondiscrimination rules. These rules are designed to ensure that your retirement plan benefits all employees, not just you. In general, the laws prohibit you from doing the following:

- making disproportionately large contributions for some plan participants (like yourself) and not for others
- unfairly excluding certain employees from participating in the plan, and
- unfairly withholding benefits from former employees or their beneficiaries.

If the IRS finds a plan to be discriminatory at any time (usually during an audit), the plan could be disqualified—that is, determined not to satisfy IRS rules. If this happens, you and your employees will owe income tax and probably penalties, as well.

Having employees also increases the plan's reporting requirements. You must provide employees with a summary of the terms of the plan, notification of any changes you make, and an annual report of contributions. And you must file an annual tax return. Because of all the complex issues raised by having employees, any business owner with employees (other than a spouse) should seek professional help when creating a retirement plan.

If you are married, you can double the contribution limits. For example, both spouses can contribute up to $6,000 per year into their IRAs, for a total of $12,000. This is true even if one spouse isn't working. To take advantage of doubling, you must file a joint tax return, and the working spouse must earn at least as much as the combined IRA contribution.

Traditional IRAs

There are two different types of IRAs that you can choose from:

- traditional IRAs, and
- Roth IRAs.

Traditional IRAs have been around since 1974. Anybody who has earned income (income from a job, a business, or alimony) can have a traditional IRA. As stated above, you can deduct your annual contributions to your IRA from your taxable income. If neither you nor your spouse (if you have one) has another retirement plan, you may deduct your contributions no matter how high your income is.

However, there are income limits on your deductions if you (or your spouse, if you have one) are covered by another retirement plan. For these purposes, being covered by another plan means you have one of the self-employed plans described below (or you or your spouse is covered by an employer plan).

These limits are based on your and your spouse's annual modified adjusted gross income (MAGI for short). Your MAGI is your adjusted gross income before it is reduced by your IRA contributions and certain other more unusual items.

	Annual Income Limits for IRA Deductions			
Tax Year	Married Filing Jointly		Single Taxpayer	
	Full Deduction	Partial Deduction	Full Deduction	Partial Deduction
2020	$104,000	$104,000–$124,000	Under $65,000	$65,000–$75,000

If you aren't covered by a retirement plan at work, but your spouse (with whom you file jointly) is covered, you get a full IRA deduction if your MAGI is under $196,000. Your deduction is phased out between $196,000 and $206,000, and eliminated completely if your MAGI is over $206,000.

You can still contribute to an IRA even if you can't take a deduction. This is called a nondeductible IRA. Your money will grow in the account tax free, and, when you make withdrawals, you'll only have to pay tax on your account earnings, not the amount of your contributions (which have already been taxed). However, figuring out how much is taxable and how much is tax free can be a big accounting headache.

For 2020 and later, there is no age limit on making contributions to IRAs.

There are time restrictions on when you can (and when you must) withdraw money from your IRA. You are not supposed to withdraw any money from your IRA until you reach age 59½, unless you die or become disabled. Under the normal tax rules, you are required to start withdrawing at least a minimum amount of your money by April 1 of the year after the year you turn 72 (but, due to the coronavirus (COVID-19) pandemic, no such withdrawals are required for 2020). Once you start withdrawing money from your IRA, the amount you withdraw will be included in your regular income for income tax purposes.

As a general rule, if you make early withdrawals, you must pay regular income tax on the amount you take out, plus a 10% federal tax penalty. There are some exceptions to this early withdrawal penalty; for example, if you withdraw money to purchase a first home or pay educational expenses, the penalty doesn't apply to withdrawals up to a specified dollar limit. To learn about these and other exceptions in detail, see *IRAs, 401(k)s & Other Retirement Plans: Strategies for Taking Your Money Out*, by Twila Slesnick and John C. Suttle (Nolo). (Penalty-free withdrawals of up to $100,000 due to the coronavirus (COVID-19) pandemic are permitted during 2020; see the "Special Retirement Account Withdrawal Rules for 2020" above.)

Roth IRAs

Like traditional IRAs, Roth IRAs are tax deferred and allow your retirement savings to grow without any tax burden. Unlike traditional IRAs, however, your contributions to Roth IRAs are *not* tax deductible. Instead, you get to withdraw your money from the account tax free when you retire.

Once you have established your account, your ability to contribute to it will be affected by changes in your income level. If you are single and your income reaches $124,000, your ability to contribute to your Roth IRA will begin to phase out. Once your income reaches $139,000, you will no longer be able to make contributions. If you are married and filing a joint return with your spouse, your ability to contribute to your account will start to phase out when your income reaches $193,000, and you will be prohibited from making any contributions at all when your income reaches $206,000. These are the 2020 limits. The limits are adjusted for inflation each year.

You can withdraw the money you contributed to a Roth IRA penalty free anytime—you already paid tax on it so the government doesn't care. But the earnings on your investments in a Roth IRA are a different matter. You can't withdraw these until after five years. Early withdrawals of your earnings are subject to income tax and early distribution penalties. You are not, however, required to make withdrawals when you reach age 72. Because Roth IRA withdrawals are tax free, the government doesn't care if you leave your money in your account indefinitely. However, your money will be tax free on withdrawal only if you leave it in your Roth IRA for at least five years.

Is the Roth IRA a good deal? If your tax rate when you retire is higher than your tax rate before retirement, you'll probably be better off with a Roth IRA than a traditional IRA because you won't have to pay tax on your withdrawals at the higher rates. The opposite is true if your taxes go down when you retire. The catch is that nobody can know for sure what their tax rate will be when they retire. You can find several online calculators that will help you compare your results with a Roth IRA versus traditional IRA at www.choosetosave.org/calculators. More information on Roth IRAs can be found at www.rothira.com.

Roth IRA Conversions

If the Roth IRA sounds attractive to you, and you already have a traditional IRA, you may convert it to a Roth IRA. This can vastly increase the amount of money in your Roth IRA.

However, when you convert to a Roth, you'll have to pay income tax on the amount of the conversion. For example, if you convert $20,000 from your traditional IRA to a Roth IRA, you'll have to add $20,000 to your taxable income for the year. If you were in the 25% bracket, this would add $5,000 to your income taxes. One way to keep these taxes down is to convert only a portion of your traditional IRAs into a Roth each year for several years instead of doing it all at once.

Whether a Roth conversion is a good idea or not depends on many factors including your age, your current tax rate, and your tax rate upon retirement. You can find an online calculator at www.dinkytown.net/retirement.html that allows you to compare the results when you convert to a Roth versus leaving your traditional IRAs alone.

You may not undo a Roth IRA conversion, called a Roth recharacterization. Thus, once you elect to convert a traditional IRA to a Roth you must pay the income tax due. You can't get out of it by changing your mind and undoing the conversion.

Employer IRAs

You can establish an employer IRA as long as you are in business and earn a profit. You don't have to have any employees, and it doesn't matter how your business is organized: You can be a sole proprietor, a partner in a partnership, a member of a limited liability company, or an owner of a regular or S corporation.

The great advantage of employer IRAs is that you can contribute more than you can to traditional IRAs and Roth IRAs. And as long as you meet the requirements for establishing an employer IRA, you can have one in addition to one or more individual IRAs.

There are two kinds of employer IRAs to choose from: SEP-IRAs and SIMPLE IRAs.

SEP-IRAs

SEP-IRAs are designed for the self-employed. Any person who receives self-employment income from providing a service can establish a SEP-IRA. It doesn't matter whether you work full time or part time. You can have a SEP-IRA even if you are also covered by a retirement plan at a full-time employee job.

A SEP-IRA is a simplified employee pension. It's very similar to an IRA except that you can contribute more money under this type of plan. Instead of a $6,000 to $7,000 annual contribution limit (2020), you can invest up to 20% of your net profit from self-employment every year, up to a maximum of $57,000 a year in 2020. You don't have to make contributions every year, and your contributions can vary from year to year. As with IRAs, you can invest your money in almost anything (stocks, bonds, notes, mutual funds, and so on).

You can deduct your contributions to SEP-IRAs from your income taxes, and the interest on your SEP-IRA investments accrues tax free until you withdraw the money. Withdrawals from SEP-IRAs are subject to the same rules that apply to traditional IRAs. If you withdraw money from your SEP-IRA before you reach age 59½, you'll have to pay a 10% tax penalty plus regular income taxes on your withdrawal, unless an exception applies. And you must begin to withdraw your money by April 1 of the year after the year you turn 72 (but, due to the coronavirus (COVID-19) pandemic, no such withdrawals are required for 2020).

SIMPLE IRAs

Self-employed people and companies with fewer than 100 employees can set up SIMPLE IRAs. If you establish a SIMPLE IRA, you are not allowed to have any other retirement plans for your business (although you may still have your own individual IRA). SIMPLE IRAs are easy to set up and administer, and you will be able to make larger annual contributions than you could to a SEP or Keogh plan if you earn less than $10,000 per year from your business.

SIMPLE IRAs may be established only by an employer on behalf of its employees. If you are a sole proprietor, you are deemed to employ yourself for purposes of this rule, and you may establish a SIMPLE IRA in your own name as the employer. If you are a partner in a partnership, an LLC member, or the owner of an incorporated business, the SIMPLE IRA must be established by your business, not by you personally.

Contributions to SIMPLE IRAs are divided into two parts. You may contribute:

- up to 100% of your net income from your business up to an annual limit—the contribution limit is $13,500 for 2020 ($16,500 if you're age 50 or over), and
- a matching contribution of up to 3% of your net business income.

If you're an employee of your incorporated business, your first contribution (called a salary reduction contribution) comes out of your salary, and the matching contribution is paid by your business.

The limits on contributions to SIMPLE IRAs might seem very low, but they could work to your advantage if you earn a small income from your business—for example, if you only work at it part time. This is because you can contribute an amount equal to 100% of your earnings, up to the $13,500 or $16,500 limits. Thus, for example, if your net earnings are only $10,000, you could contribute the entire amount (plus a 3% employer contribution). You can't do this with any of the other plans because their percentage limits are much lower. For example, you may contribute only 20% of your net self-employment income to a SEP-IRA or Keogh, so you would be limited to a $2,000 contribution if you had a $10,000 profit.

The money in a SIMPLE IRA can be invested like any other IRA. Withdrawals from SIMPLE IRAs are subject to the same rules as traditional IRAs with one big exception: Early withdrawals from SIMPLE IRAs are subject to a 25% tax penalty if you make the withdrawal within two years after the date you first contributed to your account. Other early withdrawals are subject to a 10% penalty, as with traditional IRAs, unless an exception applies.

Keogh Plans

Keogh plans—named after the congressman who sponsored the legislation that created them—are only for business owners who are sole proprietors, partners in partnerships, or LLC members. You can't have a Keogh if you incorporate your business.

Keoghs require more paperwork to set up than employer IRAs, but they also offer more options: You can contribute more to these plans and still get an income tax deduction for your contributions.

Types of Keogh Plans

There are two basic types of Keogh plans:
- defined contribution plans, in which the amount you receive on retirement is based on how much you contribute to—and how much accumulates in—the plan, and
- defined benefit plans, which provide for payment of a set amount of money upon retirement.

There are two types of defined contribution plans: profit-sharing plans and money purchase plans. These plans can be used separately or in tandem with one other.

Profit-Sharing Plans

You can contribute up to 20% of your net self-employment income to a profit-sharing Keogh plan, up to a maximum of $57,000 per year in 2020. You can contribute any amount up to the limit each year or contribute nothing at all.

Money Purchase Plans

In a money purchase plan, you contribute a fixed percentage of your net self-employment earnings every year. You decide on the percentage when you establish your plan. Make sure you will be able to afford the contributions each year because you can't skip them, even if your business earns no profit for the year. In return for giving up flexibility, you can contribute a higher percentage of your earnings with a money purchase plan—the lesser of 25% of compensation or $56,000 in 2019 (the same maximum amount applies to profit-sharing plans).

Setting Up a Keogh Plan

As with individual IRAs and employer IRAs, you can set up a Keogh plan at most banks, brokerage houses, mutual funds, other financial institutions, and trade or professional organizations. You can also choose among a huge array of investments for your money.

To set up your plan, you must adopt a written Keogh plan and establish a trust or custodial account with your plan provider to invest your funds. Your provider should have an IRS-approved master or prototype Keogh plan for you to sign. You can also have a special plan drawn up for you, but this is expensive and unnecessary for most small business owners.

Withdrawing Your Money

You may begin to withdraw money from your Keogh plan after you reach the age of 59½. If you have a profit-sharing plan, early withdrawals are permitted without penalty if you suffer financial hardship, become disabled, or have to pay health expenses in excess of 7.5% of your adjusted gross income. If you have a money purchase plan, early withdrawals are permitted if you become disabled, leave your business after you turn 55, or make child support or alimony payments from the plan under a court order. Otherwise, early withdrawals from profit-sharing and money purchase Keogh plans are subject to a 10% penalty. (However, penalty-free withdrawals of up to $100,000 due to the coronavirus (COVID-19) pandemic are permitted during 2020; see "Special Retirement Account Withdrawal Rules for 2020" above.)

Solo 401(k) Plans

Most people have heard of 401(k) plans—retirement plans established by businesses for their employees. 401(k)s are a type of profit-sharing plan in which a business's employees make plan contributions from their salaries and the business makes a matching contribution. These plans are complex to establish and administer and are generally used only by larger businesses. Until recently, self-employed people and businesses without employees rarely used 401(k) plans, because they offered no benefit over other profit-sharing plans that are much easier to set up and run.

However, things have changed. Now, any business owner who has no employees (other than a spouse) can establish a solo self-employed 401(k) plan (also called a one-person or individual 401(k)). Solo 401(k) plans are designed specifically for business owners without employees.

Solo 401(k) plans have the following advantages over other retirement plans:

- You can make very large contributions—as much as 20% of your net profit from self-employment, plus an elective deferral contribution of up to $19,500 in 2020. The maximum contribution per year is $57,000 in 2020 (the same maximum amount that applies to the Keogh plans discussed above). Business owners who are at least 50 years old may make additional contributions of up to $6,000 per year; these catch-up contributions don't count toward the $57,000 annual limit.

- You can borrow up to 50% of your vested account balance up to $50,000 from your solo 401(k) plan (100% and $100,000 for 2020 through 9/23/2020), as long as you repay the loan within five years. (You cannot borrow from a traditional IRA, Roth IRA, SEP-IRA, or SIMPLE IRA.)

As with other plans, you must pay a 10% penalty tax on withdrawals you make before the age of 59½, but you may make penalty-free early withdrawals for reasons of personal hardship (defined as an "immediate financial need" that you can't meet any other way).

You can set up a solo 401(k) plan at most banks, brokerage houses, mutual funds, and other financial institutions, and you can invest the money in a variety of ways. You must adopt a written plan and set up a trust or custodial account with your plan provider to invest your funds. Financial institutions that offer solo 401(k) plans have preapproved plans that you can use.

CAUTION

Beware of retirement account deadlines. If you want to establish any of the retirement accounts discussed in this chapter and take a tax deduction for the year, you must meet specific deadlines. The deadlines vary according to the type of account you set up, as shown in the following chart. Once you establish your account, you have until the due date of your tax return for the year (April 15 of the following year, or later if you receive a filing extension) to contribute to your account and take a deduction. (For 2020, the due date for filing individual 2019 tax returns was extended to July 15 due to the coronavirus (COVID-19) pandemic; the extended filing date remained October 15, 2020.)

Retirement Account Deadlines	
Plan Type	Deadline for Establishing Plan
Traditional IRA	Due date of tax return (April 15)
Roth IRA	Due date of tax return (April 15 plus extensions)
SEP-IRA	Due date of tax return (April 15 plus extensions)
SIMPLE IRA	October 1
Keogh Profit-Sharing Plan	December 31
Keogh Money Purchase Plan	December 31
Keogh Defined Benefit Plan	December 31
401(k) Plan	December 31

More Home Business Deductions

This chapter looks at some of the most common deductible operating expenses that you are likely to incur in the normal course of running your home business, such as advertising expenses, insurance, and legal fees. You can deduct these costs as business operating expenses as long as they are ordinary, necessary, and reasonable in amount and meet the additional requirements discussed below.

Advertising

Almost any type of business-related advertising is a currently deductible business operating expense. You can deduct advertising to sell a particular product or service, to help establish goodwill for your business, or just to get your business known. Advertising costs include what you pay for:

- business cards
- brochures
- advertisements in the local yellow pages
- newspaper and magazine advertisements
- trade publication advertisements
- catalogs
- advertisements on the Internet, including Google adwords
- fees you pay to advertising and public relations agencies
- package design costs, and
- signs and display racks.

However, advertising to influence government legislation is never deductible. And help-wanted ads you place to recruit workers are not advertising costs, but you can still deduct them as ordinary and necessary business operating expenses.

Goodwill Advertising

You can usually deduct the cost of goodwill advertising—ads intended to keep your name before the public—if it relates to business you reasonably expect to gain in the future. Examples of goodwill advertising include:

- advertisements that encourage people to contribute to charities, such as the Red Cross or similar causes

- sponsoring a little league baseball team, bowling team, or golf tournament
- giving away product samples, and
- holding contests and giving away prizes.

However, you can't deduct time and labor that you give away as an advertising expense, even though donating them often promotes goodwill. You must actually spend money to have an advertising expense. For example, a lawyer who does pro bono work for indigent clients to gain exposure for his law practice may not deduct the cost of his services as an advertising expense.

Giveaway Items

The cost of giveaway items that you use to publicize your business (such as pens, coffee cups, T-shirts, refrigerator magnets, calendars, tote bags, and key chains) are deductible. However, you are not allowed to deduct more than $25 in business gifts to any one person each year (see "Gifts," later in this chapter). This limitation applies to advertising giveaway items unless they:

- cost $4 or less
- have your name clearly and permanently imprinted on them, and
- are one of a number of identical items you distribute widely.

> EXAMPLE 1: Jay has a home business selling rare wines. He orders 1,000 ballpoint pens with his name and contact information printed on them and distributes them at wine tastings and gourmet food and wine fairs. Each pen costs Jay $1. The pens do not count toward the $25 gift limit. Jay may deduct the entire $1,000 expense for the pens.

> EXAMPLE 2: Jay buys a $200 fountain pen and gives it to his best customer. The pen is a business gift to an individual, so Jay can deduct only $25 of the cost.

Signs, display racks, and other promotional materials that you give to other businesses to use on their premises do not count as gifts.

Website Development and Maintenance

The cost of developing and maintaining a website for a business varies widely. It can be relatively inexpensive if you use a standard template you purchase from a template company. However, the cost will be much greater if you want to create a custom design for your website.

Many businesses currently deduct all website development and ongoing maintenance expenses as an advertising expense. However, some tax experts believe that the cost of initially setting up a website is a capital expense, not a currently deductible business operating expense, because the website is a long-term asset that benefits the business for more than one year. Under normal tax rules, capital expenses must be deducted over several years. Three years is the most common deduction period used for websites, because this is the period used for software.

However, even if website development costs are capital expenses, they may be currently deducted in a single year under Section 179 (see Chapter 5).

Most tax experts agree that ongoing website hosting, maintenance, and updating costs are currently deductible operating expenses. Money you spend to get people to view your website, such as SEO (search engine optimization) campaigns, is also a currently deductible advertising expense.

Business Bad Debts

Business bad debts are debts that won't be fully repaid and arise from your business activities. Examples include:

- money you lend for a business purpose
- sales you make on credit, or
- guaranteed business-related loans.

You can currently deduct business bad debts as business operating expenses when they become wholly or partly worthless. However, to claim the deduction, you must incur an actual loss of money or have previously included the amount of the debt as income on your tax return. Because of this limitation, many small businesses are unable to deduct bad debts.

Requirements to Deduct Bad Debts

You must meet three requirements to deduct a business bad debt as a business operating expense:

- You must have a bona fide business debt.
- The debt must be wholly or partly worthless.
- You must have suffered an economic loss from the debt.

A Bona Fide Business Debt

A bona fide debt exists when someone has a legal obligation to pay you a sum of money—for example, you sell goods or merchandise to a customer on credit. You will generally need some written evidence of the debt—for example, a signed promissory note or another writing stating the amount of the debt, when it is due, and the interest rate (if any)—in order to claim this deduction. An oral promise to pay may also be legally enforceable, but would be looked upon with suspicion by the IRS.

A business debt is a debt that is created or acquired in the course of your business or becomes worthless as part of your business. Your primary motive for incurring the debt must be related to your business. Debts you take on for personal or investment purposes are not business debts. (Remember, investing is not a business; see Chapter 2.)

> EXAMPLE 1: Mark, an advertising agent, lends $10,000 to his brother-in-law, Scott, to help him develop his bird diaper invention. Mark will get 25% of the profits if the invention proves successful. This is an investment, not a business debt.

> EXAMPLE 2: Mark lends $10,000 to one of his best business clients to keep the client's business running. Because the main reason for the loan is business related (to keep his client in business so he will continue as a client), the debt is a business debt.

A Worthless Debt

You may deduct a debt only if it is wholly or partly worthless. A debt becomes worthless when there is no longer any chance that it will be repaid. You don't have to wait until a debt is due to determine that it is worthless, nor do you have to go to court to try to collect it. You just have to be able to show that you have taken reasonable steps to try to collect the debt or that collection efforts would be futile. Examples include:

- You've made repeated collection efforts that have proven unsuccessful.
- The debtor has filed for bankruptcy or has already been through bankruptcy and had all or part of the debt discharged (forgiven) by the bankruptcy court.
- The debtor has gone out of business, gone broke, died, or disappeared.

Keep all documentation that shows a debt is worthless, such as copies of unpaid invoices, collection letters you've sent the debtor, logs of collection calls you've made, bankruptcy notices, and credit reports.

You must deduct the entire amount of a bad debt in the year it becomes totally worthless. If only part of a business debt becomes worthless—for example, you received a partial payment before the debt became uncollectible—you can deduct the unpaid portion that year or you can wait until the following year to deduct it. For example, if you think you might get paid more the next year, you can wait and see what your final bad debt amount is before you deduct it.

An Economic Loss

You are not automatically entitled to deduct a debt simply because the obligation has become worthless. To get a deduction, you must have suffered an economic loss. According to the IRS, you have suffered a loss only if you:

- already reported as business income the amount you were supposed to be paid
- paid out cash, or
- made credit sales of inventory for which you were not paid.

These rules make it impossible to deduct some types of business debts.

Types of Bad Debts

There are many different types of business debts that small businesses can incur. The sections that follow discuss some of the more common ones.

Sales of Services

Unfortunately, if you're a cash basis taxpayer who sells services to your clients (like many home businesses), you can't claim a bad debt deduction if a client fails to pay you. Cash basis taxpayers report income only when they actually receive it, not when they perform the services the client ordered. As a result, cash basis taxpayers don't have an economic loss (in the eyes of the IRS) when a client fails to pay.

> EXAMPLE: Bill, a home-based dog walker, works 20 hours walking a client's dogs and bills the client $250. The client never pays. Bill is a cash basis taxpayer, so he doesn't report the $250 as income because he never received it. As far as the IRS is concerned, Bill has no economic loss and cannot deduct the $250 the client failed to pay.

The IRS strictly enforces this rule (harsh as it may seem). Absent the rule, the IRS fears that businesses would inflate the value of their services in order to get a larger deduction.

Accrual basis taxpayers, on the other hand, report sales as income in the year the sales are made—not the year payment is received. These taxpayers can take a bad debt deduction if a client fails to pay for services rendered, because they have already reported the money due as income. Therefore, accrual taxpayers have an economic loss when they are not paid for their services.

> EXAMPLE: Andrea, a home-based financial consultant, bills a client $10,000 for consulting services she performed during the year. Andrea is an accrual basis taxpayer, so she characterizes the $10,000 as income on her books and includes this amount in her gross income for the year in which she billed the services, even though she hasn't actually received payment. The client later files for bankruptcy, and the debt becomes worthless. Andrea may take a business bad debt deduction to wipe out the $10,000 in income she previously charged on her books.

There's no point in switching from cash basis to the accrual method to deduct bad debts. The accrual method doesn't result in lower taxes—the bad debt deduction merely wipes out a sale that was already reported as income and taxed.

RELATED TOPIC

Cash or accrual? Read all about it in Chapter 15, which includes a detailed discussion of the cash basis and accrual accounting methods.

Credit Sales of Inventory

Most deductible business bad debts result from credit sales of inventory to customers. If you sell goods on credit to a customer and are not paid, you can take a deduction whether you are an accrual or cash basis taxpayer. You deduct the cost of the inventory at the end of the year to determine the cost of goods sold for the year. (See Chapter 10 for more on inventory deductions.)

Cash Loans

Whether you are a cash basis or an accrual taxpayer, cash loans you make for a business purpose are deductible as bad debts in the year they become worthless.

> EXAMPLE: John, an advertising agent, loaned $10,000 to one of his best clients to keep the client's business running. The client later went bankrupt and could not repay the loan. John may deduct the $10,000 as a business bad debt.

Business Loan Guarantees

If you guarantee a debt that becomes worthless, it qualifies as a business bad debt only if you:
- made the guarantee in the course of your business
- have a legal duty to pay the debt
- made the guarantee before the debt became worthless, and

- received reasonable consideration (compensation) for the guarantee—
you meet this requirement if you make the guarantee for a good-faith
business purpose or according to normal business practices.

EXAMPLE: Ling has a home business selling gourmet coffee and teas. She
guaranteed payment of a $20,000 note for Pete's Coffee Bar, one of Ling's
largest clients. Pete's later filed for bankruptcy and defaulted on the loan.
Ling had to make full payment to the bank. She can take a business bad
debt deduction because her guarantee was made for a good-faith business
purpose—her desire to retain one of her better clients and keep a sales outlet.

Loans or Guarantees to Your Corporation

If your business is incorporated, you cannot take a bad debt deduction
for a loan to your corporation if the loan is actually a contribution to
capital—that is, the money is part of your investment in the business. You
must be careful to treat a loan to your corporation just as you would treat
a loan made to a business in which you have no ownership interest. You
should have a signed promissory note from your corporation setting forth:

- the loan amount
- the interest rate—which should be reasonable
- the due date, and
- a repayment schedule.

If you are a principal shareholder in a small corporation, you'll often
be asked to personally guarantee corporate loans and other extensions
of credit. Creditors demand these guarantees because they want to
be able to go after your personal assets if they can't collect from your
corporation. If you end up having to make good on your guarantee
and can't get repaid from your corporation, you will have a bad debt.
You can deduct this bad debt as a business debt if your dominant motive
for making the loan or guarantee was to protect your employment status
and ensure your continuing receipt of a salary. If your primary motive
was to protect your investment in the corporation, the debt is a personal
debt. The IRS is more likely to think you are protecting your investment

if you receive little or no salary from the corporation or your salary is not a major source of your overall income.

Personal Debts

The fact that a debt doesn't arise from your business doesn't mean it's not deductible. However, unlike business bad debts, personal bad debts are deductible only if they become wholly worthless. A deductible nonbusiness bad debt is classified as a short-term capital loss for tax purposes. As such, it is subject to the limitations on taking short-term capital losses: You can deduct such a loss against any short- or long-term capital gains you have for the year from the sale of capital assets (such as real estate and stocks). Any remaining amount of your loss is deductible only up to $3,000 per year against your other ordinary income.

Nondeductible losses may be carried over to be deducted in future years.

Casualty Losses

Casualty losses are damage to property caused by fire, theft, vandalism, earthquake, storm, flood, terrorism, or some other "sudden, unexpected, or unusual event." There must be some external force involved in a casualty loss. Thus, you get no deduction if you simply lose property or it breaks or wears out over time.

You may take a deduction for casualty losses to business property only if—and only to the extent that—the loss is not covered by insurance. If the loss is fully covered, you can't take a deduction.

Amount of Deduction

How much you may deduct depends on whether the property involved was stolen, completely destroyed, or partially destroyed. However, you must always reduce your casualty losses by the amount of any insurance proceeds you receive (or reasonably expect to receive). If more than one item was stolen or destroyed, you must figure your deduction separately for each.

Total Loss

If the property is stolen or completely destroyed, your deduction is calculated as follows:

$$
\begin{array}{rl}
& \text{Adjusted basis} \\
- & \text{Salvage value} \\
- & \underline{\text{Insurance proceeds}} \\
= & \underline{\text{Casualty loss}} \\
\end{array}
$$

(Your adjusted basis is the property's original cost, plus the value of any improvements, minus any deductions you took for depreciation or Section 179 expensing—see Chapter 5.) Obviously, if an item is stolen, there will be no salvage value.

> **EXAMPLE:** Sean's home computer is stolen by a burglar. The computer cost $2,000. Sean has taken no tax deductions for it because he purchased it only two months ago, so his adjusted basis is $2,000. Sean is a renter and has no insurance covering the loss. Sean's casualty loss is $2,000 ($2,000 adjusted basis – $0 salvage value – $0 insurance proceeds = $2,000).

Special Rules for Losses Related to Federally Declared Disasters

The cost of repairing damaged property is not part of a casualty loss. Neither is the cost of cleaning up after a casualty. Instead, these expenses are deductible in addition to any deductible casualty loss you have. Normally, you have to depreciate over several years the cost to clean up hazardous waste on business property, or any repairs to property or equipment you make that make the property better than it was before it was repaired. However, special rules apply to damage or destruction to business property caused by a federally declared disaster. Under those circumstances, you can currently deduct costs related to the repair of business property damaged by the disaster; the abatement or control of hazardous substances released due to the disaster; or the removal of debris from, or the demolition of structures on, real property damaged or destroyed by the disaster. (I.R.C. § 198A.) You can currently deduct these expenses, even though normally you would have to depreciate these costs under the regular tax rules.

Partial Loss

If the property is only partly destroyed, your casualty loss deduction is the lesser of the decrease in the property's fair market value or its adjusted basis, reduced by any insurance you receive or expect to receive.

> EXAMPLE: Assume that Sean's computer from the example above is partly destroyed due to a small fire in his home. Its fair market value in its damaged state is $500. Because he spent $2,000 for the computer, the decrease in its fair market value is $1,500. The computer's adjusted basis is $2,000. He received no insurance proceeds. Thus, his casualty loss is $1,500.

Inventory

You don't have to treat damage to or loss of inventory as a casualty loss. Instead, you may deduct it on your Schedule C as part of the cost of your goods sold. (See Chapter 10 for more information on deducting inventory costs.) This is advantageous because it reduces your income for self-employment tax purposes, which casualty losses do not. However, if you do this, you must include any insurance proceeds you receive for the inventory loss in your gross income for the year.

Personal Property

Uninsured casualty losses to personal property—that is, property you don't use for your business—can also be deductible from your income tax. However, during 2018 through 2025, you can qualify for a personal casualty loss deduction only if your loss is caused by a federally declared disaster. Other casualty losses to personal property—for example, uninsured losses due to ordinary house fires—are not deductible. For this reason, it is wise to have adequate homeowners' or renters' insurance to fully cover such losses.

Uninsured losses caused by a federally declared disaster are an itemized deduction and are deductible only to the extent they exceed 10% of your adjusted gross income for the year. For example, if you have $10,000 in total casualty losses and 10% of your AGI is $7,000, your loss is limited to $3,000. In addition, your loss for each item of individual or personal property is deductible only to the extent it exceeds $100—in other words, you must reduce your loss for each item by $100.

Losses Due to Coronavirus (COVID-19) Pandemic

Ordinarily, casualty losses involve physical damage to tangible property such as a building. However, some losses caused by the coronavirus (COVID-19) pandemic could also be deductible casualty losses. To be deductible, such losses must:

- not be reimbursed through insurance or otherwise
- be evidenced by "closed and completed transactions," and
- be related to the disaster and sustained in the same year.

Such losses could include business inventory sold at a loss, thrown away because it spoiled or expired, or donated to charity. However, inventory losses can already be deducted as cost of goods sold. If you do so, you may not also take a casualty loss deduction. Other possible casualty deductions due to the COVID-19 pandemic include monetary losses directly attributable to the pandemic such as termination payments made to cancel contracts or loss of deposits paid for preplanned business travel or events.

Because the coronavirus (COVID-19) pandemic was declared a national disaster by the federal government, taxpayers have the option of deducting their losses in 2019 instead of 2020 and obtaining a refund for taxes paid in that year. (I.R.C. § 165(i).) You should consult with a tax professional to see if you qualify for this deduction; and, if so, when and how to take it.

Damage to Your Home Office

You may deduct losses due to damage to or destruction of your home office as part of your home office deduction. However, your loss is reduced by any insurance proceeds you receive or expect to receive.

You can deduct casualty losses that affect your entire house as an indirect home office expense. The amount of your deduction is based on your home office use percentage.

> EXAMPLE: Dana's home, valued at $500,000, is completely destroyed by a fire. Her fire insurance covered only 80% of her loss, or $400,000, leaving her with a $100,000 loss. Her home office took up 20% of her home. She can deduct 20% of her $100,000 loss, or $20,000, as an indirect home office deduction.

You can fully deduct casualty losses that affect only your home office—for example, if only your home office is burned in a fire—as direct home office expenses. However, you can't take a business expense deduction for casualty losses that don't affect your home office at all—for example, if your kitchen is destroyed by fire. See Chapter 6 for a detailed discussion of the home office deduction.

If the loss involves business property that is in your home office, but is not part of your home—for example, a burglar steals your home office computer—you can deduct the entire value of that loss directly, rather than as part of the home office deduction.

Tax Reporting

You report casualty losses to business property on Part B of IRS Form 4684, *Casualties and Thefts*, and then transfer the deductible casualty loss to Form 4797, *Sales of Business Property*, and the first page of your Form 1040. The amount of your deductible casualty loss is subtracted from your adjusted gross income for the year. However, casualty losses are not deducted from your self-employment income for purposes of calculating your Social Security and Medicare tax. These reporting requirements differ from those for other deductions covered in this chapter, which are reported on IRS Schedule C, Form 1040.

Partnerships, S corporations, and LLCs must also fill out Form 4797. The amount of the loss is subtracted when calculating the entity's total business income for the year. This amount is reported on the entity's information tax return (Form 1065 for partnerships and LLCs; Form 1120S for S corporations). C corporations deduct their casualty losses on their own tax returns (Form 1120).

If you take a casualty loss as part of your home office deduction, you must include the loss on Form 8829, *Expenses for Business Use of Your Home* (see Chapter 6).

Charitable Contributions

If, like the vast majority of home business owners, you are a sole propri-etor, a partner in a partnership, an LLC member, or an S corporation shareholder, the IRS treats any charitable contributions your business makes as personal contributions by you (and your co-owners, if any). As such, the contributions are not business expenses—you can deduct them only as personal charitable contributions. Starting in 2020, you may deduct $300 per year in cash contributions to public charities without itemizing. You may deduct additional contributions of money or property contributions (including inventory) only if you itemize your personal deductions on your personal tax return; they are subject to certain income limitations. The deduction for donated inventory is limited to the fair market value of the inventory on the date it is donated, reduced by any gain you would have realized had you sold the property at its fair market value instead of donating it.

> EXAMPLE: Barbee, who runs a crafts business out of her home, donates unsold inventory to a nursing home. The fair market value of the inventory is $1,000. Barbee spent $500 to acquire the inventory, so she would have had a $500 gain had she sold it at its fair market value. Her charitable deduction must be reduced by the amount of this gain, so she gets only a $500 deduction.

RESOURCE
For detailed guidance on tax deductions for charitable contribu-tions, refer to *Every Nonprofit's Tax Guide,* by Stephen Fishman (Nolo).

Dues and Subscriptions

Dues you pay to professional, business, and civic organizations are deductible business expenses, as long as any organization's main purpose is not to provide entertainment facilities to members. You can deduct dues paid to:

- bar associations, medical associations, and other professional organizations

- trade associations, local chambers of commerce, real estate boards, and business leagues, and
- civic or public service organizations, such as a Rotary or Lions club.

You get no deduction for dues you pay to belong to other types of social, business, or recreational clubs—for example, country clubs or athletic clubs (see Chapter 7). For this reason, it's best not to use the word "dues" on your tax return because the IRS may question the expense. Use other words to describe the deduction—for example, if you're deducting membership dues for a trade organization, list the expense as "trade association membership fees."

You may also deduct subscriptions to professional, technical, and trade journals that deal with your business field, as a business expense.

Education Expenses

What about deducting the cost of business-related education—for example, a college course or seminar? These expenses may be deductible, but only in strictly limited circumstances. To qualify for an education deduction, you must be able to show that the education:

- maintains or improves skills required in your existing business, or
- is required by law or regulation to maintain your professional status.

Because of these restrictions, it is usually not possible to deduct undergraduate and graduate tuition. Instead, this deduction is usually used by professionals like doctors and accountants who can deduct the cost of continuing professional education.

> EXAMPLE: Aliyah is a self-employed attorney who works from home. Every year, she is required by law to attend 12 hours of continuing legal education to maintain her status as an active member of the state bar. The legal seminars she attends to satisfy this requirement are deductible education expenses.

If you qualify, deductible education expenses include tuition, fees, books, and other learning materials. They also include transportation and travel (see below). You may also deduct expenses you pay to educate or train your employees.

Can You Deduct Your MBA?

Ordinarily, you can't deduct the cost of obtaining a degree that leads to a professional license or certification—for example, a law degree, medical degree, or dental degree. However, it may be possible to deduct the cost of obtaining an MBA (a master's degree in business administration) because an MBA is a more general course of study that does not lead to a professional license or certification. The decisive factor is whether you were already established in your trade or business before you obtained the MBA. If so, it is deductible.

In one highly publicized case, for example, a registered nurse was allowed to deduct her $15,000 tuition cost of obtaining an MBA with a health care management specialization. The nurse worked for many years as a quality control coordinator at various hospitals. The court held that while the MBA may have improved her skill set, she was already performing the tasks and activities of her trade or business before commencing the MBA program, and continued to do so after receiving the degree. (*Lori A. Singleton-Clarke v. Comm'r*, T.C. Summ. Op. 2009-182 (2009).)

Starting a New Business

You cannot currently deduct education expenses you incur to qualify for a *new* business or profession. For example, courts have held that IRS agents could not deduct the cost of going to law school, because a law degree would qualify them for a new business—being a lawyer. (*Jeffrey L. Weiler*, 54 T.C. 398 (1970).) On the other hand, a practicing dentist was allowed to deduct the cost of being educated in orthodontia, because becoming an orthodontist did not constitute the practice of a new business or profession for a dentist. (Rev. Rul. 74-78.)

Minimum Educational Requirements

You cannot deduct the cost required to meet the minimum or basic level educational requirements for a business or profession. Thus, for example, you can't deduct the expense of going to law school or medical school.

Traveling for Education

Local transportation expenses you pay to travel to and from a deductible educational activity are deductible. This includes transportation between either your home or business and the educational activity. Going to or from home to an educational activity does not constitute nondeductible commuting. If you drive, you may deduct your actual expenses or use the standard mileage rate. (See Chapter 8 for more on deducting the cost of local travel.)

Lifetime Learning Credit

Instead of taking a tax deduction for your business-related education expenses, you may qualify for the lifetime learning credit. A tax credit is a dollar-for-dollar reduction in your tax liability, so it's even better than a tax deduction.

The lifetime learning credit can by used to help pay for any undergraduate or graduate level education, including nondegree education to acquire or improve job skills (for example a continuing education course). If you qualify, your credit equals 20% of the first $10,000 of postsecondary tuition and fees you pay during the year, for a maximum credit of $2,000 per tax return. However, the credit is phased out and then eliminated at certain income levels: It begins to go down if your modified adjusted gross income is over $59,000 ($118,000 for a joint return), and you cannot claim the credit at all if your MAGI is over $69,000 ($138,000 for a joint return). These are the limits for 2020. The limits are adjusted for inflation each year.

You can take this credit not only for yourself, but for a dependent child (or children) for whom you claim a tax exemption, or your spouse as well (if you file jointly). And it can be taken any number of times. However, you can't take the credit if you've already deducted the education cost as a business expense.

EXAMPLE: Bill, a self-employed real estate broker with a $40,000 AGI, spends $2,000 on continuing real estate education courses during the year. He may take a $400 lifetime learning credit (20% × $2,000 = $400).

There's no law that says you must take your education courses as close to home as possible. You may travel outside your geographic area for education, even if the same or a similar educational activity is available near your home or place of business. Companies and groups that sponsor educational events are well aware of this rule and take advantage of it by offering courses and seminars at resorts and other enjoyable vacation spots, such as Hawaii and California. Deductible travel expenses may include airfare or other transportation, lodging, and meals. (See Chapter 9 for more on business travel deductions.)

You cannot claim travel itself as an education deduction. You must travel *to* some sort of educational activity. For example, an architect could not deduct the cost of a trip to Paris because he studied the local architecture while he was there—but he could deduct a trip to Paris to attend a seminar on French architecture.

Entertainment and Meals

The Tax Cuts and Jobs Act made major changes to the longstanding deductions for business-related entertainment and meals. Starting in 2018, most business-related entertainment is not deductible. However, the deductibility of certain meals is unclear.

Entertainment

For decades, taxpayers were allowed to partly deduct the cost of entertainment, amusement, or recreation if the purpose was to generate income or provide other specific business benefits. The Tax Cuts and Jobs Act eliminated all such deductions starting in 2018. (I.R.C. § 274(a).) Thus, you may not deduct country club or skiing outings; theater or sporting event tickets; entertainment at nightclubs; hunting, fishing, or similar trips; or other vacation trips. This is true even if the expenses result in a specific business benefit such as landing a new client. Nondeductible entertainment expenses also include membership fees and dues for any club organized for business, pleasure, recreation, or other social purposes, and any entertainment facility fees.

However, a few types of entertainment remain wholly or partly deductible:

- 100% of the cost of entertainment provided as part of a company recreational or social activity—for example, a picnic or holiday party for your employees
- 100% of entertainment expenses for business meetings of employees, stockholders, agents, or directors—for example, the costs of renting a conference room in a hotel for such a meeting
- 100% of expenses for entertainment goods, services, and facilities that you sell to customers
- 100% of expenses for goods, services, and facilities you or your business make available to the general public, and
- 100% of the cost of any entertainment or recreation expenses included as part of an employee's compensation and reported as such on the employee's W-2.

Meals

Business-related meals have long been a deductible expense. This continues, even after enactment of the Tax Cuts and Jobs Act. Historically, food and beverage expenses have been closely scrutinized by the IRS because of past abuses by taxpayers. For this reason, it is wise to keep good records of such expenses. See Chapter 15.

Meals With Clients, Prospects, and Others

When the Tax Cuts and Jobs Act eliminated the deduction for business-related entertainment, many feared it also eliminated deductions for client and prospect meals, since such meals were deducted as an entertainment expense. However, the IRS has adopted proposed regulations providing that most business-related food and beverage expenses remain 50% deductible. (Proposed Reg. 1.274-12.) Although these proposed regulations are technically not legally binding until they become final, taxpayers can rely on them for expenses incurred after December 31, 2017. (REG-100814-19, February 21, 2020, p. 22.)

Under the proposed regulations, 50% of food and beverage costs are deductible as a business expense if:

- the expense is not lavish or extravagant under the circumstances
- the taxpayer, or an employee of the taxpayer, is present when the items are consumed, and
- the food or beverages are provided to a business associate.

You or an employee need to be present at the meal to take this deduction. Moreover, the food or beverages must be furnished to a "business associate." This is any person you could reasonably expect to engage or deal with in the active conduct of your business. This includes current or prospective customers, clients, suppliers, employees, agents, partners, or professional advisers.

The meal need not be indispensable to be "ordinary and necessary"; it just needs to be helpful to your business. The IRS does not require that you actually close a deal or get some other specific business benefit to take this deduction.

Although the meal may not be "lavish or extravagant," there is no dollar limit on how much you can spend; nor are you barred from eating at deluxe restaurants. You must use your common sense to determine if a meal is too lavish under the circumstances. In practice, the IRS will rarely second guess you on this, especially if you have good documentation for the expense.

> **EXAMPLE:** Ivan, a sole proprietor consultant, has a meeting with a prospective client at a nice restaurant because the prospective client will like getting a free lunch. While at the lunch they discuss business, but don't close any deals. He pays $200 for the lunch, including a $35 tip. Ivan can deduct 50% of the cost of the lunch—$100—as a business expense.

What about meals you pay for during an entertainment activity, like a sporting event? These are deductible if they are purchased separately from the entertainment or listed separately on the receipt.

> **EXAMPLE:** You treat a client to a baseball game (which you also attend) and pay for beers and food while at the game. Since you paid for the beer and food separately, you can deduct 50% of the cost. You can't deduct the cost of the tickets.

What if the cost of tickets for an entertainment event like a ball game includes the cost of food and beverages? The food and beverages are not deductible unless separately listed on the bill or invoice.

Other Meals

Other types of meals that remain deductible after passage of the Tax Cuts and Jobs Act include:

- 50% of the cost of meals you consume while you travel for business—this is a business travel expense deduction, not an entertainment deduction (see Chapter 9)
- 100% of the cost of meals provided to employees as part of a company recreational or social activity—for example, food for an employee picnic or holiday party (the activity may not include only highly compensated employees)
- 50% of meal expenses for business meetings of employees, stockholders, agents, or directors (may not include food at restaurants, but may include food for offsite meetings at hotels or other places business meetings are normally held)
- 50% of the cost of meals served to employees on business premises—for example, doughnuts, bagels, or coffee
- 100% of the cost of meals sold to customers—for example, food at an event or workshop patrons pay to attend (food part of the cost), and
- 100% of the cost of meals made available to the general public— for example, a realtor provides free snacks at an open house, or a financial adviser puts on a free educational dinner seminar for potential clients.

Gifts

If you give someone a gift for business purposes, your business expense deduction is limited to $25 per person per year. Any amount over the $25 limit is not deductible. If this amount seems low, that's because it was established in 1954!

> EXAMPLE: Lisa, a self-employed marketing consultant, gives a $200 Christmas gift to her best client. She may deduct $25 of the cost.

A gift to a member of a customer's family is treated as a gift to the customer, unless you have a legitimate nonbusiness connection to the family member. If you and your spouse both give gifts, you are treated as one taxpayer—it doesn't matter if you work together or have separate businesses.

The $25 limit applies only to gifts to individuals. It doesn't apply if you give a gift to an entire company. Such company-wide gifts are deductible in any amount, as long as they are reasonable. However, the $25 limit does apply if the gift is intended for a particular person or group of people within the company.

> EXAMPLE: Bob sells products to the Acme Company. Just before Christmas, he drops off a $100 cheese basket at the company's reception area for use by all Acme employees. He also delivers an identical basket to Acme's president. The first basket left in the reception area is a company-wide gift, not subject to the $25 limit. The basket for Acme's president is a personal gift and therefore is subject to the limit.

Insurance for Your Business

You can deduct the premiums you pay for any insurance you buy for your business as a business operating expense. This includes:

- fire, theft, and flood insurance for business property
- liability insurance
- medical insurance for your employees (see Chapter 12)
- professional malpractice insurance—for example, medical or legal malpractice insurance

- credit insurance that covers losses from business debts
- workers' compensation insurance you are required by state law to provide your employees (if you are an employee of an S corporation, the corporation can deduct worker's compensation payments made on your behalf, but you must report them as part of your employee wages)
- business interruption insurance
- life insurance covering a corporation's officers and directors (unless you are a direct beneficiary under the policy), and
- unemployment insurance contributions (you deduct these either as insurance costs or as business taxes, depending on how they are characterized by your state's laws).

Homeowners' Insurance for Your Home Office

If you have a home office and qualify for the home office deduction, you may deduct the home office percentage of your homeowners' or renters' insurance premiums. For example, if your home office takes up 20% of your home, you may deduct 20% of the premiums. You can deduct 100% of any coverage that you add to your homeowners' or renters' policy specifically for your home office and/or business property. For example, if you add an endorsement to your policy to cover business property, you can deduct 100% of the cost.

Car Insurance

If you use the actual expense method to deduct your car expenses, you can deduct the cost of insurance that covers liability, damages, and other losses for vehicles used in your business as a business expense. If you use a vehicle only for business, you can deduct 100% of your insurance costs. If you operate a vehicle for both business and personal use, you can deduct only the part of the insurance premiums that applies to the business use of your vehicle. For example, if you use a car 60% for business and 40% for personal reasons, you can deduct 60% of your insurance costs.

If you use the standard mileage rate to deduct your car expenses, you can't take a separate deduction for insurance. The standard rate is intended to cover your insurance costs. (See Chapter 8 for more on vehicle deductions.)

Interest on Business Loans

Interest you pay on business loans is usually a currently deductible business expense. It makes no difference whether you pay the interest on a bank loan, personal loan, credit card, line of credit, car loan, or real estate mortgage. Nor does it matter whether the collateral you used to get the loan was business or personal property. If you use the money for business, the interest you pay to get that money is a deductible business expense. It's how you use the money that counts, not how you get it. Borrowed money is used for business when you buy something with the money that's deductible as a business expense.

> **EXAMPLE:** Max, the sole proprietor owner of a small construction company, borrows $50,000 from the bank to buy new construction equipment. He pays 6% interest on the loan. His annual interest expense is deductible.

Your deduction begins only when you spend the borrowed funds for business purposes. You get no business deduction for interest you pay on money that you keep in the bank. Money in the bank is considered an investment—at best, you might be able to deduct the interest you pay on the money as an investment expense.

How to Eliminate Nondeductible Personal Interest

Because interest on money you borrow for personal purposes—like buying clothes or taking vacations—is not deductible, you should avoid paying this type of interest whenever possible. If you own a business, you can do this by borrowing money to pay your business expenses, and then using the money your business earns to pay off your personal debt. By doing this, you "replace" your nondeductible personal interest expense with deductible business expenses.

Home Offices

If you are a homeowner and take the home office deduction, you can deduct the home office percentage of your home mortgage interest as a business expense. (See Chapter 6 for more on the home office deduction.)

Car Loans

If you use your car for business, you can deduct the interest that you pay on your car loan as an interest expense. You can take this deduction whether you deduct your car expenses using the actual expense method or the standard mileage rate, because the standard mileage rate was not intended to encompass interest on a car loan.

If you use your car only for business, you can deduct all of the interest you pay. If you use it for both business and personal reasons, you can deduct the business percentage of the interest. For example, if you use your car 60% of the time for business, you can deduct 60% of the interest you pay on your car loan.

Loans From Relatives and Friends

If you borrow money from a relative or friend and use it for business purposes, you may deduct the interest you pay on the loan as a business expense. However, the IRS is very suspicious of loans between family members and friends. You need to carefully document these transactions. Treat the loan like any other business loan: Sign a promissory note, pay a reasonable rate of interest, and follow a repayment schedule. Keep your canceled loan payment checks to prove you really paid the interest.

Loans to Buy a Business

If you borrow money to buy an interest in an S corporation, a partnership, or an LLC, it's wise to seek an accountant's help to figure out how to deduct the interest on your loan. You must allocate the money among the company's assets. Depending on what assets the business owns, the interest might be deductible as a business expense or as an investment expense, which is more limited (see "Interest on Business Loans," above).

Interest on money you borrow to buy stock in a C corporation is always treated as investment interest. This is true even if the corporation is small (also called closely held), and its stock is not publicly traded.

Interest You Can't Deduct

You can't deduct interest:
- on loans used for personal purposes
- on debts your business doesn't owe
- on overdue taxes (only C corporations can deduct this interest)
- that you pay with funds borrowed from the original lender through a second loan (but you can deduct interest on the new loan once you start making payments)
- that you prepay if you're a cash basis taxpayer (but you may deduct it the next year)
- on money borrowed to pay taxes or fund retirement plans, or
- on loans of more than $50,000 that are borrowed on a life insurance policy on yourself or another owner or employee of your business.

Points and other loan origination fees that you pay to get a mortgage on business property are not deductible business expenses. You must add these amounts to the cost of the building and deduct them over time using depreciation. The same is true for interest on construction loans if you are in the business of building houses or other real property.

Deducting Investment Interest

Investing is not a business, so you can't take a business expense deduction for interest that you pay on money borrowed to make personal investments. You may take a personal deduction for investment interest, but you may not deduct more than your net annual income from your investments. Any amount that you can't deduct in the current year can be carried over to the next year and deducted then.

> EXAMPLE: Donald borrows $10,000 on his credit card to invest in the stock market. The interest he pays on the debt is deductible as an itemized personal deduction on Schedule A, Form 1040. He cannot deduct more than he earns during the year from his investments.

Get Separate Credit Cards for Your Business and Car Expenses

If you use the same credit card for your business and nonbusiness expenses, you are theoretically entitled to a business deduction for the credit card interest on your business expenses. However, you'll have a very difficult time calculating exactly how much of the interest you pay is for business expenses. To avoid this problem, use a separate credit card for business. This can be a special business credit card, but it doesn't have to be. You can simply designate one of your ordinary credit cards for business use. If you drive for business and use the actual expense method to take your deduction, it's a good idea to use another credit card just for car expenses. This will make it much easier to keep track of what you spend on your car.

Always pay your personal credit cards first, because you can't deduct the interest you pay on those cards.

Legal and Professional Services

You can deduct fees that you pay to attorneys, accountants, consultants, and other professionals as business expenses if the fees are paid for work related to your business.

> **EXAMPLE:** Ira, a freelance writer, hires attorney Jake to represent him in a libel suit. The legal fees Ira pays Jake are a deductible business expense.

Legal and professional fees that you pay for personal purposes generally are not deductible. For example, you can't deduct the legal fees you incur if you get divorced or you sue someone for a traffic accident injury. Nor are the fees that you pay to write your will deductible, even if the will covers business property that you own.

Buying Long-Term Property

If you pay legal or other fees in the course of buying long-term business property, you must add the amount of the fee to the tax basis (cost) of the property. You may deduct this cost over several years through depreciation or deduct it in one year under I.R.C. Section 179. (See Chapter 5 for more on deducting long-term property.)

Starting a Business

Legal and accounting fees that you pay to start a business are deductible only as business start-up expenses. You can deduct $5,000 of start-up expenses the first year you're in business and any amounts over $5,000 over 180 months. The same holds true for incorporation fees or fees that you pay to form a partnership or an LLC. (See Chapter 3 for more on deducting start-up costs.)

Accounting Fees

You can deduct any accounting fees that you pay for your business as a deductible business expense—for example, fees you pay an accountant to set up or keep your business books, prepare your business tax return, or give you tax advice for your business. During 2018 through 2025, you may not deduct tax preparation fees for your personal taxes as a miscellaneous itemized deduction. Thus, you should have your tax preparer bill you separately for preparing the business portion of your tax return.

Self-employed taxpayers may deduct the cost of having an accountant or other tax professional complete the business portion of their tax returns—Schedule C and other business tax forms—but they cannot deduct the time the preparer spends on the personal part of their returns. If you are self-employed and pay a tax preparer to complete your Form 1040 income tax return, make sure that you get an itemized bill showing the portion of the tax preparation fee allocated to preparing your Schedule C (and any other business tax forms you have to file).

Taxes and Licenses

Most taxes that you pay in the course of your business are deductible.

Income Taxes

Federal income taxes that you pay on your business income are not deductible. However, a corporation or partnership can deduct state or local income taxes it pays. Individuals may deduct state and local income taxes only as itemized deductions on Schedule A, Form 1040. This is a personal, not a business, deduction.

However, you can deduct state tax you pay on gross business income as a business expense. This tax is a federally deductible business operating expense. Of course, you can't deduct state taxes from your income for state income tax purposes.

Self-Employment Taxes

If you are a sole proprietor, a partner in a partnership, or an LLC member, you may deduct one-half of your self-employment taxes from your total net business income. This deduction reduces the amount of income on which you must pay personal income tax. It's an adjustment to gross income, not a business deduction. You don't list it on your Schedule C; instead, you take it on Page One of your Form 1040.

Employment Taxes

If you have employees, you must pay half of their Social Security and Medicare taxes from your own funds and withhold the other half from their pay. Employment taxes consist of a 12.4% Social Security tax on income up to an annual ceiling. The annual Social Security ceiling for 2020 was $137,700. Medicare taxes are not subject to any income ceiling and are levied at a 2.9% rate up to an annual ceiling—$200,000 for single taxpayers and $250,000 for marrieds filing jointly; all income above that ceiling is taxed at a 3.8% rate. This combines to a total 15.3% tax on employment income up to the Social Security tax ceiling.

You may deduct half of this amount as a business expense. On your tax return, you should treat the taxes you withhold from your employees' pay as wages paid to your employees.

> **EXAMPLE:** You pay your employee $20,000 a year. However, after you withhold employment taxes, your employee receives $18,470. You also pay an additional $1,530 in employment taxes from your own funds. On your tax returns, you should deduct the full $20,000 salary as employee wages and deduct the $1,530 as employment taxes paid.

Sales Taxes

You may not deduct state and local sales taxes that you are required to collect from a buyer and turn over to your state or local government. Do not include these taxes in your gross receipts or sales.

However, you may deduct sales taxes that you pay when you purchase goods or services for your business. The amount of the tax is added to the cost of the goods or services for purposes of your deduction for the item.

> **EXAMPLE:** Jean, a self-employed carpenter, buys $100 worth of nails from the local hardware store. She has to pay $7.50 in state and local sales taxes on the purchase. She may take a $107.50 deduction for the nails. She claims the deduction on her Schedule C as a purchase of supplies.

If you buy a long-term business asset, the sales taxes must be added to its basis (cost) for purposes of depreciation or expensing under I.R.C. Section 179.

> **EXAMPLE:** Jean buys a $3,000 power saw for her carpentry business. She pays $150 in state and local sales tax. The saw has a useful life of more than one year and is therefore a long-term business asset for tax purposes. She can't currently deduct the cost as a business operating expense. Instead, Jean must depreciate the cost over several years or deduct the full cost in one year using 100% bonus depreciation or Section 179. The total cost to be depreciated or expensed is $3,150.

Real Property Taxes

You can deduct your current year's state and local property taxes on business real property as business expenses. However, if you prepay the next year's property taxes, you may not deduct the prepaid amount until the following year.

Home Offices

The only real property most home businesspeople own is their home. If you are a homeowner and take the home office deduction, you may deduct the home office percentage of your property taxes as a business deduction. This can be advantageous because the personal itemized deduction for homeowners' property taxes for a first and second home during 2018 through 2025 is limited to $10,000. Any property tax you deduct as part of your home office deduction doesn't count toward this limit. Additionally, the Tax Cuts and Jobs Act nearly doubled the standard deduction, with the result that many homeowners are unable to itemize and are therefore unable to deduct any property tax as a personal itemized deduction. You may deduct the home office portion of your property as a business deduction whether or not you itemize.

Charges for Services

Water bills, sewer charges, and other service charges assessed against your business property are not real estate taxes, but they are deductible as business expenses. If you have a home office, you can deduct your home office percentage of these items.

However, real estate taxes imposed to fund specific local benefits, such as streets, sewer lines, and water mains, are not deductible as business expenses. Because these benefits increase the value of your property, you should add what you pay for them to the tax basis (cost for tax purposes) of your property.

Buying and Selling Real Estate

When real estate is sold, the real estate taxes must be divided between the buyer and seller according to how many days of the tax year each held ownership of the property. You'll usually find information on this in the settlement statement you receive at the property closing.

Other Taxes

Other deductible taxes include:

- excise taxes—for example, Hawaii's general excise tax on businesses ranging from 0.5% to 4.5% of gross receipts
- state unemployment compensation taxes or state disability contributions
- corporate franchise taxes
- occupational taxes charged at a flat rate by your city or county for the privilege of doing business, and
- state and local taxes on personal property—for example, equipment or machinery that you use in your business.

You can deduct taxes on gasoline, diesel fuel, and other motor fuels that you use in your business. However, these taxes are usually included as part of the cost of the fuel. For this reason, you usually do not deduct these taxes separately on your return. However, you may be entitled to a tax credit for federal excise tax that you pay on fuels used for certain purposes—for example, farming or off-highway business use. See the IRS website for more information.

License Fees

License fees imposed on your business by your local or state government are deductible business expenses. For example, some cities and counties require home business owners to obtain business licenses; the fees for such licenses are deductible.

Record Keeping and Accounting

When you incur business expenses, you can take tax deductions and save money on your taxes. But those deductions are only as good as the records you keep to back them up.

This is what Alton Williams, a schoolteacher with a sideline business selling new and used books, found out when he was audited by the IRS. Over a four-year period, he claimed over $70,000 in business deductions and inventory costs from his business. Unfortunately, he had no records or receipts tracking these expenses. His excuse: "A receipt is something I never thought I would actually need." The auditor reduced his deductions for each year by 50% to 70%, and Williams ended up owing the IRS almost $10,000. (*Williams v. Comm'r.*, 67 TC Memo 2185.)

By far, the most common reason taxpayers lose deductions when they get audited by the IRS is failure to keep proper records. Any expense you forget to deduct, or lose after an IRS audit because you can't back it up, costs you dearly. Every $100 in unclaimed deductions costs the average midlevel-income person (in a 24% tax bracket) $43 in additional federal and state income and self-employment taxes.

Luckily, it's not difficult to keep records of your business expenses. This chapter shows you how to document your expenditures so you won't end up losing your hard-earned deductions.

What Records Do You Need?

If you're a sole proprietor with no employees, you need just two types of records for tax purposes:

- a record of your business income and expenses, and
- supporting documents for your income and expenses.

You need records of your income and expenses to figure out whether your business earned a taxable profit or incurred a deductible loss during the year. You'll also have to summarize your income and expenses in your tax return (IRS Schedule C).

You need receipts and other supporting documents, such as credit card records and canceled checks, in case you're audited by the IRS. These supporting documents enable you to prove to the IRS that your claimed expenses are genuine. Some expenses—travel and entertainment, for example—require particularly stringent documentation. Without this paper trail, you'll lose valuable deductions in the event of an audit. Remember, if you're audited, it's up to you to prove that your deductions are legitimate.

These aren't necessarily all the records you'll need. For example, if you make or sell merchandise, you will have to also keep inventory records. And if you have employees, you must create and keep a number of records, including payroll tax records, withholding records, and employment tax returns. Also, special record-keeping requirements must be followed if you've formed a corporation, limited liability company with two or more owners, or partnership.

Business Checkbook and Credit Cards

First of all, before you even think about what type of record-keeping system you'll use, you should set up a separate checking account for your business (if you haven't done so already). Your business checkbook will serve as your basic source of information for recording your business expenses and income.

A separate business checkbook is legally required if you've formed a corporation, a partnership, or an LLC. Keeping a separate business account is not legally required if you're a sole proprietor, but it will provide many important benefits, such as:

- Your canceled checks will serve as proof that you actually paid for your claimed expenses.
- It will be much easier for you to keep track of your business income and expenses if you pay them from a separate account.
- Your business account will clearly separate your personal and business finances; this will prove very helpful if you're audited by the IRS.
- Your business account will help convince the IRS that you are running a business and not engaged in a hobby. Hobbyists don't generally have separate bank accounts for their hobbies. This is a huge benefit if you incur losses from your business, because losses from hobbies are not fully deductible. (See Chapter 2 for more on the hobby loss rule.)

Deposit all your business receipts (checks you receive from clients, for example) into the account and make all business-related payments by check from the account (other than those you make by credit card). Don't use your business account to pay for personal expenses or your personal account to pay for business items. To withdraw money for personal use, write a check to yourself or transfer funds into your personal checking account.

Setting Up Your Bank Account

Your business checking account should be in your business name. If you're a sole proprietor (like the vast majority of home business owners), you can use your own name. If you've formed a corporation, partnership, or limited liability company, the account should be in your corporate, partnership, or company name. If you're a sole proprietor doing business under an assumed name, you'll probably have to give your bank a copy of your fictitious business name statement.

You don't have to open your business checking account at the same bank where you have your personal checking account. Shop around and open your account with the bank that offers you the best services at the lowest price. If you're doing business under your own name, consider opening up a second personal account in that name and using it solely for your business instead of creating a separate business account. You'll usually pay lower fees for a personal account than for a business account.

You may also want to establish interest-bearing accounts for your business, in which you can place cash you don't immediately need. For example, you may decide to set up a business savings account or a money market mutual fund in your business name.

When You Write Checks

If you already keep an accurate, updated personal checkbook, do the same for your business checkbook. If, however, you tend to be lax in keeping up your checkbook (as many of us are), you're going to have to change your habits. Now that you're in business, you can't afford this kind of carelessness. Unless you write large numbers of business checks, maintaining your checkbook won't take much time.

When you write business checks, you may have to make some extra notations besides the date, number, amount of the check, and the name of the person or company to which the check is written. If the purpose of the payment is not clear from the name of the payee, describe the business reason for the check—for example, the equipment or service you purchased.

You can use the register that comes with your checkbook and write in all this information manually, or you can use a computerized register. Either way works fine as long as the information is complete and up to date. (See "Records Required for Specific Expenses," below, to find out what information you need to record for various types of expenses.)

Don't Write Checks for Cash

Avoid writing checks payable to cash, because doing so makes it hard to tell whether you spent the money for a business purpose and may lead to questions from the IRS if you're audited. If you must write a check for cash to pay a business expense, be sure to include the receipt for the cash payment in your records.

Use a Separate Credit Card for Business

Use a separate credit card for business expenses instead of putting both personal and business items on one card. Credit card interest for business purchases is 100% deductible, while interest for personal purchases is not deductible at all (see Chapter 14). Using a separate card for business purchases will make it much easier for you to keep track of how much interest you've paid for business purchases. The card doesn't have to be in your business name; you can just use one of your personal credit cards. Always use your business checking account to pay your business credit card bill.

Calendar or Appointment Book

Although not required, another highly useful item is an appointment book, calendar, day planner, or tax diary. You can find inexpensive ones in any stationery or office supply store. Many electronic calendars are available as well.

Properly used, this humble item will:

- provide solid evidence that you are serious about making a profit from your business, and thereby avoid an IRS claim that your activity is a hobby (see Chapter 2)
- help show that the expenses you incur are for business, not personal, purposes
- help verify meal and travel expenses
- enable you to use a sampling method to keep track of business mileage, instead of keeping track of every mile you drive all year (see "Records Required for Specific Expenses," below), and
- if you claim a home office deduction, help show that you use your office for business.

> **EXAMPLE:** Tom, a self-employed advertising copywriter who worked out of his Florida home, kept a detailed appointment book. He devoted a page to each day, listing all of his business activities. He also kept a mileage log to record his business mileage. When he was audited by the IRS, the auditor picked out a trip from his mileage log at random and asked him the purpose of the trip. Tom looked at his appointment book entry for that day, and was able to truthfully and credibly tell the auditor that the trip was to visit a client. The auditor accepted his explanation and the rest of his business mileage deductions.

Every day you work, you should include in your calendar or appointment book:

- the name of every person you talk to for business
- the date, time, and place of every business meeting
- every place you go for business
- the amount of all travel and meal expenses that are less than $75, and
- if you claim the home office deduction, the time you spend working in your office.

Below is a sample page from an appointment book for a self-employed real estate salesperson (you'll find information in "Records Required for Specific Expenses," below, on what information you need to list for different types of expenses).

Sunday	Monday	Tuesday	Wednesday	Thursday	Friday	Saturday
	1 Meeting with Earl Crowler	*2*	*3* Show 111 Green St.	*4* Answer phones	*5* Sales Meeting	*6* Prepare for open house— Green St.
7 Open House 111 Green St.	*8*	*9* Sales Meeting	*10* Lunch Gibbons	*11*	*12* Meeting Kim Mann	*13*
14 Open House 222 Blue St.	*15*	*16* Show Gibbons 222 Blue St.	*17*	*18* Lunch Mortgage Broker	*19* Sales Meeting	*20*
21 Open House 456 Main St.	*22*	*23* Sales Meeting	*24* Lunch Mortgage Broker	*25* Breakfast Kiwanis Club	*26* Sales Meeting	*27*
28 Open House 826 3rd St.	*29* Continuing education seminar	*30*	*31*			

Records of Your Income and Expenses

When people talk about "keeping the books," they mean keeping a record of a business's income and expenses. You may be surprised to learn that, if you're a sole proprietor, the IRS does not require you to use any particular type of record-keeping system. It says that "you may choose any record-keeping system suited to your business that clearly shows your income and expenses."

Such records can take a variety of forms and be kept in a variety of ways—some simple, some complex.

Paper Versus Electronic Records

The first choice you need to make is whether to keep paper records you create by hand or to use computerized electronic record keeping. Either method is acceptable to the IRS.

Although it may seem old-fashioned, many small business owners keep their records by hand on paper, especially when they are first starting out. You can use a columnar pad, notebook paper, or blank ledger books. There are also "one-write systems" that allow you to write checks and keep track of expenses simultaneously. Go to your local stationery store and you'll find what you need.

Hiring a Bookkeeper

If you really hate record keeping, you always have the option of hiring someone to keep your records for you. You should have no problem finding a bookkeeper through referrals from friends or colleagues, sources such as Craigslist, or the phone book. However, if you decide to use a bookkeeper, you should still continue to sign all your business checks and make deposits yourself. Giving such authority to a bookkeeper can lead to embezzlement.

Manual bookkeeping may take a bit more time than using a computer, but has the advantage of simplicity. You'll always be better off using handwritten ledger sheets, which are easy to create and understand and simple to keep up to date, instead of a complicated computer program that you don't understand or use properly.

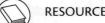 **RESOURCE**
For an excellent guide to small business bookkeeping by hand, refer to *Small Time Operator*, by Bernard B. Kamoroff (Taylor Trade Publishing).

If you want to use electronic record keeping, there are many options to choose from. These range from simple checkbook programs to sophisticated accounting software. We won't discuss how to use these programs in detail. You'll need to read the manual or tutorial that comes with the program you choose. There are also books and websites that explain how to use them. However, if you're not prepared to invest the time to use a computer program correctly, don't use it!

Create Your Own Spreadsheet

You can create your own spreadsheet to keep track of your expenses and income with a program such as *Excel*. Many templates are available to help you do this; or you can customize your own spreadsheet. See the discussion of how to track business expenses to see what you should include in your spreadsheet.

Personal Finance Software

Personal finance software such as *Quicken* may be perfectly adequate for a one-owner service business. These programs are easy to use because they work off of a computerized checkbook. When you buy something for your business, you write a check using the software. It automatically inputs the data into a check register. You'll have to input credit card and cash payments separately.

You create a list of expense categories just like you do when you create a ledger sheet or spreadsheet. Software like *Quicken* comes with preselected categories, but these are not adequate for many businesses so you'll probably have to create your own. The expense category is automatically noted in your register when you write a check.

The software can then take this information and automatically create income and expense reports—that is, it will show you the amounts you've spent or earned for each category. This serves the same purpose as the expense journal. It can also create profit and loss statements. *Quicken* provides all the tools many small service businesses need. However, if your business involves selling goods or maintaining an inventory, or if you have employees, you'll need more sophisticated software.

Small Business Accounting Software

Small business accounting programs, such as *QuickBooks* by Intuit, *AccountEdge,* and *Sage 50cloud Accounting,* can do everything personal financial software can do and much more. You can use such software to: produce bills, download credit card and bank transactions, reconcile bank accounts, generate sophisticated reports, create budgets, track inventory, track employee time and calculate payroll withholding, generate invoices and keep track of accounts receivable, and maintain fixed asset records.

These software packages are more expensive than personal finance software and are harder to learn to use. If you don't need their advanced features, there is no reason to use them.

Online Bookkeeping

Online bookkeeping relies on a Web-based computer application rather than desktop bookkeeping software. Your data is stored online in the "cloud" by the online bookkeeping service. This way you won't lose your data if your home computer is stolen or destroyed. Popular online account services that charge a monthly fee include *FreshBooks*, *Harvest*, *QuickBooks Self-Employed*, *QuickBooks Online*, *Sage*, *Zoho Books*, *Outright*, *Xero*, *Kashoo*, *FreeAgent*, *Less Accounting*, *WorkingPoint*, *Cheqbook*, *Sage Intacct*, *Clear Books*, *Wave*, and *KashFlow*.

Before You Purchase an Online App

You don't want to spend your hard-earned money on a financial app only to discover that you don't like it. Before you purchase an app, do some research:

- Talk to others in similar businesses to find out what they use; if they don't like a product, ask them why.
- Think carefully about how many features you need—the more complex the software, the harder it will be to learn and use it.
- Obtain a demo version you can try out for free to see if you like it; you can usually download one from the software company's website.

A list and comparison of most available accounting software packages and online subscription services can be found at http://en.wikipedia.org/wiki/Comparison_of_accounting_software.

Tracking Your Business Expenses

You can track your expenses by creating an expense journal that summarizes all your business expenses by category. This will show what you buy for your business and how much you spent. It's very easy to do this. You can create your journal on paper or you can set up a computer spreadsheet program, such as *Excel*, to do it. Or, if you already have or would prefer to use a financial computer program such as *Quicken*, you can do that instead.

To decide what your expense categories should be, sit down with your bills and receipts and sort them into categorized piles. IRS Schedule C,

Profit or Loss From Business, the tax form sole proprietors must use to claim their deductions, lists common categories of business expenses. These categories are a good place to start when you devise your own list, because you'll have to use them when you complete your Schedule C for your taxes. The Schedule C categories include:

- advertising
- bad debts
- car and truck expenses
- commissions and fees
- depletion (rarely used by most small businesses)
- depreciation and Section 179 expense deductions
- employee benefit programs
- insurance (other than health)
- interest
- legal and professional services
- meals
- office expenses
- pension and profit-sharing plans
- rent or lease—vehicles, machinery, and equipment
- rent or lease—other business property
- repairs and maintenance
- supplies
- taxes and licenses
- travel
- utilities, and
- wages.

The Schedule C list of business categories is by no means exclusive. (In fact, it used to contain more categories.) It just gives you an idea of how to break down your expenses. Depending on the nature of your business, you may not need all these categories or you might have others. For example, a graphic designer might have categories for printing and typesetting expenses, or a writer might have a category for agent fees. Be sure not to use multiple categories for the same expenses—for example, you don't need both an "office supplies" and an "office expenses" category; one will do.

You should always include a final category called "miscellaneous" for various and sundry expenses that are not easily pigeonholed. However, you should use this category sparingly, to account for less than 10% of your total expenses. Unlike travel or advertising, miscellaneous is not a type of business expense. It's just a heading under which you can lump together different types of expenses that don't fit into another category.

Entertainment Expenses No Longer Deductible

As a result of the Tax Cuts and Jobs Act, entertainment expenses are no longer deductible starting in 2018. For example, you may not deduct athletic or theater tickets for clients. There is no need to document these nondeductible expenses. (See Chapter 14 for more details.)

Expense Journal

Date	Check No.	Transaction	Amt.	Advertising	Outside Contractors	Utilities	Supplies	Rent	Travel	Equipment	Meals & Entertainment	Misc.
5/1	123	ABC Properties	500					500				
5/1	124	Office Warehouse	150				150					
5/10	VISA	Computer World	1,000							1,000		
5/15	VISA	Café Olé	50								50	
5/16	Cash	Sam's Stationery	50				50					
5/18	125	Electric Co.	50			50						
5/30	126	Bill Carter	5,050		500							
Total This Page			6,850		500	50	200	500		1,000	50	
Total Year to Date			7,900	200	2,000	250	400	2,500	300	1,500	250	500

You can add or delete expense categories as you go along—for example, if you find that your miscellaneous category contains many items for a particular type of expense, add it as an expense category. You don't need a category for automobile expenses, because these expenses require a different kind of documentation for tax purposes.

In separate columns, list the check number, date, and name of the person or company paid for each payment. If you pay by credit card or check, indicate it in the check number column.

Once a month, go through your check register, credit card slips, receipts, and other expense records and record the required information for each transaction. Also, total the amounts for each category when you come to the end of the page and keep a running total of what you've spent for each category for the year to date.

The example above shows a portion of an expense journal.

Supporting Documents

The IRS lives by the maxim that "figures lie and liars figure." It knows very well that you can claim anything in your books and on your tax returns, because you create or complete them yourself. For this reason, the IRS requires that you have documents to support the deductions you claim on your tax return. In the absence of a supporting document, an IRS auditor may conclude that an item you claim as a business expense is really a personal expense, or that you never bought the item at all. Either way, your deduction will be disallowed.

The supporting documents you need depend on the type of deduction. However, at a minimum, every deduction should be supported by documentation showing:

- what you purchased for your business
- how much you paid for it, and
- whom (or what company) you bought it from.

You must meet additional record-keeping requirements for local transportation, travel, entertainment, meal, and gift deductions, as well as for certain long-term assets that you buy for your business ("Records Required for Specific Expenses," below, covers these rules).

You can meet the basic requirements by keeping the following types of documentation:

- canceled checks
- sales receipts
- account statements
- credit card sales slips

- invoices, and
- petty cash slips for small cash payments.

Keep your supporting documents in a safe place. If you don't have a lot of receipts and other documents to save, you can simply keep them all in a single folder. If you have a lot of supporting documents to save or are the type of person who likes to be extremely well organized, separate your documents by category—for example, income, travel expenses, or equipment purchases. You can use a separate file folder for each category or get an accordion file with multiple pockets.

Make Digital Copies of Your Receipts

According to an old Chinese proverb, the palest ink is more reliable than the most retentive memory. However, when it comes to receipts, ink is no longer so reliable. Receipts printed on thermal paper (as most are) fade over time. By the time the IRS audits your return, you may find that all or most of the paper receipts you've carefully retained in your files are unreadable.

Because of the fading problem, you should photocopy your receipts if you intend to rely on hard copies. Obviously, this is time consuming and annoying. But there is an easier alternative: Make digital copies of your receipts and throw away the hard copies.

There are many inexpensive smartphone applications you can use to copy and keep track of receipts. Two of the most popular are Shoeboxed.com and Expensify.com. Using these and other similar apps, you can add notes and then upload the digital photos to an online account for permanent storage. These apps can even automatically categorize your expenses, and you can export your data to *QuickBooks*, *Quicken*, *Excel*, *Freshbooks*, and other accounting software.

Canceled Check + Receipt = Proof of Deduction

Manny, a self-employed photographer, buys a $500 digital camera for his business from the local electronics store. He writes a check for the amount and is given a receipt. How does he prove to the IRS that he has a $500 business expense?

Could Manny simply save his canceled check when it's returned from his bank? Many people carefully save all their canceled checks (some keep them for decades), apparently believing that a canceled check is all the proof they need to show that a purchase was a legitimate business expense. This is not the case. All a canceled check proves is that you spent money for something. It doesn't show what you bought. Of course, you can write a note on your check stating what you purchased, but why should the IRS believe what you write on your checks yourself?

Does Manny's sales receipt prove that he bought his camera for his business? Again, no. A sales receipt only proves that somebody purchased the item listed in the receipt. It does not show who purchased it. You could write a note on the receipt stating that you bought the item, but you could easily lie. Indeed, for all the IRS knows, you could hang around stores and pick up receipts people throw away to give yourself tax deductions. There are also websites that, for a fee, will create legitimate-looking fake receipts.

However, when you put a canceled check together with a sales receipt (or an invoice, a cash register tape, or a similar document), you have concrete proof that you purchased the item listed in the receipt. The check proves that you bought something, and the receipt proves what that something is.

This doesn't necessarily prove that you bought the item for your business, but it's a good start. Often, the face of a receipt, sales slip, or the payee's name on your canceled check will strongly indicate that the item you purchased was for your business. But if it's not clear, note the purpose of the purchase on the document. Such a note is not proof of how you used the item, but it will be helpful. For some types of items that you use for both business and personal purposes—cameras are one example—you might be required to keep careful records of your use. (See "Records Required for Specific Expenses," below, for the stricter rules that apply to these types of expenses.)

Credit Cards

Using a credit card is a great way to pay business expenses. The credit card slip will prove that you bought the item listed on the slip. You'll also have a monthly statement to back up your credit card slips. You should use a separate credit card for your business.

Proving Payments With Bank Statements	
If payment is by:	**The statement must show:**
Check	Check number
	Amount
	Payee's name
	Date the check amount was posted to the account by the bank
Electronic funds transfer	Amount transferred
	Payee's name
	Date the amount transferred was posted to the account by the bank
Credit card	Amount charged
	Payee's name
	Transaction date

Account Statements

Sometimes, you'll need to use an account statement to prove an expense. Some banks no longer return canceled checks, or you may pay for something with an ATM card or another electronic funds transfer method. Moreover, you may not always have a credit card slip when you pay by credit card—for example, when you buy an item over the Internet. In these situations, the IRS will accept an account statement as proof that you purchased the item. The chart above shows what type of information you need on an account statement.

Records Required for Specific Expenses

The IRS is particularly suspicious of business deductions people take for local transportation, travel, meals, gift, and entertainment expenses. It knows that many people wildly inflate these deductions—either because they're dishonest or because they haven't kept good records and instead estimate how much they think they must have spent. For this reason, special record-keeping requirements apply to these deductions. Likewise, there are special requirements for long-term assets that can be used for both personal and business purposes. If you fail to comply with the requirements discussed below, the IRS may disallow a deduction, even if it was legitimate.

Automobile Mileage and Expense Records

If you use a car or another vehicle for business purposes, you're entitled to take a deduction for gas and other auto expenses. You can either deduct the actual cost of your gas and other expenses or take the standard rate deduction based on the number of business miles you drive. (See Chapter 8 for more on car expenses.)

Either way, you must keep a record of:
- your mileage
- the dates of your business trips
- the places you drove for business, and
- the business purpose for your trips.

The last three items are relatively easy to keep track of. You can record the information in your appointment book, calendar, or day planner. Or, you can record it in a mileage log.

No Documentation Needed for Utilitarian Vehicles

All this documentation is not required for vehicles that ordinarily are not driven for personal use—for example, ambulances, hearses, trucks weighing more than 14,000 pounds, cement mixers, cranes, tractors, garbage trucks, dump trucks, forklifts, moving vans, and delivery trucks with seating for only the driver (with or without a folding jump seat). But you still need to keep track of your gas, repair, and other expenses.

Calculating your mileage takes more work. The IRS wants to know the total number of miles you drove during the year for business, commuting, and personal driving other than commuting. Commuting is travel between home and your office or other principal place of business. If you work from a home office, you'll have no commuting mileage. Personal miles include, for example, trips to the grocery store, personal vacations, or visits to friends or relatives.

Claiming a Car Is Used Solely for Business

If you use a car 100% for business, you don't need to keep track of your personal or commuting miles. However, you can successfully claim to use a car 100% for business only if you:
- work out of a tax-deductible home office
- have at least two cars, and
- use one car just for business trips.

To keep track of your business driving, you can use either a paper mileage logbook that you keep in your car or an electronic application. Logbooks are available in any office supply store and there are dozens of smartphone apps that you can use to record your mileage. Many of these apps use GPS tracking to automatically calculate your mileage for each trip.

Whichever you choose, there are several ways to keep track of your mileage; some are easy and some are a bit more complicated.

Fifty-Two-Week Mileage Book

The hardest way to track your mileage—and the way the IRS would like you to do it—is to keep track of every mile you drive every day, 52 weeks a year, using a mileage logbook or business diary. This means you'll list every trip you take, whether for business, or personal reasons. If you enjoy record keeping, go ahead and use this method. But there are easier ways.

Tracking Business Mileage

An easier way to keep track of your mileage is to record your mileage only when you use your car for business. If you record your mileage with an electronic app, check the manual to see how to implement this system. If you use a paper mileage logbook, here's what to do:

1. Note your odometer reading in the logbook at the beginning and end of every year that you use the car for business. (If you don't know your January 1 odometer reading for this year, you might be able to estimate it by looking at auto repair receipts that note your mileage.)
2. Record your mileage and note the business purpose for a trip every time you use your car for business.
3. Add up your business mileage when you get to the end of each page in the logbook (this way, you'll only have to add the page totals at the end of the year instead of all the individual entries).

At the end of the year, your logbook will show the total business miles you drove during the year. You calculate the total miles you drove during the year by subtracting your January 1 odometer reading from your December 31 reading.

If you use the actual expense method, you must also calculate your percentage of business use of the car. You do this by dividing your business miles by your total miles.

> EXAMPLE: Yolanda uses her car extensively for her home business. At the beginning of the year, her odometer reading was 34,201 miles. On December 31, it was 58,907 miles. Her total mileage for the year was therefore 24,706. She recorded 62 business trips in her mileage logbook for a total of 9,280 miles. Her business use percentage of her car is 38% (9,280 ÷ 24,706 = 0.376).

Sampling Method

There is an even easier way to track your mileage: Use a sampling method. Under this method, you keep track of your business mileage for a sample portion of the year and use your figures for that period to extrapolate your business mileage for the whole year.

This method assumes that you drive about the same amount for business throughout the year. To back up this assumption, you must scrupulously keep an appointment book showing your business appointments all year long. If you don't want to keep an appointment book, don't use the sampling method.

Your sample period must be at least 90 days—for example, the first three months of the year. Alternatively, you may sample one week each month—for example, the first week of every month. You don't have to use the first three months of the year or the first week of every month; you could use any other three-month period or the second, third, or fourth week of every month. Use whatever works best for you—you want your sample period to be as representative as possible of the business travel you do throughout the year.

You must keep track of the total miles you drove during the year by taking odometer readings on January 1 and December 31 and deducting any atypical mileage before applying your sample results.

EXAMPLE: Tom, a traveling salesman, uses the sample method to compute his mileage, keeping track of his business miles for the first three months of the year. He drove 6,000 miles during that time, and had 4,000 business miles. The business percentage of his car use was 67%. From his January 1 and December 31 odometer readings, Tom knows he drove a total of 27,000 miles during the year. However, Tom drove to the Grand Canyon for vacation, so he deducts this 1,000 mile trip from his total. This leaves him with 26,000 total miles for the year. To calculate his total business miles, he multiplies the yearlong total by the business use percentage of his car: 67% × 26,000 = 17,420. Tom claims 17,420 business miles on his tax return.

Keeping Track of Actual Expenses

If you take the deduction for your actual auto expenses instead of using the standard rate (or if you are thinking about switching to this method), keep receipts for all of your auto-related expenses, including gasoline, oil, tires, repairs, and insurance. You don't need to include these expenses in your ledger sheets; just keep them in a folder or an envelope. At tax time, add them up to determine how large your deduction will be if you use the actual expense method. Also add in the amount you're entitled to deduct for depreciation of your auto. (See Chapter 8 for more on using the actual expense method, including vehicle depreciation.)

Use a Credit Card for Gas

If you use the actual expense method for car expenses, you should use a credit card when you buy gas. It's best to designate a separate card for this purpose. The monthly statements you receive will serve as your gas receipts. If you pay cash for gas, you must either get a receipt or make a note of the amount in your mileage logbook.

Costs for business-related parking (other than at your office) and for tolls are separately deductible whether you use the standard rate or the actual expense method. Get and keep receipts for these expenses.

Travel and Gift Expenses

Deductions for business-related meals and travel (including meals while traveling), and gifts are hot-button items for the IRS because they have been greatly abused by many taxpayers. You need to have more records for these expenses than for almost any others, and they will be closely scrutinized if you're audited.

Whenever you incur an expense for business-related travel (including meals while traveling) or gifts, you must document the following facts:

- **The amount.** How much you spent, including tax and tip for meals. Document the amount of each separate travel expense, such as airfare, lodging, and meals. However, the cost of meals and incidental expenses may be combined on a daily basis by category—for example, daily meal, gas, taxi, or Uber expenses.
- **The date and place.** The location and dates of departure and return for travel, the date and place of meals, or the date and description of gifts.
- **The business purpose.** The business reason for travel or the business benefit derived (or expected to be derived) from it. The business benefit derived (or expected to be derived) as a result of a gift.
- **The business relationship:** If meals or gifts are involved, you should record the business relationship with the people at the meal or receiving the gift—for example, list their names and occupations and any other information needed to establish their business relation to you.

The IRS does not require you to keep receipts, canceled checks, credit card slips, or any other supporting documents for travel expenses (including meals while traveling) meals or gifts that cost less than $75. However, *you must still document the facts listed above.* This exception does not apply to lodging—that is, hotel or similar costs—when you travel for business. You do need receipts for these expenses, even if they cost less than $75.

CAUTION

Unclear status of business meal deduction. The Tax Cuts and Jobs Act appeared to eliminate deductions for most business meals (except those while traveling) starting in 2018 (see Chapter 14). The act also eliminated the special requirements for documenting such expenses—requirements that remain applicable to travel and gift expenses. However, it is expected that action will be taken to restore the deduction for business meals. Thus, the prudent course is to continue to document them and follow the rules for travel and gift expenses covered above.

Business Meals Not When Traveling

Meals and beverages you purchase other than while traveling on business are no longer subject to the strict substantiation rules described above. Instead, they are now subject to the same record-keeping rules as any business deduction. This means you are still supposed to have records of the amount and business purpose. But, if you lack adequate records, you can ask the IRS and/or Tax Court to permit you at least a partial deduction under the *Cohan* rule (see "What If You Don't Have Proper Tax Records?" below). Under this rule, taxpayers who lack all required records are permitted to make an estimate of how they must have spent the money. The IRS has discretion to allow such taxpayers to deduct all or part of the estimated amount. But, you must provide at least some credible evidence on which to base this estimate, such as receipts, canceled checks, notes in your appointment book, or other records.

Receipts to Keep

Type of Expense	Receipts to Save
Travel	Airplane, train, or bus ticket stubs; travel agency receipts; rental car; and so on
Meals While Traveling	Meal check, credit card slip
Lodging	Statement or bill from hotel or other lodging provider; your own written records for cleaning, laundry, telephone charges, tips, and other charges not shown separately on hotel statement

All this record keeping is not as hard as it sounds. You can record the facts you have to document in a variety of ways, and the information doesn't have to be all in one place. Information that is shown on a receipt, a canceled check, or another item need not be duplicated in a log, an appointment book, a calendar, or an account book. Thus, for example, you can record the facts with:

- a receipt, credit card slip, or similar document alone
- a receipt combined with an appointment book entry, or
- an appointment book entry alone (for expenses less than $75).

However you document your expense, you are supposed to do it in a timely manner. You don't need to record the details of every expense on the day you incur it. It is sufficient to record them on a weekly basis. However, if you're prone to forgetting details, it's best to get everything you need in writing within a day or two.

Using Electronic Records to Document Travel Deductions

These days, many of us fly without an actual airline ticket, using "paperless travel." When you book a flight this way, you will receive a receipt and an itinerary (via download from a website, in an email, or by fax), but no actual ticket. The IRS says it's perfectly fine to use copies of these types of electronic records to document a travel deduction, as long as they show the amount spent, date, location, and business purpose of the expenditure. Make sure you save these records, in either digital or hard copy format. (Ltr. Ruling 98050007.)

Listed Property

Listed property refers to certain types of long-term business assets that can easily be used for personal as well as business purposes. Listed property includes:

- cars, boats, airplanes, motorcycles, and other vehicles, and
- any other property generally used for entertainment, recreation, or amusement—for example, cameras and camcorders.

Because all listed property is long-term business property, you cannot deduct it like a business expense. Instead, you must depreciate it over several years or deduct it in one year, unless you can deduct it in one year with the de minimis safe harbor, bonus depreciation, or Section 179 expensing. (See Chapter 5 for detailed information on deducting listed property.)

Special Record-Keeping Requirements

The IRS fears that taxpayers might claim business deductions for listed property, but use it for personal reasons. That's why you're required to document how you use listed property. Keep an appointment book, or a logbook, business diary, or calendar showing the dates, times, and reasons for which the property is used—both business and personal. You also can purchase logbooks for this purpose at stationery or office supply stores.

> **TIP**
> **Rules for cellphones.** Cellphones and similar personal communication devices are no longer considered listed property. Thus, the strict record-keeping requirements for listed property do not apply to these devices. In addition, you don't have to include the fair market value of a cellphone provided to an employee for business purposes in the employee's gross income for tax purposes, as long as the cellphone is provided to the employee for noncompensatory purposes (meaning business purposes not related to providing additional compensation).

How Long to Keep Records

You need to have copies of your tax returns and supporting documents available in case you are audited by the IRS or another taxing agency. You might also need them for other purposes—for example, to get a loan, a mortgage, or insurance.

You should keep your records for as long as the IRS has to audit you after you file your returns for the year. These statutes of limitation range from three years to forever—they are listed in the table below.

To be on the safe side, you should keep your tax returns indefinitely. They usually don't take up much space, so this shouldn't be a big hardship. Your supporting documents probably take up more space. You should keep these for at least six years after you file your return. If you file a fraudulent return, keep your supporting documents indefinitely (if you have any). If you're audited, they will show that at least some of your deductions were legitimate.

Storing Your Records Electronically

If you don't want to keep paper copies of your tax records, you can make digital copies and store them on your computer or "in the cloud." The IRS has approved the use of electronic storage systems for this purpose. (Rev. Proc. 97-22, 1997-1 CB 652.)

Keep your long-term asset records for three years after the depreciable life of the asset ends. For example, keep records for five-year property (such as computers) for eight years. You should keep your ledger sheets for as long as you're in business, because a potential buyer of your business might want to see them.

IRS Statutes of Limitations

If:	The limitations period is:
You failed to pay all the tax due	3 years
You underreported your gross income for the year by more than 25%	6 years
You filed a fraudulent return	No limit
You did not file a return	No limit

What If You Don't Have Proper Tax Records?

Because you're human, you may not have kept all the records required to back up your tax deductions. Don't despair, all is not lost—you may be able to fall back on the *Cohan* rule. This rule (named after the Broadway entertainer George M. Cohan, who was involved in a tax case in the 1930s) is the taxpayer's best friend. The *Cohan* rule recognizes that all businesspeople must spend at least some money to stay in business, and so must have at least some deductible expenses, even if they don't have adequate records to back them up.

If you're audited and lack adequate records for a claimed deduction, the IRS can use the *Cohan* rule to make an estimate of how much you must have spent, and allow you to deduct that amount. However, you must provide at least some credible evidence on which to base this estimate, such as receipts, canceled checks, notes in your appointment book, or other records. Moreover, the IRS will allow you to deduct only the smallest amount you must have spent, based on the records you provide. In addition, the *Cohan* rule cannot be used for travel, meal, entertainment, or gift expenses, or for listed property.

If an auditor claims you lack sufficient records to back up a deduction, you should always bring up the *Cohan* rule and argue that you should still get the deduction based on the records you do have. At best, you'll probably get only part of your claimed deductions. If the IRS auditor disallows your deductions entirely or doesn't give you as much as you think you deserve, you can appeal in court and bring up the *Cohan* rule again there. You might have more success with a judge. However, you can't compel an IRS auditor or a court to apply the *Cohan* rule in your favor. They have discretion to decide whether to apply the rule and how large a deduction to give you.

> **EXAMPLE:** Ajuba Gaylord had a part-time business as a home-based salesperson. One year, she took a $474 deduction for postage and over $1,100 for meals and entertainment. The IRS disallowed both deductions because she had no documentary evidence showing that the expenses were for her business. However, the tax court applied the *Cohan* rule and

allowed her a $75 deduction for postage. It reasoned that this was the least that she must have spent, given the nature of her business. However, the court would not use the *Cohan* rule to grant her a deduction for meal and entertainment expenses. (*Gaylord v. Comm'r.*, TC Memo 2003-273.)

Reconstructing Tax Records

If you can show that you possessed adequate records at one time, but now lack them due to circumstances beyond your control, you may reconstruct your records for an IRS audit. Circumstances beyond your control include acts of nature, such as floods, fires, earthquakes, or theft. (Treas. Reg. 1.275.5(c)(5).) If you lose your tax records while moving, that doesn't constitute circumstances beyond your control. Reconstructing records means you either create brand new records just for your audit or obtain other evidence to corroborate your deductions—for example, statements from people or companies from whom you purchased items for your business.

Accounting Methods

An accounting method is a set of rules used to determine when and how your income and expenses are reported. Accounting methods might sound like a rather dry subject, but your choice about how to account for your business expenses and income will have a huge impact on your tax deductions. You don't have to become as expert as a CPA on this topic, but you should understand the basics.

You must choose an accounting method when you file your first tax return. If you later want to change your accounting method, you must get IRS approval. The IRS requires some types of businesses to use the accrual method. If your business doesn't fall into this group, you are free to choose the method you want, as long as it clearly shows your income and expenses. If you operate two or more separate businesses, you can use a different accounting method for each. (A business is separate for tax purposes only if you keep a separate set of books and records for it.)

There are two basic methods of accounting: cash basis and accrual basis. Most home businesses can use either method, with the cash method by far the more popular.

Personal and Business Accounting Methods May Differ

You can account for business and personal items using different accounting methods. For example, you can figure your business income under an accrual method, even if you use the cash method to figure personal items. Almost everyone uses the cash basis method of accounting for personal finances, so it might be convenient to continue to use it for personal items even if you use the accrual method for your business.

Cash Method

The cash method is the simplest method. It is used by individuals who are not in business and by most small businesses. The cash method is based on this commonsense idea: You haven't earned income for tax purposes until you actually receive the money, and you haven't incurred an expense until you actually pay the money. Using the cash basis method, then, is like maintaining a checkbook. You record income only when the money is received and expenses only when they are actually paid. If you borrow money to pay business expenses, you incur an expense under the cash method only when you make payments on the loan.

> **EXAMPLE 1:** Helen, a home-based marketing consultant, completes a market research report on September 1, 2020 but isn't paid by the client until February 1, 2021. Using the cash method, Helen records the payment as income in February 2021—when she receives it.

> **EXAMPLE 2:** On December 1, 2020, Helen goes to the Acme electronics store and buys a laser printer for her consulting business. She buys the item on credit from Acme—she's not required to make any payments until March 1, 2021. Helen does not record the expense until 2021 when she actually pays for the printer.

The cash method is by far the most popular because it is the simplest and easiest to understand and apply. It can also save on taxes because taxable income can be deferred by postponing billings to the following year. Deductions can be speeded up by buying things before year end. For these reasons, the IRS has not been in favor of the cash method. Before 2018, there were restrictions on the ability to use the cash method by C corporations and businesses that produced, bought, or sold merchandise and were required to maintain an inventory. However, the Tax Cuts and Jobs Act greatly expanded the number of businesses that may use the cash method. Any business with no more than $26 million in average gross receipts during the prior three tax years can use the cash method. Businesses other than regular C corporations can use the cash method even if their gross receipts exceed $26 million provided that the method clearly reflects their income.

The Cash Method of Paying Expenses

Although it's called the cash method, this method for paying business expenses includes payments by check, credit card, or electronic funds transfer, as well as by cash. If you pay by check, the amount is deemed paid during the year in which the check is drawn and postal mailed or emailed— for example, a check dated December 31, 2020 is considered paid during 2020 only if it has a December 31, 2020 postmark or it's electronically paid by that date.

Constructive Receipt

Under the cash method, payments are "constructively received" when an amount is credited to your account or otherwise made available to you without restrictions. Constructive receipt is as good as actual receipt. If you authorize someone to be your agent and receive income for you, you are considered to have received it when your agent receives it.

EXAMPLE: Interest is credited to your business bank account in December 2020, but you do not withdraw it or enter it into your passbook until 2021. You must include the amount in gross business income for 2020.

No Postponing Income

You cannot hold checks or other payments from one tax year to another to avoid paying tax on the income. You must report the income in the year the payment is received or made available to you without restriction.

EXAMPLE: On December 1, 2020, Helen receives a $5,000 check from a client. She holds the check and doesn't cash it until January 10, 2021. She still has to report the $5,000 as income for 2020 because she constructively received it that year.

No Prepayment of Expenses

The general rule is that you can't prepay expenses when you use the cash method—you can't hurry up the payment of expenses by paying them in advance. An expense you pay in advance can be deducted only in the year to which it applies.

EXAMPLE: Mia pays $1,000 in 2020 for a business insurance policy that is effective for one year, beginning July 1. She can deduct $500 in 2020 and $500 in 2021.

However, there is an important exception to the general rule called the 12-month rule. Under this rule, you may deduct a prepaid expense in the current year if the expense is for a right or benefit that extends no longer than the earlier of:
- 12 months, or
- until the end of the tax year after the tax year in which you made the payment.

EXAMPLE 1: You are a calendar year taxpayer and you pay $10,000 for a business insurance policy that is effective for one year beginning July 1, 2020. The 12-month rule applies because the benefit you've paid for—a business insurance policy—extends only 12 months into the future. Therefore, the full $10,000 is deductible in 2020.

EXAMPLE 2: You are a calendar year taxpayer and you pay $3,000 in 2019 for a business insurance policy that is effective for three years, beginning July 1, 2019. This payment does not qualify for the 12-month rule because the benefit extends more than 12 months. Therefore, you must use the general rule: $500 is deductible in 2020, $1,000 is deductible in 2021, $1,000 is deductible in 2022, and $500 is deductible in 2023.

There is one small catch: If you previously followed the old rule, under which expenses prepaid beyond the calendar year were not currently deductible, you must get IRS approval to use the 12-month rule. Approval is granted automatically by the IRS upon filing of IRS Form 3115, *Application for Change in Accounting Method*. You should attach one copy of the form to the return for the year of the change and send another copy to the IRS national office (not the service center where you file your return). The address is on the instructions for the form.

It is a good idea to get a tax pro to help you with this form because it may require some adjustment of the deductions you've taken for prepaid expenses in previous years under the old rule.

Accrual Method

In accrual basis accounting, you report income or expenses as they are earned or incurred, rather than when they are actually collected or paid. The accrual method can be difficult to use because complex rules determine when income or expenses accrue. You recognize income when it is earned, due, or received—whichever is earlier. Expenses are deductible only when liability is fixed, the amount can be determined with reasonable accuracy, and economic performance has occurred.

Obtaining IRS Permission to Change Your Accounting Method

You choose your accounting method by checking a box on your tax form when you file your tax return. Once you choose a method, you can't change it without getting permission from the IRS. Permission is granted automatically for many types of changes, including using the 12-month rule to deduct prepaid expenses. You must file IRS Form 3115, *Application for Change in Accounting Method*, with your tax return for the year you want to make the change (if the change is automatically granted).

Automatic approval can also be obtained to change to the cash method if you've been using the accrual method and come within one of the exceptions discussed above. However, changing your accounting method can have serious consequences, so consult a tax professional before doing so.

Tax Years

You are required to pay taxes for a 12-month period, also known as the tax year. Sole proprietors, partnerships, limited liability companies, S corporations, and personal service corporations are required to use the calendar year as their tax year—that is, January 1 through December 31.

However, there are exceptions that permit some small businesses to use a tax year that does not end in December (also known as a fiscal year). You need to get the IRS's permission to use a fiscal year. The IRS doesn't want businesses to use a fiscal year, but it might grant you permission if you can show a good business reason for it.

One good reason to use a fiscal year is that your business is seasonal. For example, if you earn most of your income in the spring and incur most of your expenses in the fall, a tax year ending in July or August might be better than a calendar tax year ending in December because the income and expenses on each tax return will be more closely related. To get permission to use a fiscal year, you must file IRS Form 8716, *Election to Have a Tax Year Other Than a Required Tax Year.*

Businesses Owned by Spouses

Many home businesses are run by married couples. Most often, married couples don't give much thought about how the IRS will characterize their ventures for tax purposes. After all, unless they form C corporations (which is unusual) all the business income will end up on their joint tax returns anyway. However, this is a mistake. If you're in business with your spouse, you have some options on how to structure your business that unmarried people don't have that can lead to significant tax savings.

An Employer-Employee Arrangement

A married person can be a sole proprietor for tax purposes if he or she is the only person who owns, manages, and controls the business. For tax purposes, a sole proprietor personally owns the business and reports its income and expenses on Schedule C. A sole proprietor can hire any number of employees to work in the business, including family members. If you hire your spouse as your bona fide employee (or vice versa), you both receive the same tax treatment as any other employer and employee. If this option works for you, it is the one that will likely save you the most in taxes.

The salary and benefits paid to the employee-spouse are tax-deductible business expenses for the employer-spouse (see Chapter 11). Even more important, various employee fringe benefits are tax free to the employee-spouse. Chief among these are health insurance and a medical reimbursement plan to reimburse the employee-spouse for out-of-pocket health expenses. Health benefits an employer provides to an employee may cover the employee's spouse and children as well as the employee-spouse. Thus, the health insurance and medical reimbursement plan can cover the employee-spouse, employer-spouse, and their children. This is a unique benefit you obtain by hiring your spouse as an employee. (See Chapter 12.)

Think of the employee fringe benefits you pay your employee-spouse as noncash wages. Given how much health insurance and other medical expenses cost, these can be substantial. The IRS says that paying an employee with noncash benefits alone is permissible as long as the spouse's total compensation is reasonable.

EXAMPLE: Joe has a public relations business he runs from home as a sole proprietor. His wife, Jean, works as his employee performing administrative tasks. Joe pays Jean no wage salary. Instead, he covers her with a medical reimbursement plan. During the year, he reimburses her $25,000 for family medical insurance, family dental expenses, family co-pays and deductions, and expenses for over-the-counter drugs and supplies related to sickness and injury. Joe deducts the $25,000 as an employee welfare benefit on his Schedule C and Jean doesn't have to pay any tax on the tax-free medical reimbursements.

However, at certain income levels, the pass-through tax deduction is based wholly or partly on how much W-2 wages you pay your employees. If you fall into this category, you may wish to pay your spouse more wages. (See Chapter 7.)

Social Security Tax Savings

The sole proprietor-employee arrangement can also save substantial Social Security taxes if your business income exceeds the Social Security tax ceiling. The Social Security tax is a 12.4% tax up to an annual ceiling. Net self-employment income above the ceiling is not subject to the tax. For 2020, the annual ceiling is $137,700. (In contrast, you must pay Medicare taxes on all your net self-employment income, no matter how high.)

Let's say your business generates $200,000 of self-employment income (and you and your spouse have no other SE or salary income). If you and your spouse each have a 50% interest in the business, you'll each file a Schedule SE reporting $100,000 self-employment income and pay $12,400 in Social Security taxes (12.4% x $100,000 = $12,400). Your total self-employment tax bill will be $24,800. On the other hand, if you have a 100% interest in the business and your spouse works as your employee and receives no cash wages, you'll report $200,000 in self-employment income on your Schedule SE and your spouse will have no taxable income. You'll pay $17,075 in Social Security tax on your self-employment income up to $137,700 and your spouse will pay $0.

The total tax savings is $7,775.

Bona Fide Employee Requirement

The one catch to this arrangement is that the nonowner spouse must be a bona fide employee. This means that the owner-spouse must manage the business while the nonowner spouse works under his or her direction and control. A spouse cannot be treated as an employee if he or she has an equal say in the affairs of the business, provides substantially equal services to the business, and contributes substantial capital to the business.

Obviously, this arrangement won't work if both spouses want to have an equal say in how the business is run. All bank accounts, contracts, and government filings should be in the proprietor-spouse's name alone.

Reasonable Compensation Requirement

The employee-spouse's total compensation must be reasonable and actually paid. Total compensation means the sum of any salary and all the fringe benefits the employer-spouse pays the employee-spouse, including health insurance and medical expense reimbursements, if any. Reasonableness is determined by comparing the amount paid with the value of the services performed. If the IRS or Social Security Administration concludes that the employee-spouse is being paid unreasonably low compensation, it could conclude that the employee-spouse is not a bona fide employee. In this event, it would reallocate the business income equally between spouses, resulting in additional Social Security taxes.

In our example above, Joe paid his wife Jean $25,000 in medical reimbursements to work in his business. If she worked 1,500 hours per year, this would come out to $16.67 per hour. If this is much less than the average salary for such work, Joe might need to pay her more. He could provide a small salary in additional to the medical reimbursements. Income taxes and payroll taxes would have to be paid on the salary, but they would still pay much less than if they were partners in the business.

You should document the reasonableness of your employee-spouse's compensation. There is a vast amount of salary information available on the Internet; some for free, some for a fee, including the following:

- The Economic Research Institute maintains a massive commercial database of salary information at www.erieri.com.
- The Society for Human Resource Management publishes an annual compensation survey. Online compensation reports for specific positions are also available for a fee. Its website may be found at www.shrm.org.
- Local surveys for a particular city, state, or region may be available— for example, the National Capitol Human Resources Association publishes an annual survey of compensation in Washington, DC.

Your Spouse Won't Qualify for Social Security? So What!

Paying the employee-spouse little or no cash wages could mean that he or she won't qualify for Social Security benefits due to lack of sufficient Social Security earnings. This is not such a big deal. If the employee-spouse does not qualify for benefits on his or her own, he or she will be entitled to a spousal benefit equal to half of the benefits of the employer-spouse. You need be married just one year to qualify for the spousal benefit. Alternatively, you can be divorced and receive the benefit based on the divorced spouse's earnings if the marriage lasted at least ten years.

When you factor in the amount of money you can earn if you invest your annual Social Security savings by paying the employee-spouse little or no wages, you'll both come out far ahead.

What About Limited Liability?

Sole proprietorships do have one big drawback: They offer no limited liability protection. When you own your business as a sole proprietor, you have unlimited personal liability for your business debts. Corporations, LLCs, and LLPs provide limited liability, which is the main reason why many business owners use them. If this concerns you, you can always form a one-person limited liability company to run the business. This will give you the same degree of limited liability as a corporation.

However, for tax purposes, a single-member LLC is a "disregarded entity." This means that, as far as taxes go, it's treated as if it doesn't exist. You can continue to file your Schedule C, just like you do as a sole proprietor. To maintain your limited liability, you'll need to run your business in the name of the LLC and your spouse will be employed by the LLC, not by you personally.

Establish a Qualified Joint Venture

In 2007, Congress decided to give married business owners a break and allow them to elect to have their jointly owned businesses treated as qualified joint ventures (QJVs) for tax purposes. With QJV status, both spouses are treated as sole proprietors for tax purposes—the simplest tax treatment for a business. Before Congress introduced the QJV election, spouses who co-owned a business had to file a partnership tax return— the most complicated tax filing—unless they formed a business entity (a corporation or limited liability company, for example).

Qualifying for QJV Status

Not all married couples who own businesses together qualify for QJV status. To file a joint venture election, you and your spouse must:
- be the only owners of the business
- file a joint return
- both elect not to be treated as a partnership, and
- both materially participate in the business.

To materially participate in the business, each spouse must work in the business at least 500 hours during the year, or each must work at least 100 hours with no one else working more (including employees or nonemployees).

In addition, married couples cannot make a qualified joint venture election if the business is owned and operated through a state law entity— this includes a limited liability company, limited liability partnership, or corporation. Thus, you cannot make this election if you've formed an LLC or a corporation to limit your personal liability.

To make the election, you and your spouse file two Schedules C for your business. Your business income, gains, losses, deductions, and credits are divided between the two of you in accordance with your respective interests in the venture. For example, if you and your spouse are equal owners of the business, you each list 50% of these amounts on your individual Schedule C. You then report your total Schedule C income or loss on your joint Form 1040.

You'll also have to file two Schedules SE to report self-employment tax for both of you. Your self-employment income on each Schedule SE is allocated in the same way as on your Schedules C. Each spouse receives credit for Social Security and Medicare coverage purposes.

Community Property Sole Proprietorships

If your business is located in one of the nine community property states (Arizona, California, Idaho, Louisiana, Nevada, New Mexico, Texas, Washington, and Wisconsin), you can choose to have your business elect to be treated as a QJV. However, you have another—often better— option. Because of the impact of state community property laws, the IRS allows married co-owners in a community property state to treat their business as a sole proprietorship for tax purposes. This treatment is allowed if your business is a "qualified entity," which means:

- It is owned only by you and your spouse as community property under state law.
- No person other than one or both spouses is an owner for federal tax purposes.
- The entity is not a corporation. (Rev. Proc. 2002-69.)

If you choose sole proprietorship status, a single Schedule C is filed in the name of one spouse. If both spouses jointly operate the business, a Schedule SE must be filed for each spouse. To make the election, simply start filing a single Schedule C and the Schedule SE, as appropriate.

For many couples, this is easier than a qualified joint venture election because there is no material participation requirement. In fact, neither spouse has to materially participate in the business.

Form a Business Entity

Like any business, you and your spouse can establish a formal business entity to own and run your business—this can be a formal partnership, a limited liability company, or a corporation. In this event, your business will be treated the same as a business owned by unmarried people. (See Chapter 1.)

Do Nothing

Many married couples do nothing in terms of establishing a formal legal status for their jointly owned business. Instead, they simply run the business together in their own names as individual co-owners. However, if you do this, you are automatically considered a partnership for tax purposes. As such, you're supposed to file a partnership tax return which can be a complex and expensive endeavor. Because they don't understand the rules, many couples treat their businesses like sole proprietorships instead and file one Schedule C reporting their business income and expenses.

This practice became so common that the IRS decided to stop actively enforcing the partnership tax filing rules for businesses owned by spouses. It issued a revenue procedure waiving the applicable penalty if the spouses reported all their business income on their Schedule C and paid all taxes due. (Rev. Proc. 84-3.)

While it may be tempting to file taxes this way, it's probably not a good idea. There are certain assumptions underlying this treatment that the IRS or Social Security Administration could decide to look into at any time. For example, if the IRS determines that the spouses in the business are 50-50 partners, it might decide to reallocate their business income for self-employment tax purposes. This could end up costing additional Social Security taxes. Or, the IRS might decide that you are not entitled to claim certain business expenses of the spouse not listed as a sole proprietor because that person was neither an employee who incurred employee expenses nor an owner who incurred deductible business expenses.

Eight Tips for Avoiding an IRS Audit

H ere are eight things you can do to minimize your chances of getting audited.

Tip #1: Be Thorough and Exact

Your return should be thorough and exact. Your math should be correct. Avoid round numbers on your return (like $100 or $5,000). This looks like you're making up the numbers instead of taking them from accurate records. You should include, and completely fill out, all necessary forms and schedules. Moreover, your state tax return should be consistent with your federal return. If you do your own taxes, using a tax preparation software will help you produce an accurate return.

Tip #2: Don't File Early

Unless you're owed a substantial refund, you shouldn't file your taxes early. The IRS generally has three years after April 15 to decide whether to audit your return. Filing early just gives the IRS more time to think about whether you should be audited. You can reduce your audit chances even more by getting an automatic extension to file until October 15. (Partnerships and S corporations may receive an automatic extension only until September 15.) Note, however, that filing an extension does not extend the date by which you have to pay any taxes due for the prior year—these must be paid by April 15.

Tip #3: Form a Business Entity

The audit rate statistics show that partnerships and small corporations are audited far less often than sole proprietors. In 2018, for example, the IRS audited 0.2% of partnerships, 0.2% of S corporations, and only 0.4% of regular C corporations with assets worth less than $250,000. In contrast, 2.4% of sole proprietors earning $100,000 to $200,000 were audited. Ninety percent of home business owners are sole proprietors, but no law says they have to be. Incorporating your business or forming a limited liability company will reduce your audit risk. However, you must balance this against the time and expense involved in forming a corporation or an LLC. Moreover, in some states—most notably California—corporations and LLCs have to pay additional state taxes.

Tip #4: Explain Items the IRS Will Question

If your return contains an item that the IRS may question or that could increase the likelihood of an audit, include an explanation to help show everything is on the up and up. For example, if your return contains a substantial bad debt deduction, explain the circumstances showing that the debt is a legitimate business expense. This won't necessarily avoid an audit, but it may reduce your chances.

Such explanations ("disclosures" in tax parlance) can be made on plain white paper and attached to your return if you file by postal mail or you can use special IRS forms. IRS Form 8275, *Disclosure Statement*, can be used to explain or disclose any information that there isn't room to include on your other tax forms. Another IRS form, Form 8275-R, *Regulation Disclosure Statement*, must be used to disclose tax positions that are contrary to IRS regulations or other rules. You shouldn't file Form 8275-R without professional help.

Tip #5: Avoid Ambiguous or General Expenses

Don't list expenses under vague categories such as "miscellaneous" or "general expense." Be specific. IRS Schedule C lists specific categories for the most common small business expenses. If an expense doesn't fall within one of these classifications, create a specific name for it.

Tip #6: Report All of Your Income

The IRS is convinced that self-employed people, including many home business owners, don't report all of their income. Finding such hidden income is a high priority. IRS computers compare 1099 forms with tax returns to determine whether there are any discrepancies. Not all income home business owners receive is reported to the IRS on Form 1099 —for example, if you sell a product to customers rather than providing a service, your receipts will not be reported on Form 1099. However, if you are audited, the auditor may examine your bank records to see whether you received any unreported income.

Tip #7: Watch Your Income-to-Deduction Ratio

Your income-to-deduction ratio can be an important audit flag. One statistical study of more than 1,200 returns that were audited concluded that if your total business expenses amount to less than 52% of your gross business income, you are "not very likely" to be audited. If your business expenses are 52% to 63% of your business income, there is a "relatively high probability" that the IRS computer will tag you for an audit. Finally, if your expenses are more than 63% of your income, the study found you are certain to be computer tagged for audit. Of course, this doesn't necessarily mean that you will be audited. Less than 10% of returns that are computer tagged for audit are actually audited. But being tagged considerably increases the odds that you'll be audited.

Whether these precise numbers are correct or not is anyone's guess. However, the basic conclusion—that your income-to-deduction ratio is an important factor in determining whether you'll be audited—is undoubtedly true.

Tip #8: Beware of Abnormally Large Deductions

It is not just the total amount of your deductions that is important. Very large individual deductions can also increase your audit chances. How much is too much? It depends in part on the nature of your business. A $2,000 foreign travel deduction might look abnormal for a plumber, but not for a person in the import-export business.

Index